D0903857

WAYFINDING IN ARCHITECTURE

ENVIRONMENTAL DESIGN SERIES

Series Editor: Richard P. Dober, AICP

Related Titles

I define the term "environmental design" as an art larger
than architecture, more comprehensive than planning,
more sensitive than engineering. An art pragmatic, one
that preempts traditional concerns. The practice of this
art is intimately connected with man's ability to function,
to bring visual order to his surroundings, to enhance and
embellish the territory he occupies.

> Richard P. Dober
> *Environmental Design*

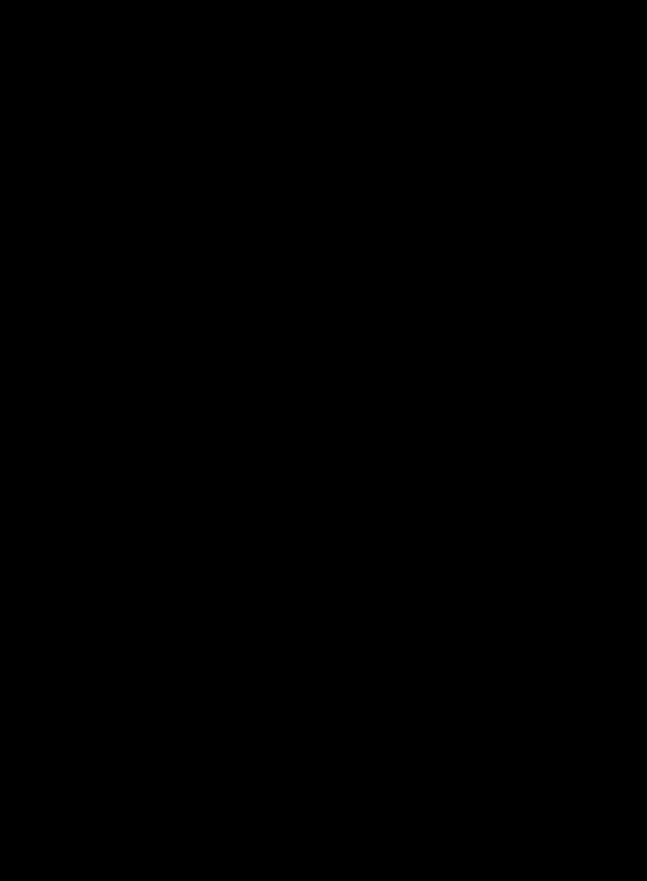

WAYFINDING IN ARCHITECTURE

Romedi Passini

Université de Montréal

VNR VAN NOSTRAND REINHOLD COMPANY

NEW YORK   CINCINNATI   TORONTO   LONDON   MELBOURNE

WILLIAM MADISON RANDALL LIBRARY UNC AT WILMINGTON

Copyright ©1984 by **Van Nostrand Reinhold Company Inc.**
Environmental Design Series, Volume 4
Library of Congress Catalog Card Number: 83-27393
ISBN: 0-442-27590-0

All rights reserved. No part of this work covered by the copyright hereon
may be reproduced or used in any form or by any means—graphic, electronic,
or mechanical, including photocopying, recording, taping, or information
storage and retrieval systems—without permission of the publisher.

Manufactured in the United States of America.

Published by Van Nostrand Reinhold Company Inc.
135 West 50th Street
New York, New York 10020

Van Nostrand Reinhold Company Limited
Molly Millars Lane
Wokingham, Berkshire RG11 2PY, England

Van Nostrand Reinhold
480 Latrobe Street
Melbourne, Victoria 3000, Australia

Macmillan of Canada
Division of Gage Publishing Limited
164 Commander Boulevard
Agincourt, Ontario MIS 3C7, Canada

15 14 13 12 11 9 8 7 6 5 4 3 2 1

Library of Congress Cataloging in Publication Data
Passini, Romedi, 1939-
    Wayfinding in architecture.
    (Environmental design series; v. 4)
    Includes bibliographical references and indexes.
    1. Space (Architecture)—Design and plans.   2. Archi-
tectural design.   3. Space perception.   4. Architecture—
Decision-making.   I. Title.   II. Series: Environmental
design series (New York, N.Y.); v. 4.
NA2765.P37   1984   711   83-27393
ISBN 0-442-27590-0

NA2765
.P37
1984

Contents

251826

Series Editor's Foreword

The built environment may be likened to a pageant, with designers orchestrating experiences and sequences to achieve certain ends. Romedi Passini terms these structured arrangements "wayfinding," an aspect of design conceptualization he explores in great depth in this illuminating book.

Design for wayfinding contributes to environmental quality in two ways. First is journey clarification—the psychological ease of connecting origins and destinations. Second is the spatial and visual enhancement of designated routes.

As Romedi Passini explains, these aspects of environmental design have a rich historic tradition. Indeed, they begin with the most elemental of human and cultural transactions, which in a defined sense are so fundamental that they transcend style and fashion.

Here then is a practical book. It addresses pragmatic matters, outlines design methods and modes useful in everyday practice, and does all this in a context that is scholarly and thought provoking.

RICHARD P. DOBER, AICP

Preface

What is more annoying than the feeling of having wasted time and energy in a futile attempt to reach a destination; what more exasperating than searching for information on displays giving everything but that which is needed? What is more bizarre than the twinge of fear or excitement and the second of panic when momentarily lost? Wayfinding difficulties are common in contemporary architectural settings. The consequences for individual users may be minimal or they may be harmful, costly or, at the extreme, disastrous. Some environments—hospitals, airports, institutional buildings, urban commercial complexes, underground transportation and parking facilities—are particularly well known for their wayfinding difficulties. The large scale of these examples certainly exacerbates the difficulties. However, the fundamental causes transcend the question of size because they are the result of a basic planning neglect. It is the purpose of this book to sensitize designers to the issues by developing the concept of wayfinding, by presenting research results that reveal wayfinding pitfalls and successes, and by proposing a method of designing for wayfinding. In short, the book has been written to serve as a general reference on the subject and as a design aid to the practitioner. It will also interest people who have a tendency to get lost and people who wonder why others get lost.

Viewing a phenomenon from its opposite often provides greater insight into its characteristics. The history of the labyrinth, the artifact most closely related to being disoriented and lost, brings to light the meaning and emotion associated with wayfinding and the companion concept of spatial orientation from which it cannot be dissociated. It discloses a profound and universal interest in man's relation to the unknown, be it in a spiritual or spatial sense, which has intricate ramifications for environmental design. The fields of architecture, urbanism, anthropology and mythology contribute to the discussion in the first chapter. A brief review of travel records and research done in anthropology and psychology is the basis for the second chapter, which investigates various beliefs about the spatial orientation, often erroneously held by the most rational thinkers. The investigation concludes with a general definition of wayfinding and spatial orientation in terms of a spatial problem solving process.

Wayfinding data collected in Montreal's downtown commercial centers is the core around which spatial problem solving is examined in the third and fourth chapters. Three main components of this process are studied: user information processing, decision making, and decision execution. A general conceptual framework is evolved that explains many common and less common observations about wayfinding. Information essential to decision making and decision execution has its source not only in spatial characteristics of the environment, but also in signs, maps, and information booths. Analysis of the shortcomings in the design of these support systems is linked to user information processing capacities, that is, perception, image formation, memory, and learning.

Designing for wayfinding, to which the final chapter is devoted, starts at the architectural and urban conception and provides challenging problems from the planning of large scale spaces to the design and placement of signs, maps, supergraphics, and even the installation of information booths.

Adequate wayfinding design is not synonymous with simplicity and simpleness; environmental complexity stimulates interest, curiosity and exploration. Wayfinding is a dynamic affair. It involves movement through space and a continuous involvement in reading, interpreting, and representing space. Being lost can certainly provoke fear. Sometimes, though, people seek orientation challenges for excitement and pleasure. Wayfinding is closely linked with experiencing space in a physical, mental, and emotional sense. It is no doubt an essential ingredient in architectural appreciation.

A special effort has been made to keep the main argument as simple as possible. The quantity of illustrations and, in particular, the marginal figures complement the written presentation. The extensive use of notes is intended to elaborate a given subject under discussion. This arrangement, it is hoped, leaves the main argument unencumbered and offers different reading choices.

ACKNOWLEDGMENTS

The gestation of this book has been a long but exciting one. The foundations were laid during graduate school at the Pennsylvania State University. I would like to thank in particular Roger Downs, who has been an exceptional teacher and tutor. In 1976 I returned to the University of Montreal where I teach a course on wayfinding and continue my own research. Many graduate students participated in the various projects, and they contributed a great deal in focusing and clarifying my own ideas. In particular I am thinking of Jean-François Bénet, Antoine Boiridy, Louis Canac-Marquis, Gilbert Sauvé, and Fuad Sayad. The manuscript was reviewed by Colin Davidson, Roger Downs, Sylvie Jutras, Amos Rapoport, and Robert Sommer. Their suggestions were stimulating and immensely helpful. I would also like to thank André Corboz and Gwen Shiels who commented on individual chapters.

ROMEDI PASSINI

1

Of Labyrinths and Disorientation

> The advice about turning always to the left reminded me that such was the common formula for finding the central courtyard of certain labyrinths. I know something about labyrinths. Not for nothing am I the great-grandson of Ts'ui Pen. He was Governor of Yunnan and gave up temporal power to write a novel with more characters than there are in the *Hung Lou Meng*, and to create a maze in which all men would lose themselves. He spent thirteen years on these oddly assorted tasks before he was assassinated by a stranger. His novel had no sense to it and nobody ever found his labyrinth.
>
> Borges, "The Garden of Forking Paths" in *Ficciones*.

Jorge Luis Borges, master of intrigue, captures the air of mystery and oddity surrounding labyrinths. The strange task of contriving the perfect maze where all men would lose themselves kept Ts'ui Pen occupied for thirteen years, and men were denied finding the labyrinth even before being denied finding their way in it. A provocative quality characterizes these strange configurations called mazes and labyrinths, and rather contradictory sensations are evoked by the thoughts of getting lost and being disoriented. The maze-maker Ts'ui Pen was something of a bewitched genius commanding attention and even admiration — he was assassinated (?). As will be seen later in this chapter, his assassination, though, is not without meaning.

What can labyrinths tell us about the topic of this book? Spatial orientation and wayfinding subsume an ensemble of complex mental processes. They allow people an idea of surrounding space, of their positions in that space, and they allow purposeful movement within that space. People must reach a great number of destinations during a typical day, and they are normally quite aware of their positions in the surrounding space and in the larger environmental context. Not only are people quite efficient at these movements, but they execute them often in an automatic or semiautomatic fashion. When everything works according to plan, the mental operations required will pass unnoticed. However, the state of being disoriented, of being confused about one's position in a surrounding space and the actions necessary to get out of it, is a deeply felt experience. Such experiences are thought provoking and make the labyrinth, which is the natural symbol of disorientation, an object of contemplation that finds expression in art and folklore. In this sense the labyrinth is a key not so much to the mental process underlying spatial orientation and wayfinding but to its affective significance. A second consideration justifies an interest in labyrinths. Any phenomenon that has gone through some form of evolution is more fully understood if its development over time can be studied. The history of a concept, since it is an abstraction, is not always readily apparent. The best that can be done is to find artifacts that have some constant and important relation to the concept. Given an interest in spatial orientation and wayfinding, what artifact could be more to the point than the labyrinths?

In this introductory chapter I therefore propose a brief historical survey of labyrinths. This overview aims at showing the extent of man's preoccupation with labyrinths and disorientation, and at providing the basis for the subsequent interpretive argument on the nature of that preoccupation; the meanings and sensations associated with complex, labyrinthine environments and the inherent phenomenon of spatial orientation will be the key issues under consideration. By showing the relevance of these issues to existing urban and architectural environments I hope to demonstrate the significance of the topic to planners and users alike.

THE FASCINATION

Etymological Dead End

A method of inquiry, taking into account the historical development of a concept or artifact, is to follow its linguistic formation and meaning. The term "orientation", according to dictionary definitions, has its root in "orient" and the custom in some cultures of situating certain buildings or entrances facing the east. The oldest known building of this type dates from the Egyptian pharaohs of the first dynasty (Rykwert, 1976).

The origin of "Labyrinth" is less clear. From etymological studies emerge four major interpretations. The oldest one, still referred to by most dictionaries, traces the provenance to Greek *Labrus*, "double axe." The sign of the double axe appeared on labyrinthine caverns in Crete and on the palace of Knossos.

This complex palace, called the Palace of the Double Axe *(laburinthos),* is thought to be the source of the term. A second interpretation of "Labyrinth" lies in a dance pattern for the worship of Ariadne or a more ancient earth goddess. As the dance pattern tended to be intricate, it was marked on the ground and referred to as the labyrinth. It is assumed that such a dance pattern may have existed at the palace of Knossos and that it was the origin of the name.[1] In a third interpretation the etymological analysis hinges on the syllables *lab* and *labor,* signifying work, effort, and difficulty. The supporters of this etymology remind us that the Latin spelling *Labor*inthus contains the crucial syllables. A fourth interpretation derives "labyrinth" from some residue of an ancient pre-European language. This analysis links the meaning of the word to stone, a place of stone, or a quarry. Thus labyrinths would come from cave and megalithic cults of a population ancestral to most European cultures.[2]

None of the above theories has been able to muster enough evidence to argue convincingly and exclusively its case. The origin of the labyrinth is further obscured by many popular alternative expressions that are not easily interpreted. "Maze" in English and "Dédale" in French are common alternatives.[3] Others are miz maze, Brower, Troy town, shepherd's race, chemin de Jérusalem, Babylon, Troeborg, Wunderberg, Irrweg.[4] Some are of local usage, some apply only to specific types of labyrinth. So, for example, shepherd's race refers to a maze cut in turf, particular to England, while a chemin de Jérusalem is a church labyrinth found almost exclusively in France and Italy. There may be some consolation in the view that despite the linguists and archaeologists, labyrinths have been able to maintain some of their impenetrable nature. In this spirit Bord (1976) writes that nothing could seem more vain than the attempt to reduce labyrinths to an exclusive definition.

A historical review of labyrinths as manifested in drawings, engravings, buildings, gardens, and in almost every form of human creativity, brings out two striking observations. Labyrinths seem to have appeared continuously in one form or another, from prehistoric times to the present. Furthermore, they have not been limited to one culture or one geographic area. On the contrary, they have appeared on almost all continents in what would seem to be an independent fashion.[5]

Timelessness

Among the oldest known labyrinths are stone engravings found in various parts of Europe. Val Camonica in northern Italy is well known for its rock sites, which exhibit engraved hunting and war scenes, illustrations of various animals, and schematic habitations as well as labyrinthine figures. The example on the

Rock engraving in Tumulus, County Meath, Ireland. *(After Bord, 1976, 26)*

Egyptian labyrinth according to Canina. *(After Matthews, 1970, 15)*

right of Figure 1.1 is of a traditional Cretan form. It has been dated at 500 B.C. The other example might be much older. The incisions in Val Camonica were made over an extensive period from Neolithic, and perhaps even Paleolithic, times up to the Roman conquest. According to Anati (1961), labyrinths represent all major periods of Camunian incision. Probably even older are the labyrinthine incisions discovered in a funeral chamber of Slievena-Calliah, county Meath, Ireland. Radiocarbon analysis has dated them from 3000 to 3500 B.C. (Bord, 1976, 34).

Entrances to Egyptian pyramids were laid out in complex arrangements of underground passages. As can be seen from the plan of the entrance to the pyramid of Mazghuna (twelfth dynasty), the use of meandering paths and heavy granite plugs weighing up to 100 tons were among the devices to delude intruders (Fig. 1.2). Classical scholars, among them Herodotus, describe an actual labyrinth building still intact in 450 B.C. According to these authors, the sepulchral monument for the ruling class and the sacred crocodiles contained many courts and innumerable chambers distributed on two to three levels and linked by winding passages. The layout of approximately 200 by 170 meters was so successfully confusing that an uninitiated visitor could not find a way in or out unless assisted by a guide. The only plan existing today is a rather free restoration by the architect Canina, made during the first part of the nineteenth century.[6]

Ancient Greece probably created the most famous labyrinth myth. The engraving by a member of the Finiguerra school (Fig. 1.3) illustrates the

Figure 1.1
Rock engravings, Capo di Ponte (Val Camonica), Italy.

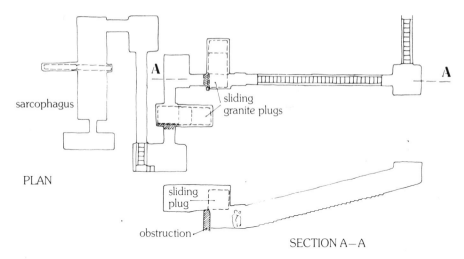

sarcophagus

PLAN

sliding
granite plugs

sliding
plug

obstruction

SECTION A—A

Figure 1.2
Layout of entrance to the pyramid at Mazghuna, Egypt. *(After Badawy, 1966, 110)*

Figure 1.3
Theseus and the Minotaur, engraving from the Finiguerra school.

Coin from Knossos. *(After Matthews, 1970, 44)*

Church labyrinth, cathedral of Chartres.

Wall labyrinth, cathedral of Lucca.

major episodes in which Theseus, aided by Ariadne, combats the dreaded Minotaur inhabiting the labyrinth constructed by the master builder Daedalus.[7] Other examples of Greek labyrinth designs are on coins originating from Knossos. They are dated at around 400 B.C.

In the twelfth and thirteenth centuries, labyrinths had their place in Romanesque and Gothic churches. Magnificent pavement labyrinths exist in the cathedral of Amiens (Fig. 1.4) and in the cathedral of Chartres. The latter has a diameter of almost 13 meters: the length of the complex path is 250 meters. Displayed in the center was probably a figurine or a copper engraving of Theseus and the Minotaur (Villette, 1971). It was not uncommon in the Middle Ages to borrow icons from antiquity and to adapt them to a Christian interpretation.[8]

Church labyrinths were also drawn and sculpted in miniature. A small wall labyrinth displayed in the portico of the cathedral in Lucca is no more than half a meter in diameter.

Hedge or topiary mazes were commonly used in garden architecture of palaces and parks during the post-Renaissance period[9]. Figure 1.5 shows a rather large rectangular maze, of more recent origin, located on the outskirt

Figure 1.4
Church labyrinth; cathedral of Amiens.

Figure 1.5
Hedge maze in Barcelona.

of Barcelona. The hedges are generally tall enough not to allow for the use of reference points outside the maze, and sufficiently uniform to efface reference points inside the maze. A particularly challenging design was proposed for the gardens of Chantilly. Once arrived at the center, only one of the eight paths will lead out again. All the others return to the center, which, perfectly symmetrical and uniform, gives no clues as to the paths already tried. The labyrinth exists today only in the form of a stone engraving.

Turf and stone mazes are more difficult to situate historically. Being cut in turf or marked with rocks or pebbles they had less chance of surviving intact. Usually composed of a single path, their pattern can still be quite complex. Figure 1.6 illustrates an example from Somerton in Oxford Shire. It measures approximately 16 by 18 meters; its path totals 400 meters.

Labyrinth lore is also part of the twentieth century. Not only are references to mazes and labyrinths common in everyday language, but they are still a source of inspiration to writers and artists as a metaphor of contemporary value or as a means of entertainment (Fig. 1.7).[10]

Hedge maze for Chantilly. *(After Bord, 1976, 123)*

Figure 1.6
Turf maze in Oxfordshire. *(After Matthews, 1970, 89)*

Figure 1.7
Contemporary labyrinth by Greg Bright. *(From G. Bright*, Labyrinths, *Latimer, London, labyrinth 23; copyright © 1975 by G. Bright)*

Placelessness

The previous sample of labyrinthine and mazelike patterns has been taken from Mediterranean and European cultures. In China, mortuary urns and pots over 3,000 years old were decorated with labyrinth motifs. A massive bronze container recently discovered from the Zhou dynasty (eleventh century B.C.) shows a decorative frieze in labyrinth patterns (Brinker and Goepper, 1980). India also has a tradition of labyrinths. Layard (1937) reported such motifs in tattoos and in threshold designs. These were originally intended to keep bad spirits from entering a person or a house. Similar threshold designs have also been found in places as distant as Scotland.

Detail from a decorative frieze of an urn, China, Zhou dynasty. *(After Brinker, 1980, 70)*

An intriguing Indian labyrinth example from the Halebid temple at Mysore (Fig. 1.8) describes the battle of a Pandava hero Abhimanyu. He has penetrated the labyrinth constructed by his enemies, the Kaurava warriors, but is losing the fight because he is unable to find his way out (Brooke, 1953).

Labyrinths also exist on the African continent. The Zulus appear to have a game using labyrinth patterns drawn on the ground by players individually or in groups to find a given destination. The game is said to lead to much teasing if a player is unsuccessful. A sacred labyrinth forest in Lome, Togo, has been described to me by an African student. This virgin woods, still in existence, contains intricate trails known only to initiates and dynastic priests. The complexity is said to be such that the intruder may never find his way out.

Evidence of labyrinths on the American continent are less plentiful than in Europe or Asia. There is a legend among the Pima Indians that describes a hero who chose to have his home in a labyrinth. (Heros are known not to be easily found when needed.) Matthews (1922) noted a labyrinth pattern used in various games played by the Pima Indians, but the author was uncertain whether they were of pre-Colombian origin. Since his publication other labyrinths have been found. A copper relief from Argentina, for example, shows a number of labyrinth motifs dated between 700 and 1000.

Relief showing labyrinth patterns, Argentina. *(After Bord, 1976, 150)*

Figure 1.8
Detail from a frieze of the Halebid temple at Mysore. *(After Bord, 1976, 146)*

THE INTERPRETATION

Labyrinths have survived, even if in slightly altered form, the history of at least 5,000 years. They have not just been linked to one cultural group or one geographic area but are truly universal. If one agrees that a most evident and fundamental function of labyrinths is to disorient, one realizes the extent to which mankind has been preoccupied with the phenomena of spatial orientation and wayfinding.[11] In order to get an insight into the nature of this interest, it is necessary to understand what labyrinths meant to the people using them. This is no easy task as the evidence only manifests itself in an indirect way, through the customs associated with the use of labyrinths, through the symbols attached to them in legends and mythology, and to a certain extent, through the physical form of the labyrinth itself.

Fear and the Unknown

The physical form of the labyrinth determines the nature of the orientation task. In this respect, it is possible to differentiate between two types of labyrinth design. The first is characterized by a more or less complex but unique path that, if followed, leads to the center and out again. The challenge in such a design is not to find one's way but to understand the spatial configuration and one's position in it. The simplest version of this type is the spiral design. Such a design, it should be said, appears simple when seen as a figure, but walking in a spiral pattern without ever seeing the total pattern is confusing. Labyrinths of this type developed into the varied and intriguing configurations seen in church labyrinths and turf mazes. Labyrinths composed of a unique path are referred to as unicursal. By contrast, the multicursal type is composed of a number of paths, forking, intersecting, and possibly leading to impasses or dead ends. Here one is not only confronted with the difficulty of identifying one's position in the maze but also of finding the way into a destination and, more important, of finding a way out again. Unicursal labyrinth designs are of older origin; the typical multicursal design only really developed after the Italian Renaissance in the form of hedge mazes.

During antiquity and the Middle Ages, labyrinth designs were currently used as symbols that could mean more than was actually represented. As late as the fifteenth century, the time of the engraving of the Minoan myth by the Finiguerra school, the unicursal design sufficed to communicate the idea of not being able to find one's way, although only one path leads to the center and out again. If the physical form is taken as real, Ariadne's thread was redundant.

Even a labyrinth of the simplest form, such as a spiral, can be said to represent a spatially complex path. Complexity is by definition not easily

Unicursal labyrinth.

Multicursal labyrinth.

grasped; it is associated with unpredictability, the unknown, and the mysterious. It has been assumed that the spiral labyrinth of prehistoric man often represented events that appeared mysterious, such as the cycle of the sun, the events of growing and dying, and so on; the rock engravings illustrated in Figure 1.1 can be seen in that perspective.

When a complex path is taken, not by deities embodying natural events but by man himself, one cannot remain dispassionate. An unpredictable, unknown, and mysterious path is not a sure path; the destination may not be reached. Getting lost and being disoriented are distinct possibilities. The myth of Theseus and the Minotaur is illustrative. The prime characteristic of the labyrinth is to disorient. The Minoan myth is quite specific on that score. Not even Daedalus could escape without resorting to the bird's way. The labyrinth is the dwelling place of the Minotaur. He alone knows its ways, and he represents its danger. It can be argued that the Minotaur stands for the fear, the anxiety, and even the terror of being lost. The image is no doubt a strong one even today. What indeed could be more frightening than a monster, half man, half beast, chasing the disoriented victims along endless paths. Theseus and Ariadne, on the other hand, can be seen as forces combating fear and anxiety. The heroic nature of Theseus stands for the courage needed to fight fear, but courage is evidently not sufficient; to avoid death, Ariadne's knowledge and cunning is also needed. It is, after all, only because of Ariadne's thread that Theseus is able to emerge from the labyrinth after having killed the Minotaur.[12]

Labyrinth incisions of Val Camonica often contain figures associated with demons and monsters. Anati (1961) even assumes the Minotaur myth to have drawn its origin from such prehistoric images. Monster labyrinths show interesting variations: sometimes the monster is being pictured within the labyrinth, sometimes he is himself the labyrinth. The link between disorientation and fear would seem to be even more direct in the latter design.

Comparable ideas have emerged in different sociocultural contexts. Malekula is an island in the northern New Hebrides whose megalithic culture has long attracted anthropologists. A labyrinth myth first published by Layard (1936) describes the path a dead person's spirit has to take to reach the land of death, which is also the land of rebirth. This path is fashioned in the form of a labyrinth, devious and often bewildering. Watching the path is a Guardian Ghost, who obliterates half the labyrinth at a critical moment. In order not to get lost the dead person's spirit has to visualize and remember the pattern of the missing part. The test is crucial. If he fails he will be eaten by the Guardian Ghost.[13] The dead man's journey is unforeseeable and fraught with difficulties. There is even a possibility that he will not arrive at the desired destination, as is symbolized by the path in the form of a labyrinth. The analogy between the Guardian Ghost and the Minotaur is possible on two accounts. Both represent danger, both can be defeated. The Guardian Ghost is powerless against

Double spiral, interpreted as a sun symbol.

Monster labyrinth from Val Camonica. (After Anati, 1961, 216, 217)

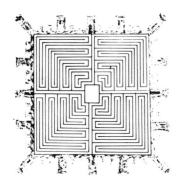

Labyrinth city, Roman floor mosaic.
(After Bord, 1976, 79)

knowledge, the dead man's understanding of the path, while the Minotaur dies by the hand of a hero.

Labyrinths evoke the fear of being lost and the danger associated with not finding one's way. This fear can, however, be put to good use. In antiquity labyrinths were applied in real and symbolic form to exclude the unwanted or at least the uninitiated. The Egyptian pyramids and the labyrinth building referred to by Herodotus are such concrete physical applications aimed at protecting funeral chambers from hostiles or predatory incursions.

The idea of exclusion and conditional passage also found use in the protection of urban agglomerations. The labyrinth served here as a defensive system.[14] Winding, narrow access to cities and complex layers of walls are frequently mentioned in literature. A Roman floor mosaic of late Republican date illustrates a labyrinth enclosed by what look like city walls. The labyrinth has a rather uncommon disposition of paths representing city streets.

The most interesting aspect of the labyrinth was magical or, as expressed in modern terminology, psychological. A city that was seen as a labyrinth or protected by a labyrinth was understood by the enemy to be difficult or impossible to enter. A labyrinth was indeed a protective device of some magical strength. According to Knight (1935) and Hildburgh (1945), the magic was kept alive and perhaps advertised by ritual labyrinth dances, which may explain some common terms to describe labyrinths.[15]

Labyrinths in Romanesque and Gothic church architecture have had various contradictory interpretations. Doublet de Boisthibault (1851) proposed that the creation of these designs was merely intended as a monument to the builders of the cathedrals or even as a pastime.[16] Ainé Dideron (1852) rejected this hypothesis and proposed a deeper religious significance. In his opinion the labyrinth symbolized the difficult and unpredictable path of life on earth that a person's soul had to travel before reaching the heavenly home.[17]

The labyrinth is again the ideal metaphor. The many detours that at times approach the center and at times move off correspond to the Christian idea of trials and struggles against temptation. The unicursal nature of the labyrinth reinforces at the same time the idea that Christians must follow the one and only route to salvation. The church labyrinth represents, still according to Dideron, a means for devotion, a form of prayer and penitence in which the believer undertakes a spiritual journey to the Holy Land.[18]

The church labyrinths were not always used for penitence, and the clergy did not always approve of their existence. The canon Jean-Baptiste Souchet, who died in 1654, wondered why these labyrinths had a place in churches when they served for nothing but crazy games in which those who have nothing to do spend their time turning and running.[19] The canon was specifically referring to the cathedral of Chartres.

Dideron (1852) also records that the labyrinths, having lost their pious meaning, became a favorite game for children, who ran it with a great deal of noise, interfering with the church service.[20] This all led to the destruction of

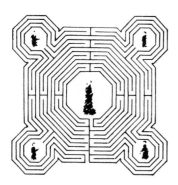

Destroyed church labyrinth of Rheims.
(After Matthews, 1970, 61)

many labyrinths by order of the church. The beautiful labyrinth in Rheims, for example, was torn out and paved over after 500 years of existence.

The use of church labyrinths for penitence does not deviate greatly from the meaning given to the mazes of antiquity. They still symbolize a difficult unpredictable path, strewn with danger. To run the maze for entertainment gives it quite a different meaning.

Hedge maze at Hampton Court.

Pleasure and the Unknown

If church labyrinths were misused by running around for thrills, turf mazes and the somewhat related stone mazes were built for that very purpose. An antiquarian writing in the eighteenth century, comments on the popularity of turf mazes and refers, somewhat disparingly, to the joy they gave the "inferior classes." "They always speak of 'em [the turf mazes] with great pleasure, as if there was something extraordinary in the thing, though they cannot tell what" (Matthews, 1970, 77). Turf mazes must have provided stimulation for people. It is hardly coincidence that turf mazes were also called "shepherd's race." To tread a maze while the flock was grazing provided an acceptable relief from boredom.

Mazelike figures are also found in childrens' play, fulfilling a similar stimulating function. These figures are often drawn on pavements or traced in sand. Pliny, in the *Natural History* (XXXII.5), mentions the existence of such labyrinths. In describing the labyrinth supposedly built by Daedalus in Crete Pliny praises its intricacy and its superior quality that was not to be compared with those drawings the Roman boys made in the sand.

Inscription in the center of the maze, Hampton Court.

Hedge mazes were also designed for amusement and entertainment. They were very popular in all parts of Europe. During the sixteenth century books illustrating the design and plantation of hedge mazes were published.[21] Some mazes are still in existence and even used today. The famous maze at Hampton Court outside London is one such example. It is of an irregular trapezoidal shape and, like most hedge mazes, of a multicursal nature. The total length is about 800 meters. The clipped hedges lining the path are more than a man's height and over half a meter thick in average. In the center of the labyrinth is a little square with two trees. For good reasons they are each protected by a wooden fence. On this fence people can express their feelings without damaging the trees. Retained is one graffito that expressed well my own feelings: "Getting there is only half the problem."

The maze is still immensely popular with children and also with adults of all ages. Children get particularly excited. Twenty children in the maze sound just like a crowded public swimming pool on a hot school-free afternoon. Not only are they excited, but they also get annoyed and a bit anxious when they do not find their way out. While trying to find my own way I could not help overhearing "I'm lost. This is ridiculous . . . Let's climb over the fence . . . Help, help. I have been in here for half and hour. I'm going to starve."

Children at the exit of Hampton Court.

Adults in the maze are, of course, less demonstrative and a bit more cautious. According to the superintendent, many adults inquire whether they will actually get lost before they decide to purchase a ticket.[22] It also happens that the management has to open a special gate to let someone out. Even a little observation tower is provided for emergencies, and occasionally they occur. It is particularly the elderly who tend to need help. An unfortunate incident ended with a broken leg when a panic-stricken senior gentleman tried to climb the hedge.

Hedge mazes, by disorienting people, by getting them momentarily lost, and by allowing for the unexpected, are a source of enjoyment of a rather complex sort. Hennebo (1962), in a discussion of garden labyrinths, links the feeling of pleasure with sensations of confusion, fear, surprise, curiosity, and anxiety.[23]

What emerges is a second major meaning of the labyrinth expressed in the way it is used to provoke excitement, stimulation and curiosity. Complex environments that challenge wayfinding can be highly valued by the user. Even the sensations associated with being lost or with not finding the way can be an exciting experience. It has to be specified that in the labyrinth example certain conditions that might be crucial are met. The person is prepared and chooses to undergo such an experience. He or she knows that the time during which they will feel lost will be limited, and that no real danger awaits. Even so, as the Hampton Court example shows, the Minotaur has been known to appear. Probably the most important aspect of the labyrinth as a source of entertainment is the challenge it offers to cope against all odds and despite the rascally master builder.

LABYRINTHS IN DISGUISE

Labyrinths may be seen to belong to the realm of mythology, the arts, the churches of the Middle Ages, and eccentric gardens. But do they? The following pages are devoted to a few selected urban and architectural examples chosen for their complicated and confusing layouts. No attempt will be made to assess their defaults or merits. The reader, who will most certainly recall similar examples, is asked to view the predominantly pictorial presentation by simply keeping in mind the Minotaur and pleasure gardens.

Ancient Cities

Palombara Sabina is a small town located approximately half an hour's drive northeast of Rome. The settlement of less than 10,000 people has grown around a castle occupying the top of a cone-shaped hill. Founded in the eleventh century, it reached its full intermural development during the seventeenth century.[24]

The town plan is composed of a more or less concentric or spiral street system winding around a hill. Figure 1.9 shows the oldest part of Palombara with its castle in the center. It will be noticed that the streets do not follow a clear pattern; they frequently fork, and as is not visible from the plan, they go up and down hill. Steep passages are the irregular links from one street to the other. All traffic turns in a clockwise direction. The houses are built close together, and streets are sufficiently narrow to prevent a view up to the castle or down into the Roman *campagna*. A comparison between Palombara and a classical circular labyrinth such as is shown in Figure 1.10 is suggestive.

An Italian town morphologically quite different from Palombara is Martina Franca, a historical center of about 20,000 inhabitants, located in Puglia. Its foundation dates back to the tenth century when the slightly elevated plateau was chosen as its site. The houses are close together, as can be seen from the aerial view of Figure 1.11. What surprises most though is the apparent chaos of the street network. The streets are often narrow, always crooked, and

Typical street in Palombara.

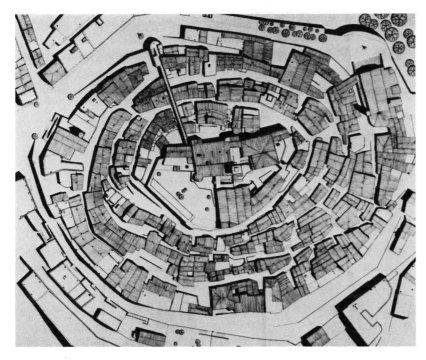

Figure 1.9
Nucleus of Palombara Sabina. *(Drawing by Lorenzo di Paolis)*

Figure 1.10
Juxtaposition of aerial view of Palombara and a labyrinth engraving by Hieronymus Cook.
(Aerial view of Palombara from E. Guidoni, La Città Europea, Electa, Milan, 1978, p. 89;
copyright © 1978 by Electa)

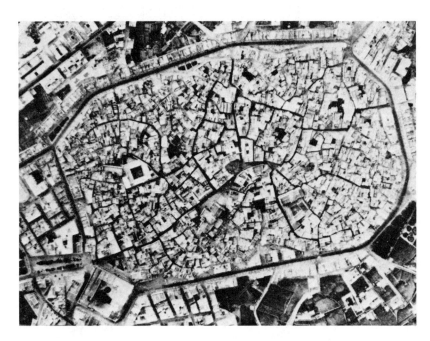

Figure 1.11
Martina Franca, aerial view of the old city. *(From E. Guidoni,* La Città Europea, Electa, Milan,
1978, p. 86; copyright © 1978 by Electa)

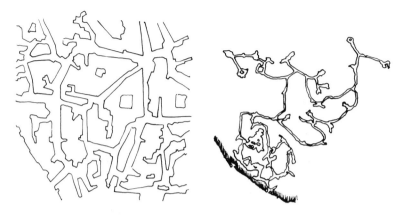

Figure 1.12
Juxtaposition of streets in Martina Franca and labyrinth caves of Gortyna, Crete.

Typical dead-end street in Martina Franca.

usually end in impasses. The evolution of Martina Franca and the origin of its morphology is a disputed subject, although, as will be seen in Chapter 4, the street pattern is of a distinctly Islamic nature.[25]

How closely a street layout from Martina Franca drawn to scale ressembles the labyrinth pattern of Gortyna on Crete is evident from Figure 1.12. The labyrinthine nature of Martina Franca has also been evoked by the Italian historian Montuori:

Getting lost in this labyrinth is a natural occurrence. Only a few reference points mark the urban fabric there is only one square, two major churches. The door and window decorations of residences belonging to the bourgeoisie, although different from one another, seem all to be made by the same family of artisans. (Free translation from the Italian, Montuori, 1969, 126)[26]

Contemporary Buildings

If it is possible to compare city plans to labyrinths, the resemblance is even more evident at the building scale, though graphically perhaps more difficult to show. The regular pattern of highly complex labyrinths, such as that drawn by Greg Bright, for example, cannot be found in any building. The reader should keep in mind that, unlike a drawing, no overall view is offered when a person walks along a corridor. Not only is it impossible to see what is happening on the other side of the wall, but the conditions are repeated on other visually inaccessible levels. In the following examples, only the circulation routes and the public spaces are drawn. This unusual way of drawing an interior corresponds to the space viewed and experienced by the visitor. No doors are indicated on the plan.

Section of a Labyrinth drawing by Greg Bright. *(From G. Bright,* Labyrinths, *Latiwer, London, labyrinth 8; copyright © 1975 by G. Bright*

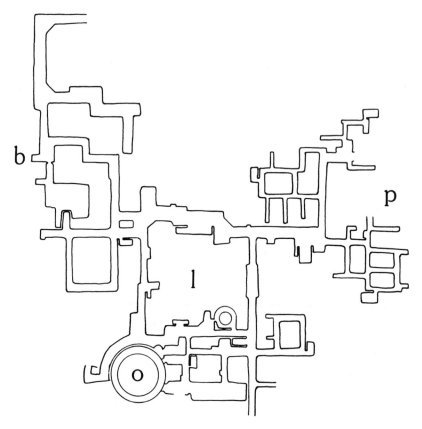

Figure 1.13
Circulation system of ground floor of Life Science Center, Halifax.

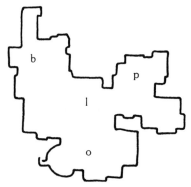

Building form corresponding to Figure 1.13.

The Life Science Center of Dalhousie University in Halifax (Nova Scotia) accommodates three departments: biology (b), oceanography (o), and psychology (p). Linking the three departments are the central lecture halls (l). Each departmental section is characterized by specific space requirements for the laboratories. Small experimental rooms surrounded by control rooms, each with individual access, lead to the complicated corridor system exemplified in Figure 1.13. Because of strict controls for temperature, light, and sound, very few windows were provided. The departmental buildings are up to six stories high, amplifying the complexity shown on the plan.

Other examples of labyrinthine layouts are often found in hospitals. Having a tendency to grow in a piecemeal fashion, the paths can be extremely

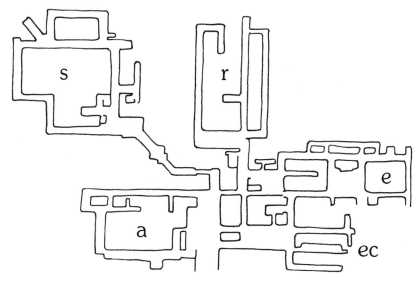

Figure 1.14
Circulation system of ground floor of Hospital Charles Le Moyne, Montréal.

complex, intricate and unpredictable. The Hospital Charles Le Moyne in Montreal, shown in Figure 1.14, has the following services on the ground floor: emergency (e), external clinic (ec), radiology (r), sismotherapy (s), and administration (a). All these services are accessible to the public, if it can find them. Routes often end in cul-de-sacs, there are parallel passages difficult to distinguish, open angles, and considerable distances to be walked to reach certain destinations.

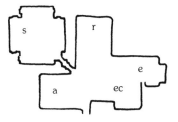

Building form corresponding to Figure 1.14.

Architecture of Contemplation

Labyrinths in disguise are also present in Islamic architecture. The mosque in Cordoba, constructed and expanded over several centuries, presents the viewer with a complex arrangement of columns and vaults. It is the decorative motifs found outside and inside, on the facade (Fig. 1.15), on windows and doors, and also on ceilings, panels, and ceramic tiles, that evoke the strongest associations with labyrinths. The motifs are often composed in continuous bands, intricately woven in three dimensions. Figure 1.15 illustrates these characteristics; Figure 1.16 compares a contemporary labyrinth design with a decorative wall panel of the mosque.

Inside view of mosque in Cordoba.

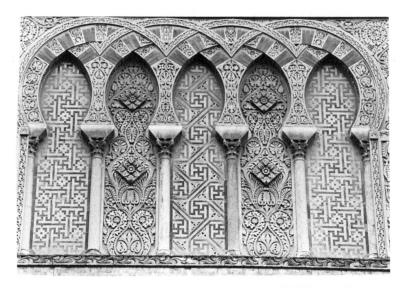

Figure 1.15
Mosque in Cordoba, decorative detail of elevation.

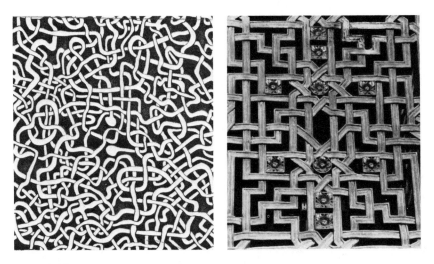

Figure 1.16
Juxtaposition of labyrinth drawing by Greg Bright and decorative panel at mosque in Cordoba.
(Labyrinth drawing from G. Bright, Labyrinths, *Latimer, London, Labyrinth 8; copyright ©1975 by G. Bright)*

CONVERGING PATHS

The maze builder Ts'ui Pen was assassinated by a stranger; the Minotaur and the Guardian Ghost still exert their symbolic grip over the labyrinth and the labyrinth in disguise. Disorientation is a problem that has preoccupied mankind in the past and as the built environment has grown in size and complexity, it has intensified. Disorientation can provoke frustration and stress and may have disastrous consequences. Kevin Lynch takes a particularly strong stand in his *Image of the City*. He notes that to get completely lost is a rare occurrence but:

Let the mishap of disorientation occur and the sense of anxiety and even terror that accompanies it reveals to us how closely it is linked to our sense of balance and well being. The very word "lost" in our language means much more than simple geographical uncertainty: it carries a tone of utter disaster. (Lynch, 1960, 4)

In light of the discussion on labyrinths, this statement would seem to reflect only one side of the argument. Nevertheless, many instances demonstrate how strongly the sensation of being lost is felt. During studies on orientation carried out in Montréal, it was a common occurrence to find people who would not frequent certain shopping complexes for no other reason than their fear of getting lost. Others disliked underground multilevel parking lots. They would not use them, or if they really had no alternative, they would try always to find the same spot, "their spot," or a place in its immediate vicinity. The experience of being lost tends also to engender feelings of incompetence. It has not been uncommon for our subjects to return to the experimenter after a test just to chat—and to let him know that they do not usually get so lost.

Problems of disorientation and wayfinding can be seen from an individual emotional basis and also in terms of a person's efficient functioning in a setting and the effort, physical and mental, to find places. In this perspective it is possible to evaluate the functional efficiency of the built environment for wayfinding. Stea and his collaborators (Stea, 1979), for example, used a cost factor as an efficiency criterion to assess a large hospital complex in Los Angeles. This cost factor was established by direct disorientation cost (time lost finding one's way, time spent giving directions to other users, time spent learning new routes) and by indirect disorientation cost (stress and the concomittant effects on absenteeism and personnel turnover). The building's complexity as well as the regular relocation of departments and services in the hospital were responsible for high inefficiency costs.

Problems of spatial disorientation have led to disastrous consequences. Fatalities have actually been attributed to the difficulty of finding an address in a residential development. Downs and Stea (1977) report the incident of an ambulance incapable of locating a given apartment in an emergency. That

MONTRÉAL TRANSPORT LIMITÉ
PRÉSENTE : « TRANSPORT MENTAL »

NOWHERE.

MONTRÉAL TRANSPORT LIMITÉE

TRANS TL
DE L'HÔTEL NELSON
PLACE JACQUES-CARTIER

DU MERCREDI 22 AU DIMANCHE 26
A 21 H 30 SAUF SAMEDI ET DIMANCHE A 22 H
ENTRÉE : 5 $

A show inspired by the "Nowhere" bus. *(From* la Presse, *April 25, 1981, p. C10, reprinted with permission)*

the situation is not more reassuring on the hospital's side, is evident from the labyrinth in disguise (Charles Le Moyne, described above). Buildings are often difficult for wayfinding under normal conditions, but very particular and often critical wayfinding problems occur when buildings have to be urgently evacuated as in the case of fire.[27]

The built environment, whether at the city or building scale, has to be safe and has to function efficiently. Wayfinding and spatial orientation are important aspects of an efficient environment. However, there is a distinct danger of falling into a simplistic functionalism, a movement that has led to so many uninspiring, even monotonous, environments. The meaning of "misused" church labyrinths or turf and hedge mazes and the many other forms of maze is that people are far from disliking a certain level of spatial complexity and the presence of a certain challenge to wayfinding.[28] Spatial complexity and the unknown awaken curiosity and the desire to explore. The factors of surprise, of discovery, all contribute to a full spatial experience. Significant in this context was the popularity of a bus service in Montréal called "Nowhere." It took people on an unspecified itinerary for an evening's entertainment.

Labyrinths in disguise will have shown, if indeed such a demonstration was necessary, that many environments do have distinct labyrinthine features. Some historic towns like Polombara Sabina and Martina Franca may have been built with the idea of a labyrinth as a psychological and defensive device in mind. Today this meaning, if ever it was an important factor, is most certainly lost. To an unaccustomed visitor the mazelike disposition of the layout may be bewildering, but soon the joy of exploring the sinuous streets of these towns becomes one of their exciting aspects. The irregular curves and open-angled intersections make it very difficult for the visitor to situate himself. At moments he will wonder where the streets will lead him and, when finally recognizing one landmark or another, there is the thrill of the puzzle solved or the surprise of the unexpected: "Ah . . . that's where we are." The architecture of the mosque in Cordoba will not get anyone lost, but it may well allow a person to be absorbed by its forest of columns and the intricacies of its decorations. In this sense the mosque allows the worshiper to "lose himself" in contemplation and meditation. In contrast to these profound effects that labyrinthine designs can have, the chosen examples of contemporary public buildings are no doubt labyrinthine by mistake and ignorance. Although not consciously designed to get people lost, they achieve it to a remarkable degree but only to the dismay of the user.

The reader will agree that no simple design recommendation and certainly no building norm can be formulated to do justice to the intricate experience that wayfinding and spatial orientation represent. It would be just as erroneous to advocate a simple environment as to opt for any complex one. The process of spatial orientation and wayfinding has to be understood before questions of physical planning can be broached. This understanding may also benefit all those who have problems getting around in today's complex environment. They may become better wayfinders by knowing where the major difficulties lie and what to look for to get a better grasp of the place they are in. The knowledge of the labyrinth pattern was after all an essential requirement to bypass the Guardian Ghost.

A priority for urbanists, architects, and designers of sign systems is no doubt to achieve a workable, efficient environment. Chapter 4 will show all too clearly that even places designed with a certain awareness and knowhow leave much to be desired on the level of wayfinding. It is hoped, however, that this book may assist in going a little further. The real challenge for the planner is to provide for an efficient as well as an interesting, stimulating environment where people feel at ease.

NOTES

1. De Vries (1957) argues that many of the hopping games children play can be traced to these ritual dances.
2. For an etymological argument based on *labrus*, the double axe, see Evans (1921); for the dance pattern interpretation see Layard (1936), and De Vries (1957); for megalithic origins see Guentert (1932) and Cagiano de Azevedo (1958).
3. It is interesting that the verb "to amaze" carries overtones of wonder and of being over-whelmed. The French "Dédale," on the other hand, is associated with Daedalus, derived from *dai-dalos*, which signifies to work artfully. It could be argued that if the term "maze" tends to view the labyrinth from the perspective of experience and sensations, *dédale* emphasizes the labyrinth as artifact. This distinction is hardly made in everyday language.
4. For a detailed etymological discussion of labyrinths and many of the alternative terms mentioned, see Matthews (1970), chapter 20 (pp. 170-181), and Cagiano de Azevedo (1958). For the etymology of Troy town see Knight (1935).
5. For a general review, the reader is advised to consult the attractive publication by Bord (1976) and a classic in labyrinthology by Matthews (1922, reprinted in 1970).
6. The construction of the original labyrinth is attributed to the reign of Amenemhat III (twelfth dynasty). Unfortunately, nothing remains of it. During the Roman occupation it served as a convenient stone quarry to build a nearby village.
7. At the lower right-hand corner of the engraving, Theseus receives the saving thread from Ariadne. To the left, the hero is seen disappearing into a tower leading to the labyrinth and to the combat with the Minotaur; the thread is carefully fixed on the outside of the tower. Having killed the Minotaur, the hero returns to Athens in company of Ariadne, but somehow he leaves her on the island of Delos (upper left). The sailing boat is shown heading for Athens. Having failed to replace the black sails for white ones, as previously agreed, the Athenians believe the hero dead. At the top corner to the right, the hero's father, Aegeus, can be seen throwing himself from a tower into the sea.
8. For an analysis of various icon adaptations during the Middle Ages, see Panofsky (1939, reprinted in 1972).
9. The term "topiary" is of Roman origin. It is possible that these mazes already existed during Roman times, although none of the classical chronicles specifically noted their existence.
10. In literature see J. L. Borges in most of his writing and particularly in *Ficciones* (1962) and Durrell in *Dark Labyrinth* (1947); among the many contemporary painters and sculptors

interested in the labyrinth metaphor are Michael Ayrton, Friedensreich Hundertwasser, André Masson, Marie-Hélenè Vieira da Silva.

11. Labyrinths also served for rites of initiation and moral purification. Often these different functions overlap and intermingle. Artifacts and vocabulary of one function become adopted for another. Many expressions related to labyrinths and wayfinding, such as "to be amazed," "to be lost," "to turn in circles," are used in a figurative sense.

12. For a quite different interpretation of the Minoan myth, see Knight (1935).

13. It is hardly a coincidence that the phenomenon of getting lost, which is one of the great dangers to a seafaring population, is also present in the expression of man's last journey.

14. The idea has reemerged in contemporary planning. Abraham Moles (1978) suggests labyrinthine dwelling layouts to assure adequate privacy (access control) with a minimum of security devices.

15. The Troy legend has been interpreted by Knight (1935) and Hildburgh (1945) in these terms. In order to break the magic spell of the labyrinth protecting Troy, a counterspell had to be devised by the conqueror. This took the form of the wooden horse. Troy, Troy town, Troy wall, and many other derivations may be traced to this legend.

16. The argument was based on a few selected cases. A church labyrinth in Rheims indeed showed four figures in each corner and one in the center which were identified with the builders of the cathedral. Similarly, in Amiens the center is supposed to represent the bishop and three architects in charge of construction.

17. "L'emblème de la route, difficile et féconde en égarements, que l'âme, placée au seuil de la vie, doit parcourir avant d'arriver au céleste séjour" (Dideron, 1852, 150).

18. "Un moyen de dévotion, une forme spéciale de prières dans laquelle le chrétien s'acquittait en esprit du voyage de la terre sainte" (Dideron, 1852, 147).

19. "Labyrinthe de plomb, que je m'étonne qu'on ait mis, n'étant qu'un amuse fol, auquel ceux qui n'ont rien à faire, perdent leur temps à tourner et à courir" (from Villette, 1971, 265).

20. "Ayant perdu de vue l'idée pieuse qui avait donné lieu à leur établissement, ils étaient devenus un obstacle à la solemnité des offices, les enfants les parcourant sans cesse avec grand bruit" (Dideron, 1852, 147).

21. Two examples are Thomas Hyll, *A Moste Briefe and Pleasant Treatyse Teachinge How to Dress, Sowe and Set a Garden* (1563), later republished as *The Gardener's Labyrinth,* and Jan Vredeman de Vries, *Hortorum Viridarioumque Formae* (1583).

22. The superintendent, whom everyone trusts, has never been in the maze and has no intention of ever going there herself, I was told. She suffers from claustrophobia.

23. "Bei den Irrgärten, den wirklichen Gartenlabyrinthen lag das eigentliche Ziel (jetzt) darin, Verwirrung und Schrecken, Üeberraschung, Neugier und Angst zu erwecken" (Hennebo, 1962; I, 106-107).

24. I am grateful to the town architect Lorenzo de Paolis and the cultural center Il Cenacolo for their hospitality and the abundance of information.

25. The Islamic origin of many southern European cities founded around the tenth century, and particularly Martina Franca, has been argued by Guidoni (1978); see also Brandi (1968) and Montuori (1969).

26. "Perdersi in questo labirinto e la cosa più facile del mondo. I punti fermi della trama urbanistica sono pochi; la piazza e una sola, le chiese importanti due. I portali dei palazzi, pur deversi l'uno dall'altro, sembrano fatti tutti della stessa famiglia di artigiani" (Montuori, 1969, 126).

27. Relatively little information is available on how people behave when faced with fires in buildings, and even less is known on how they find their way in such conditions. Interviews with people who have experienced major fires show no evidence of the commonly accepted irrational and panic-induced behavior (Wood, 1980). Various authors argue that the association of panic and fires does not hold as long as an escape route appears feasible to the victim (Sime, 1980; Canter et al., 1980). Legislation and building codes

are often based on such false behavioral premises that are not only overcautious but can actually reduce chances of escape. Delays in warning and ambiguous messages, often used in public places to avoid mass panic, are examples.

28. In the literature, complexity has been treated as a phenomenon of perception. Attempts have been made to establish desired levels of stimulation (see Wohlwill, 1968, and Berlyne, 1966). Complexity has also been discussed as a design requirement. Venturi (1966) and Rapoport (1967) have argued for ambiguity of form as a means to achieve complexity.

REFERENCES

Anati, E., 1961, *Camonica Valley,* Alfred Knopf, New York.

Badawy, A., 1966, *A History of Egyptian Architecture,* University of California Press, Berkeley.

Berlyne, D. E., 1966, "Curiosity and Exploration," *Science* **153**(3731):25-33.

Bord, J., 1976, *Mazes and Labyrinths of the World,* Latimer New Dimensions, London.

Borges, J. L., 1962, *Ficciones,* Grove Press, New York.

Brandi, C., 1968, *Martina Franca,* Guido le Noci, Milano.

Bright, G., 1975, *Labyrinths,* Latimer, London.

Brooke, S. C., 1953, "The Labyrinth Pattern in India," *Folk-Lore* **64**(4):463-472.

Brinker, H., and R. Goepper, 1980, *Kunstschätze aus China,* Kunsthaus Zürich, Zürich.

Cagiano de Azevedo, M., 1958, *Saggio sul Labirinto,* Vita e Pensiero, Milan.

Canter, D., ed., 1980, *Fires and Human Behavior,* John Wiley and Sons, New York.

Canter, D., J. Breaux, and J. Sime, 1980, "Domestic, Multiple Occupancy, and Hospital Fires," in *Fires and Human Behavior,* D. Canter, ed., John Wiley and Sons, New York, pp.117-136.

De Boisthibault, D., 1851, "Notice sur le labyrinthe de la cathédrale de Chartres," *Revue Archéologique,* Septième annèe, première partie, pp. 437-447.

De Vries, J., 1957, "Untersuchung über das Hüpfspiel," Helsinky," *FF Communications* **70**(173):51-83.

Dideron, A., 1852, "Essai sur le pavage des églises antérieurement au 15e siècle," *Annales Archéologiques* **12**:233-305.

Downs, R., and D. Stea, 1977, *Maps in Minds,* Harper and Row, New York.

Durrell, L., 1947, *The Dark Labyrinth,* Faber, London.

Evans, A. J., 1921, *The Palace of Minos at Knossos,* Macmillan, London.

Fusco, V., and M. Roberti, 1976, *Guida Illustrata del Parco Nacionale delle Incisioni Rupestri,* Erregi, Milan.

Guentert, H., 1932, *Labyrinth,* Sitzungsberichte der Heidelberger Akademie der Wissenschaften, Heidelberg.

Guidoni, E., 1978, *La Città Europea,* Electa, Milano.

Hennebo, D., 1962, *Geschichte der deutschen Gartenkunst,* Broschek Verlag, Hamburg.

Hildburgh, W. L., 1945, "The Place of Confusion and Indeterminability in Mazes and Maze-Dances," *Folk-Lore* **56**(1):188-192.

Knight, W. F. J., 1935, "Myth and Legend at Troy," *Folk-Lore* **46**(2):98-121.

Layard, J., 1936, "Maze-Dances and the Ritual of the Labyrinth in Malekula," *Folk-Lore* **42**(2):123-170.

Lynch, K., 1960, *The Image of the City,* MIT Press, Cambridge, Mass.

Matthews, W. H., 1970, *Mazes and Labyrinths: Their History and Development,* Dover Publications, New York.

Moles, A., and E. Rohmer, 1978, *Psychologie de l'espace,* Casterman, Paris.

Montuori, E., 1969, "La città murata di Martina Franca," *L'Architettura, Cronache e Storia,* no. 164.

Panofsky, E., 1972, *Studies in Iconology,* Harper and Row, New York.

Rapoport, A., and R. E. Kantor, 1967, "Complexity and Ambiguity in Environmental Design," *Journal of the American Institute of Planners* **33:**210-221.

Rykwert, J., 1976, *The Idea of Town*, Princeton University Press, Princeton, N.J.

Sime, J. D., 1980, "The Concept of 'Panic,'" in *Fires and Human Behavior*, D. Canter, ed., John Wiley and Sons, New York, pp. 3-81.

Stea, D., ed., 1979, *Hospital Orientation Project*, School of Architecture and Urban Planning, UCLA, Los Angeles.

Venturi, R., 1966, *Complexity and Contradiction in Architecture*, Museum of Modern Art, New York.

Villette, J., 1971, "Quand Thesée et le Minotaure ont-ils disparu du labyrinthe de la cathédrale de Chartres?" *Mémoires de la Société Archéologieque d'Eure et Loir* **25:**255-270.

Wohlwill, J., 1968, "Amount of Stimulus Exploration and Preference or Differential Functions of Stimulus Complexity," *Perception and Psychophysics* **4**(5):307-312.

Wood, P. G., 1980, "A Survey of Behaviors in Fires," in *Fires and Human Behavior*, D. Canter, ed., John Wiley and Sons, New York, pp. 83-95.

2

What Are Spatial Orientation and Wayfinding?

Frédérique stopped his yellow Beetle at the edge of a vast forest, stretching over an undulating landscape. Equipped with our knives and baskets, we bashed through the wood, up and down small gullies looking for mushrooms during the greater part of the afternoon. On our return, we were again surprised at the ease by which we found our point of origin, and at the precision by which we walked toward the yellow Beetle . . . , as if guided by a sixth sense. *(Author's personal notes)*

ORIENTATION, IN SEARCH OF A SENSE

The reader does not have to run the risks of the amateur mycologist to experience similar surprises and feelings of satisfaction at the relatively effortless accomplishment of a seemingly difficult wayfinding task. Not everybody has the same confidence in this ability. Indeed, some pride themselves in having a good sense of orientation; others may admit that their sense is not always good or that they lack it altogether. It is common in everyday language to refer to a sense of orientation. We have to ask ourselves what is meant by such a sense and whether its existence is borne out by concrete evidence.

Sense of Direction

A sense of orientation is usually equated with a sense of direction, that is, an ability to maintain a direction while moving, or to point to a direction independently of one's location in space and independently of cues originating from the environment. By a sense of orientation people describe a supposed reliance on themselves and not on the environment to perform tasks that necessitate a knowledge of direction.

Darwin, in an essay on instincts published posthumously in 1883, probed the mystery of migration in animals.[1] He distinguished between the instinct impelling the animal to migrate at a certain period and "the unknown means by which they can tell one direction from another, and by which, after starting, they are able to keep their course" (Darwin in Romanes, 1883, 356). This astonishing capability is described as an "unknown power" by which not only many animals but also "savage men" can keep on course. Although, to my reading, Darwin does not specifically explain these observed performances of wayfinding as instinct, he does quote travel reports in which such an innate sense is postulated.[2] In particular, he refers to a Russian explorer, Admiral Ferdinand Wrangell, who commanded an expedition to the polar sea in 1820: "the experienced navigator Wrangell expatiates with astonishment on the 'unerring instinct' of the natives of northern Siberia, by which they guided him. Wrangell was . . . trying to reason the true route, the native had always a perfect knowledge of it instinctively"[3] (Darwin in Romanes, 1883, 357).

Other explorers have commented in their journals on the surprising abilities of indigenous people to find their way in what appeared difficult environments. George Grey, governor of South Australia, reported from an expedition in western Australia that "the natives have a faculty, even in the trackless woods which they have never before been in, of returning direct to any spot they have left, by however circuitous a course they may have travelled after quitting it" (Grey, 1841, 72).

A careful reading of these accounts often reveals alternative explanations of the native's wayfinding performances. Wrangell, in describing the skillful piloting of his sledge driver, noted:

In the midst of the intricate labyrinths of ice, turning sometimes to the right and sometimes to the left, now winding round a large hummock, now crossing over a smaller one, among such incessant changes of direction he seemed to have a plan of them all in his memory. (Wrangell, 1845, p. 140)

Even more important, the explorer enumerates the various landmarks used to maintain a constant direction, which comprised remarkable pieces of ice in the distance, wavelike ridges, and snowdrifts formed by known prevailing winds. Far from relying on themselves, the sledge drivers were referring extensively to environmental cues for wayfinding.

Despite these observations, the idea of an instinctive sense of orientation prevailed even among scientists. At the turn of the century, some psychologists set out to prove its existence. Again they postulated that some people had an unfailing sense of direction, a kind of internal compass, upon which they could rely in all situations. Howard and Templeton (1966) summarize the disappointing outcome in the following manner:

Warren (1908) described a boy with what he called a "magnetic sense of direction." He attempted to disorient him but was not successful. Twenty two years later De Silva (1931) located this person who disclaimed ever having had any special magnetic sense. (Howard and Templeton, 1966, 266)

Other claims for a sense of direction have been shown to be unfounded when the data was checked. A Russian psychologists (Shemyakin, 1962), for example, notes that the "pure" sense of direction attributed to Australian aborigines was no more than an excellent memory of places visited.

If man was equipped with a sense of direction he should be able to maintain a direction without relying on cues from the environment. He should be able to walk straight ahead when blindfolded. This again has been shown to be impossible. Shemyakin (1962) records one of these experiments:

100 trainee pilots were lined up. They were all blind-folded and ordered to march directly forward. At first they walked straight ahead, then some of them began to turn to the right, others . . . to the left and gradually began to walk in circles and back track. (Shemyakin, 1962, 193-194)

The wayfinding performance that most people are capable of is rather astonishing, if the magnitude of certain tasks is taken into consideration. From an evolutionary perspective, it is quite evident that humans had to be good at it to survive as a species. Hunters and gatherers had to get around in an environment that seemed rather undifferentiated, and finding their way was a question of life and death.

The extraordinary ease and efficiency by which chosen destinations can be reached is probably the key reason for the popular association between wayfinding and an innate, special sense of orientation. However, other difficult tasks are executed in a similarly effortless fashion. The analogy with driving a car is illustrative. During our first driving lesson were we not all painfully aware of all the operations needed to get the car moving: accelerating, decompressing the clutch, shifting gears, turning the blinker on, looking in the rear view mirror, remembering to brake, and so on? Once experienced, a task as complicated as driving through a traffic-congested city while talking to a friend happens almost as if we, as drivers, had little to do with it. Again, a claim for a sixth, or by now seventh, sense of driving is thinkable, were it not for our memory of the learning process. We do not normally remember how we learned to find our way, and that is probably the crucial difference.

Reliance on Direction

Fine, the reader may say, there is no such thing as an innate sense of direction, nevertheless people rely on a direction-giving capacity when finding their way. In reply, I would argue that some may refer to directions more than others, but on the whole, this reliance has been overrated. When in doubt, I propose the following experiment. It will not take long; all that is needed is a local map, which should not be opened as yet. The first part of the experiment consists in pointing to a well-known location within a range of, let us say, 1 to 10 kilometers; the home, the work place, a school, or any other prominent building can be chosen. The direction should now be recorded by aligning any straight object with the location and comparing them to the real direction on the map. If within an error margin of 5°, the reader may consider himself fairly accurate.

As Figure 2.1 shows, 5° error is not very much; the outstretched arm can only be moved by about half the width of the hand to stay within that limit. If the reader is approaching the 180° error margin, he should not be ashamed but keep on reading. Even an error of only 5° misses the destination by about 100 meters for one kilometer and by 1,000 meters for 10 kilometers distance. We all know, we can find our way much more precisely than that.

From the time children have had to go to geography lessons, they also have had to learn the cardinal directions. Despite the teaching, children, as well as many adults, are found to have great difficulty indicating compass directions even when they find themselves in places they know very well. The geographer Gregg (1940) observed that most people made small directional movements with their heads or arms when referring to cardinal directions. He thought these movements to be an important aspect in the process of recording

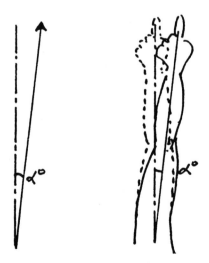

Figure 2.1
A directional error of 5°.

directions. As a teaching device he recommended that pupils should regularly stand up, point in a given direction, and make the accompanying small body movement. Howard and Templeton (1966) refer to the questionable success of the method: "[Gregg] gave no evidence that such a procedure improves orientation ability, and several children whom he asked to do this thought it was silly, which is scarcely surprising" (Howard and Templeton, 267).

One of the first thorough scientific studies on spatial orientation was undertaken by Lord in 1941. She used over 300 elementary school children to test their ability in pointing to local and distant cities. She was also interested in the children's ability to maintain a sense of direction while they were driven in a bus on a given route. The conclusions were not different from the classroom experiences discussed above. The children, in general, did not have a good notion of cardinal directions. When traveling on the bus, the children were often lost before the first test was administered. Needless to say, under normal circumstances the children did not have any trouble getting around in their daily environment; they were no more disoriented than their teachers.[4]

The aborigines of central Australia are known for their remarkable way-finding performances. Living in a relatively undifferentiated environment where water is scarce, they have been forced to move regularly from waterhole to waterhole. To find water is a question of life and death.

Lewis (1976), who had previously done extensive studies on Pacific navigation, traveled with Australian aborigines to get an insight into their skill. Among various tasks, he asked them to point out directions to places of importance in the life of the people. Lewis considered the results disappointing; the directions were sometimes correct, but more often they were imprecise and even wrong. Lewis found errors of 60° and more for people who depend on wayfinding to survive.

While traveling with aborigines, Lewis witnessed remarkable wayfinding skills, but generally the performers were not able to point accurately to destinations. A rather colorful description of a hunting scene is chosen as an illustration:

Pinta Pinta, who is a very good hunter though an atrocious shot, tracked an emu 4-5 km through flat spinifex until he killed it at very short range with a shotgun. He returned direct to the camp and guided me in the Landrover, also in a straight line, except for a detour round a creek bed, straight to the spot where the emu's body was hidden out in the spinifex plain. (Lewis, 1976, p. 260)

How did he find the bird's position? By remembering its direction? Most unlikely; Pinta Pinta, when questioned would not give any direction but explained, "I know where I go to the place." This reply will be elucidated as our discussion progresses.

Wayfinding performances of children as well as of adults have been shown

Orientation Générale
—le nord est de l'autre côté du sud et vice-versa. Pour l'est et l'ouest, c'est pareil excepté que c'est le contraire (from Croc).

to be superior to their ability to give directions. These performances cannot therefore be explained by a sense of direction, innate or learned. Giving directions has to be seen as an independent task. The knowledge of directions is not so much a prime information relied upon to orient or to find a way but a result of these capacities. Having negated the existence of a sense of direction, it will be necessary to replace this convenient explanation of wayfinding. To do this, we shall look at some early experimental studies in psychology.

BACK TO MAZES

Maze Behavior in Rats

A group of psychologists working in the early part of this century was particularly interested in mazes and rats. Some of this research, identified with behaviorism or operant psychology, is well known in its vulgarized version, even to the layman. It may be worthwhile to recall that behaviorists of the time had a rather simplistic idea of rats and more or less the same idea of humans. Their idea states essentially that stimulation emanating from the environment determines behavior. They differentiated between two types of stimulation, the first impinging on the organism before it responded and the second occurring after the response. The latter they considered particularly important: if the stimulus was positive (reward), the organism would tend to repeat its behavior.

This observation led to the theory of reinforcement. It stated that behavior could be controlled by adjusting the stimulus. All that was needed to explain the behavior of rats and humans was a simple model, where links between stimuli and responses were established and reinforced if the consequences were positive. Within this perspective, a behavioral repertory could be built up on a sequential additive basis.

The behaviorists used mazes to study how rats build up their behavior repertory, what sensory modalities were involved in this learning process, and what the effects of reinforcers were. One of the oldest devices used by Small (1900) was a 6 by 8 foot rectangular version of the Hampton Court maze, discussed in Chapter 1. Later, more regular mazes were constructed in the form of repetitive T or Y junctions. They contained choices of routes that the rat had to learn to find the reward, usually in the form of food for an appropriately starved animal. A well-learned route through a maze was seen as a chain reflex (Watson, 1914), or as a series of reinforced choices (Hull, 1932). Some data showed that rats could take shortcuts if partitions in the maze were removed (Honzik, 1933; Hebb and Williams, 1946). These observations, not fully accountable by the behaviorist's model, remained somewhat incidental, and a little, but telling, anecdote has survived. Some silly rats, it is reported, instead of repeating the responses they learned to

Hampton Court maze as used for maze learning studies with rats by Small, 1900. *(After Woodworth and Schlosberg, 1965, 614)*

reach the food chamber, tried to climb out of the maze to get there more directly! "Eye witnesses" have claimed that the annoyed experimenter would push the deviant beast back into the maze, telling it to "behave."

Of significance here is that the stimulus-response model in its simple form does not allow for such shortcut behavior. The learned stimulus-response connections would not lead the animal to climb out of the maze in the first place, nor would it provide for the development of alternative routes to a destination.

The Tolman Experiment

Observations, like the one reported by Hebb and Williams and maybe even the anecdote, triggered a series of most interesting experiments by a psychologist in the forties. In these now classic studies, Tolman (1948) showed first that rats learned even without reinforcement. Indeed, when rats were allowed to roam a maze prior to the experiment, that is, prior to being rewarded with food, they had a net advantage over rats that were not allowed to roam the maze. This meant that rats of the first groups had learned something about the maze on their own initiative. Second, Tolman showed that rats were more active than expected not only in terms of learning but also in terms of perception. Tolman and his group observed that rats often engage in head movements to size up the place where they have been put. It meant to Tolman that the animals actively observed the environment rather than simply being impinged upon by the environment. Third, he found that rats were much more intelligent than had generally been assumed.

The experiment involved two mazes, illustrated in Figure 2.2. The training maze on the left (maze A) shows a circular platform with the rat's entrance at

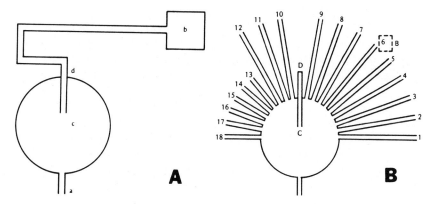

Figure 2.2
Tolman's maze for learning experiments with rats. *(After Downs and Stea, 1977, 33, 34)*

the bottom and a path leading to a food chamber at the top. In the first part of the experiment, the rat, after roaming for a while, eventually found the food chamber along the path. At no time could he see the food chamber directly nor the configuration of the path. After repeating the experiment a few times over a few days, the rat learned to reach the box directly without any roaming or hesitation. The big question was what had the rat learned? Was it just the behavioral sequences triggered by certain stimuli or was it more than that?

The answer is neatly contained in the second part of the experiment. Once the rat had been trained to reach the food box, he was placed in a different maze (Fig. 2.2, maze B). Entering the circular platform at the same place, the rat found the exit leading to the food box barred. Instead he was confronted by 18 exits from which to choose. Here is the clue; over one third of all the rats chose the exit (no. 6) that would have led directly to the food box.

Half of all the animals are accounted for if the adjacent exits 5 and 7 are included. The conclusion of the study is important; rats are able to do more than establish stimulus-response links that tend to be reinforced. By performing this task, rats proved to be capable of complicated mental operations that enable the accumulation and integration of information about the environment into a spatial organization. They had to combine into a whole what they perceived in parts. Tolman referred to this organized information as a cognitive map, although he emphasized that the term should be understood as a metaphor rather than an artifactual map. It should be noted that Lord (1941), in the previously described study, and Trowbridge (1913) had already proposed the notion of a cognitive or imaginary map.

A rather vivid illustration of the essential difference between the two schools of thinking has been proposed by Tolman (1948). Within the first framework, that of the behaviorists, the central nervous system is seen as somewhat like an old-fashioned telephone exchange room where incoming calls (stimuli) are connected by simple one-to-one switches to outgoing lines (responses). Within the second framework proposed by Tolman, that of a cognitive school of thinking, the central nervous system is seen as rather like a "map control room."[5] Incoming information is worked over and integrated into a tentative map or a simplified model showing, among other things, the key elements of the environment and their geometric relations in space. It is on the basis of this map or model that actions are taken.

Pinta Pinta and his emu story can be understood if viewed in the light of cognitive mapping. Being a good hunter, he registered his tracking the emu into a spatially organized maplike structure that incorporated not only his spatial moves but also information about the surrounding environment. From this maplike structure he could devise alternative routes to reach the hidden bird. If Lewis had insisted long enough, Pinta Pinta could probably have given him some approximate directions too, but he would have deduced them from his cognitive map.

Toward a Definition of Orientation

At this point in the discussion the following observations should be retained. Spatial orientation and wayfinding cannot be explained by a special innate sixth sense, nor by any acquired sense of direction. Instead, mental or cognitive processes have to be assumed that are capable of organizing perceived parts of the environment into a maplike ensemble respecting certain geometric properties. Spatial orientation could, therefore, be described as a *person's ability to mentally determine his position within a representation of the environment made possible by cognitive maps.* In this first definition, therefore, spatial orientation is equated with *"knowing where one is"* and with *"having an adequate cognitive map."* Seen from this perspective, the study of cognitive maps would seem to be the most promising approach to the comprehension of spatial orientation.

COGNITIVE MAPS AND ORIENTATION

Tolman's study demonstrating the cognitive mapping ability of rats in mazes dates back to 1948. One would expect little to remain unresearched on this topic. Almost the contrary is true, however. Interest in researching cognitive maps started only in the sixties, while specific research on orientation and wayfinding emerged sporadically.[6]

Two publications were probably responsible for the general rediscovery of cognitive maps as a concept worth investigating, *The Image* by Boulding in 1958 and *The Image of the City* by Lynch in 1960. Boulding's main purpose can be summarized as follows: in order to understand what people do, one has to understand what people know or, more precisely, what they believe they know. The subjective and often simplified ideas people have about their physical and nonphysical environment are brought together by the image. The understanding of this image, Boulding argued, is essential in understanding human behavior. The major contribution by Lynch in popularizing the concept of the image or the cognitive map was to link it to environmental design, particularly at the urban scale.[7] In doing so, he emphasized the spatial characteristics of the cognitive map. Clear images of an environment, he argued, contribute to a person's efficient functioning, in particular to his wayfinding performances. Lynch identified the common elements people tend to select from the environment to build up their images. The visual accessibility and impact of such elements he thought to be the design criteria for a highly "legible" or "imageable" environment.[8] Both, psychologists and planners were now interested in the same concept, even if for quite different reasons.

A cognitive map cannot be observed directly. The researcher has to content himself with indirect manifestations such as sketch maps, pictorial drawings, verbal descriptions, modeling, and other forms of spatial manipulations. These manifestations are influenced by the chosen channel of communication and limited by the person's ability to communicate. Nevertheless, consistent results have emerged from research done during the sixties and early seventies. This research has been reviewed extensively (Beck and Wood, 1976; Saarinen, 1976; Canter, 1977; Moore, 1979; Evans, 1980; Gärling, 1980). The discussion here will be limited to major characteristics of cognitive maps having a particular bearing on orientation and wayfinding.

Most of the research on cognitive maps revolved around three key questions: what are cognitive maps like in content and organization; what intervening variables affect the content and organization of maps; how do cognitive maps compare to the geometric reality of the physical environment.

Map Typology

The early research efforts in this field led to the identification of variations in maps and to a general typology. Although the designating term may vary, two types of map have generally been recognized (see Shemyakin, 1962; Appleyard, 1970; Tolman, 1948; Lord, 1941). One map type relates to a person's movement in space. The map is actually re-created by remembering what has been seen when walking through a given setting. The sketch map on the left of Figure 2.3 represents a subject's view of the ground floor of the commercial center Bonaventure in downtown Montréal.[9]

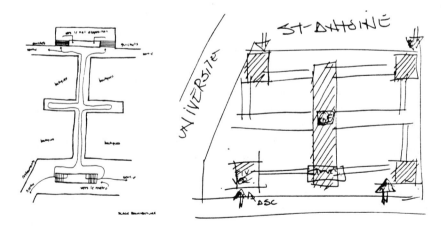

Figure 2.3
Example of a linearly and spatially organized map at the building scale.

The person's imaginary trip is actually shown on the drawing. Only the space viewed from that trip is drawn. This type of organization is called linear or sequential, and the map is referred to as a route map. A great number of people organize information about the physical environment in such a linear or sequential fashion. Route maps can be seen as a result of a temporal organization of space. Time provides a means of ordering environmental information (one thing after another) and of dealing with complexities (one at a time).

The sketch map on the right is quite different. The plan here is composed without resorting to a specific position of the person, and his movement in the imagined setting. The environment is understood as a spatial entity. In such a sketch map, the person may first draw the circulation system or the building form, then he may indicate the four elevators, the four entrances, the streets, and so on. This type of organization is called spatial, and the ensuing map is referred to as being a survey map. Survey and route maps, then, are the manifestations of two basically different representations of macro-spaces. The descriptors "linear" and "spatial" refer only to the way the information is organized. Even a route map is a representation of space from which information of a distinctly spatial nature, such as the relative position of locations or directions to locations, can be extracted.

The same types of map are found at the urban scale, where most of the mapping research has actually been done. The linearly organized sketch map in Figure 2.4 on the left shows the path of an excursion and the places viewed from that path, while the sketch map on the right gives directly the spatial

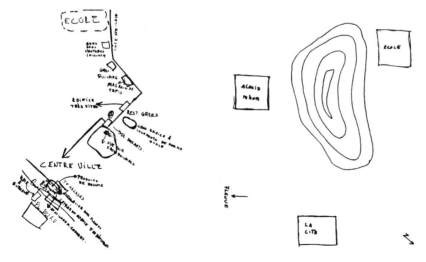

Figure 2.4
Example of a linearly and spatially organized map at the urban scale.

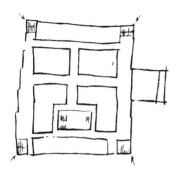

Spatial organization of the shopping complex Bonaventure after only two visits.

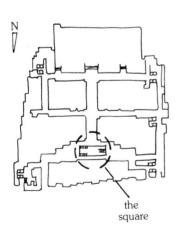

the square

True-to-scale plan of shopping level at complex Bonaventure.

location of the places visited, the mountain, the direction of the St. Lawrence, and a cardinal direction. The example shows that the spatially organized map is not necessarily richer or more complete.[10]

Cognitive maps express the way information about the spatial environment is organized. Underlying this organization are three basic frames of reference, which are egocentric, fixed, and coordinate. The term "abstract frame" is also used for the latter. Within the egocentric frame, elements in the environment are positioned in respect to the viewer, while within a fixed frame, elements of the environment as well as the viewer are related to a particular point in the environment, such as in one's home. Finally, within a coordinate frame, elements in the environment are positioned in relation to some abstract system. The egocentric frame is relied upon in sequential, route-type representations, while the fixed and, in particular, the coordinate frames are more extensively used in spatial, survey-type representations. The three systems involve levels of abstraction that increase from egocentric to fixed to coordinate. The systems also appear in this order during the development of the child.[11]

Intervening Variables

Certain factors are known to influence the type of cognitive organization identified as linear-sequential and spatial. Among the most important are: (1) the developmental stage of a child—young children up to the age of seven organize space only in a linear-sequential fashion (Hart and Moore, 1973); (2) the extent of an experience in a given setting—the first contact with an unknown place results generally in a linear-sequential map—some people quickly arrive at a spatial organization and others remain linear-sequential;[12] (3) the modes of experiencing the environment—an active exploration by walking and driving tends to produce more detailed and structured maps than a passive explanation by being shown or driven around. A tendency to produce more spatially organized maps is also associated with active exploration (Appleyard, 1970). This variable is often reflected in social and occupational traits (Orleans; 1973; Rand, 1969).

The Question of Accuracy

Of particular interest for spatial orientation as defined above is the accuracy of cognitive maps in respect to the geometric properties of a setting. Although sketch maps and other forms of description vary greatly from one person to another, certain characteristics are universal. Maps contain typical distortions in respect to scale. Places well known to a person are seen as more important in size. This is particularly evident if people draw geographic maps, but it is also observable at the building scale. The shopping complex Bonaventure, still serving as an illustration, contains a great number of shops, boutiques, restaurants, cinemas, an exhibition hall, in fact any kind of facility one would expect to find on a downtown city street. The slightly irregular circulation system divides the space into five zones. A split level on the southern side of the building contains bazaar-like stalls on the lower level and a large exhibition hall on the upper level. The bazaar and the exhibition halls attract fewer people and are less familiar than the central shops, with the result that in the sketch maps the corresponding surface is reduced or the space is left out altogether. A square and a small well leading to the metro system are located toward the opposite northern side of the building. This square is seen by many as the most important place of Bonaventure. The access to the metro is well known and is generally drawn out of proportion. Many sketch maps show nothing but the central square even if the task was to represent Bonaventure as a whole.

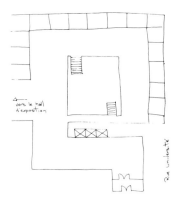

Sketch map emphasizing the square.

Metric distortions in cognitive maps manifest themselves in differences between cognitive and real distances. Cognitive distances, again, can only be measured indirectly as they appear in sketch maps or more commonly in distance estimates to specific places or in estimates of travelled routes.[13] Studies have shown that, on the whole, people are not very accurate in estimating routes in metric units, although they may be quite able to judge relative distances. Even when distances are compared in nonmetric terms, certain complicated but relatively consistent distortions occur.[14] Routes appear generally longer if they contain, for example, many intersections, many barriers, or distinctive features such as curves, reference points, and so on (Sadalla and Staplin, 1980; Byrne, 1979; Canter, 1977). Intervening points on a route increase distance estimates. Hartley (1977) referred to this factor as the "clutter effect." The more cluttered a route, the greater the resulting cognitive distance. A second powerful distortion is introduced by the degree of a person's liking or disliking of a place. This factor is referred to as valence. Positive valence, that is, liking a place results in a shortening of estimated distance (Briggs, 1973; Golledge and Zannaras, 1973). It is, of course, possible that with certain routes, the two factors compensate for each other. A trip downtown may evoke high valence and a high clutter effect.

Large spaces are often mapped by regrouping spatial elements into distinct areas. A person may, for example, visualize a continent in terms of countries, a city in terms of districts, and an interior space in terms of functional areas that can appear as clearly enclosed forms. If two elements are situated within the same area, the distance will tend to be assessed as being shorter than if the elements are in two distinct areas (Rapoport, 1977). Coren and Girgus (1980) have shown that perceptual organization of stimuli according to Gestalt principles leads to distortions in the perceived spatial relationships.[15]

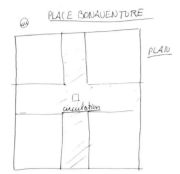

Highly schematized sketch map.

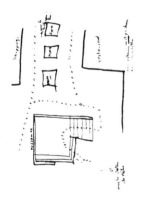

Selection and deformation; the well leading to the metro.

Again, elements within a figure appear closer together than if they span two figures.

Distance and time are often used interchangeably.[16] To the question of how far away a place is, one might conceivably get an answer in terms of the time needed to get there. When referring to time, on the other hand, people use distance descriptors such as short, long, and so on. It has been suggested that time expresses the experience of moving through space, and distance is an abstraction thereof. There is little evidence, though, that distance estimates are based on time estimates or the reverse. Canter (1977) compared estimates of time and distance with actual time and distance of a chosen route on the London Underground. A rather confusing picture of relationships between time and distance emerged from that study.[17] The author suggested that people tend to have a more consistent idea of distance than time.

Cognitive maps, we have seen, represent an organization of the physical environment in simplified form. Cognitive maps contain distortions of distances, and they also tend to be more or less schematic. Open angles, for example, are often transformed into rectangles or multiples thereof, curved lines are straightened, and spatial configurations are simplified to basic geometric forms.[18] A highly schematic map of Bonaventure might just show a central circulation system in the form of a cross with a square.

Another way to simplify is to select certain elements and to omit others. The selected elements usually have a particular meaning to the person; they can also represent particular experiences, or they reflect the elements most often used. A sketch map of Bonaventure contains, for example, only one of the two stairs in the central square. On the other hand, elements have also been shown that do not exist. To accentuate the importance of the central well, additional stairs and even additional floors have been drawn.[19]

Cognitive maps undergo transformations. Downs and Stea (1973) have identified three types: accretion, diminution, and reorganization. Accretion and diminution refer to small changes in a cognitive map when new elements are perceived and incorporated or when old elements are forgotten. Cognitive maps are generally resistent to total reorganization. This guarantees a certain stability of the known environment. The resistence to reorganization can take surprising forms. During my first visit to Manhattan, I imagined the island upside down. What is south in reality, the financial district, appears as being north in my map. Even today, while I write this text, my map is not properly reorganized. That first image has to be rotated by 180° to get it in place.

The structure and content of cognitive maps, their evolution and transformations, as well as the reference systems in use to establish spatial relations are relevant to the study of how people comprehend and mentally represent their surrounding physical environment. The question remains whether cognitive maps adequately explain spatial orientation?

Most of the sketch-maps of Bonaventure shown above were selected among the more accurate representations in my sample. Even so, the deviations from the actual plan are important. If spatial orientation is defined as a person's ability to determine his position in a mental representation of the environment, the required prerequisite would have to be an adequate representation of the environment, that is, an adequate cognitive map.[20] Over half of the approximately one hundred subjects who drew sketch maps of Bonaventure do not fulfill this basic requirement. Should they, therefore, be considered disoriented? Surely not. Even those who cannot muster a sketch or give a verbal description that renders a place halfway recognizable are generally able to get around quite efficiently. Furthermore, they would not consider themselves to be disoriented or lost.

This incongruity is important. It indicates that the definition of spatial orientation as a person's ability to determine his position in a mental representation of the environment is insufficient to account for all observable situations. Even if the concept of cognitive maps is important and indeed essential in determining how spaces are understood and mentally organized, in themselves they are inadequate as vehicles to comprehend spatial orientation.[21]

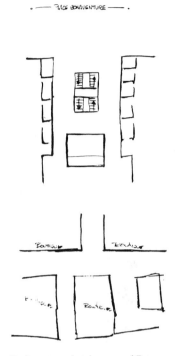

Rudimentary sketch maps of Bonaventure.

THE LESSON FROM HIPOUR

Lynch (1960), in an appendix to the *Image of the City,* gives an extensive review of the anthropological literature dealing with orientation and imagery in various cultures. The Arunta of central Australia, the Eskimo of Greenland, the inhabitants of the Sahara desert, the Micronesians and Polynesians, all undertake extensive travels in what are to us undifferentiated environments. Even more important, the vastness and uniformity of the environment makes it extremely difficult to achieve an adequate representation.[22] The travel and navigation of these populations provide for an insight into spatial orientation when a cartographic-type representation cannot be assumed.

Landfinding in the Pacific

One of the most extreme navigation examples and at the same time one of the best documented is to be found in the South Seas, in particular within the Caroline Islands.

Figure 2.5 gives the geographic disposition of the inhabited islands. The question that intrigues anthropologists is how the islands were settled in the first place. The question is particularly relevant if one considers that the inhabitants had no compasses at their disposition nor any other navigational aids.

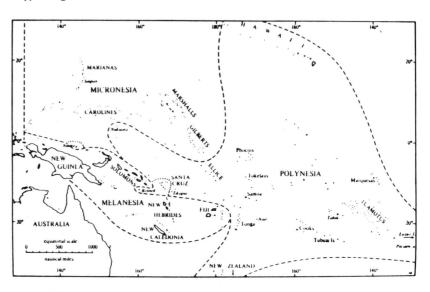

Figure 2.5
South Sea Islands. *(From D. Lewis,* We, the Navigators, *University Press of Hawaii, Honolulu, 1975, p. 14; copyright © 1975 by Australian National University Press, Canberra)*

Hipour, the navigator. *(From D. Lewis, We, the Navigators, University Press of Hawaii, Honolulu, 1975, p. 41; copyright © 1975 by Australian National University Press, Canberra.)*

Some authors (Sharp, 1964; Akerbloom, 1968) have argued that the inhabitants could not navigate accurately over long distances, since they were unable to determine the position of their vessels while traveling on the open sea. They argued for a one-way settlement pattern based on chance rather than controlled exploration. This meant that those who were not favored by chance would starve at sea.

This seems a neat way out, but the argument did not hold up in the light of extensive and rich data collected by two anthropologists, first Gladwin (1970) and later Lewis (1975).[23] Apart from demonstrating the navigational skills of some older inhabitants, among whom was a most capable navigator named Hipour who sailed the open sea over 1,000 miles test distance, Gladwin and Lewis showed that the Polynesians did not need to know the position of the vessel in a geographic sense. Contrary to the system of Western navigation, which localizes both destination and the vessels' position within a system of coordinates, Micronesian navigation operated on the knowledge of how to get to a destination. That is, they knew the process involved in reaching a destination.[24] The two authors give a full account of the navigation in use; they refer to it as a dead reckoning system. It implies three distinct parts: identifying initial course directions or establishing an initial course plan; executing the plan, keeping on course, and correcting for lateral drift; and homing on the destination.

Course plans were conceived mainly in relation to stars, especially to the position of setting and rising stars on the horizon. One can well imagine that plans for long open sea voyages contained a large amount of directional information. In addition, each destination was associated with a set of stars that varied with the island of departure. If one takes into account Gladwin's observation that navigators remembered star directions for 55 commonly made there-and-back-again trips, one appreciates the amount of information that had to be memorized. The islands and reefs that were major seamarks also had to be memorized; finally, the major sea currents and wave directions (and their seasonal changes) were added. As a perfect knowledge of this information was crucial to successful navigation, it is not surprising that this knowledge was a jealously kept secret within the different navigational schools and that it was constantly kept alive by being made the major topic of conversation.

In order for a dead reckoning system to work, it is necessary for the navigator to estimate those lateral forces that lead to drifting. Many examples are given by Lewis (1975) where he experienced course corrections made by the navigators. On the basis of changes in wave patterns, navigators were able to identify changes of currents while at sea. Although some of these changes were constant and known in advance, others occurred unexpectedly, and thus the original course plan had to be adjusted. Given an original course plan, the voyages must be seen composed of a series of sequential steps for which appropriate corrections were made whenever the need arose.

For successful landfall, particular knowledge was necessary to increase the chances of success. The nearby existence of land was perceived long before the island was visible. Wave patterns, color of water and sky, as well as animal and plant life were indicators of land and allowed the navigators to increase their homing ground perceptually by some 50 miles on either side.

What is the lesson from Hipour? Navigation in the South Seas is probably one of the most remarkable feats of seamanship. The magnitude of the task and the gravity of the risks do not need emphasizing. A repertory of course directions, navigational strategies for keeping on course, and the various means to estimate sea currents as well as to perceive close-by islands, all have to be seen as an integral part of South Sea navigation. Although the navigators were incapable of determining their exact position on an open sea voyage and therefore could not be said to have been oriented in the terms described above, they knew perfectly well what to do in order to reach a destination. To consider navigators like Hipour disoriented would not only contradict common sense but would actually amount to an insult.

An Extended Definition

Here we reach a critical point in the discussion. The definition of spatial orientation as being the ability of a person to determine where he is within a physical setting has to be extended to include an alternative ability that consists in determining *what to do in order to reach a place.* Instead of relying on a spatial representation of the physical environment to situate himself, the person may rely on a plan of action or a strategy to go somewhere. The first definition can be called static in nature, while the second is dynamic. Only if deprived of both, will the person have the sensation of being lost or disoriented.[25]

One definition does not exclude the other; rather, they have to be seen as complementary. The first emphasizes mental representations, cognitive maps or images; the second, actions or behaviors. In order to arrive at a general conceptualization of spatial orientation and wayfinding that can encompass both definitions, we will have to reconsider how images relate to behavior.

IMAGE AND BEHAVIOR

The Planning Link

To understand human behavior, it is essential to study what people know, that is, to study their image of the physical and nonphysical environment. This was the argument of the cognitive school of thinking, as expressed by Boulding (1958). An image is a complex and often vague body of knowledge. Even if a full understanding of such an image were possible, it would not suffice to fully comprehend or predict behavior. Something is needed to make the link from the image to behavior. This critical issue was outlined and studied by Miller, Galanter, and Pribram only two years after Boulding's publication (Miller et al., 1960). The three authors, whose contribution has probably not received the attention it merits, proposed a planning or decision-making process as the all important link between image and behavior.

A concrete example might be useful at this point. Let us assume a person envisaging a vacation trip by car. The most obvious thing to do is to plan an itinerary foreseeing where to go, when, and how. This itinerary is composed of a series of decisions and can be seen to represent a plan of action. In order to make up this itinerary, the person has probably relied on information obtained from a travel office, from geographic maps, from previous experiences, and even from what he imagines to be there. All this information is integrated into an image or a cognitive map he has about the area. In this example it is the itinerary, that is, the outcome of planning and decision making that leads to behavior. A person's image or cognitive map of an area provides the necessary background information.

Process and Product

A second conceptual step is required to prepare the ground for a comprehensive definition of spatial orientation and wayfinding. We will return to the vacation illustration. Before setting off on a trip a person might have a general plan of action, but he will hardly have a full and detailed plan. After all, the knowledge about the place to be visited is only sketchy. New information will be acquired during travel that will alter the image or cognitive map. Cognitive maps, therefore, are not to be seen as something stable. They change when new information is acquired and when other information is forgotten. A cognitive map is a product at a particular moment in time of a more general cognitive-mapping process. Downs and Stea (1977), who were probably the first authors to emphasize the process of cognitive mapping rather than the product, the cognitive map, defined this process as "an abstraction concerning those cognitive or mental abilities that enable us to collect, organise, store, recall and manipulate information about the spatial environment" (Downs and Stea, 1977, 6). During the vacation trip, the cognitive map is completed and altered according to new incoming information. As the cognitive map changes, the plan may change too and in turn affect what the person is doing and where he is going.

In the previous discussion I have formulated two complementary definitions of spatial orientation. The first emphasized a person's understanding of his position within a mental representation of the environment. Conditions of "knowing where one is" and of "having an adequate cognitive map" are usually equated with spatial orientation. The second definition focused on a person's behavior and on his coping with the problem of reaching a spatial destination. Conditions of "knowing what to do to go places" are linked with this second, more dynamic definition of spatial orientation. A comprehensive conceptualization would, therefore, have to include ongoing information processing in the form of cognitive mapping to do justice to the first definition and a process of planning or decision making to satisfy the second definition.

Spatial Orientation in Contrast to Wayfinding

It could be argued that the term "spatial orientation" should be used to describe a person's ability to understand the space around him and to situate himself, while wayfinding would be reserved for the ability to reach a place. This differentiation is ambiguous. A person who cannot establish his position in space but knows how to find his way is still oriented. Wayfinding, on the other hand, can include, among various cognitive processes, the ability to process information and in particular to organize information about the physical environment into a cognitive map. The two terms express, if anything different, two approaches or two emphases of the same phenomena. In order to underline the dynamic and comprehensive aspects of the concept, preference will be given to the term "wayfinding."

SPATIAL ORIENTATION AND WAYFINDING:
COMPLEX COGNITIVE PROCESSES

This chapter started with a discussion of what spatial orientation is not. It is not an innate sixth sense of direction. Also, it has been suggested that direction is derived from a spatial understanding of the environment rather that being the prime knowledge on which spatial orientation and wayfinding are based. This spatial understanding requires a cognitive-mapping process, the product of which at a particular moment in time is a cognitive map or image. We have seen that an understanding of the cognitive map is difficult. Even if we could clearly identify such a map, we would still not know how people manage to reach a destination. What is needed is a planning process that leads from the image to behavior; cognitive maps contain information needed to plan. As a person continually acquires new information in interacting with the environment, these cognitive maps are changing too. Hence the importance of emphasizing the study of the process rather than the product.

Given these observations, I propose that spatial orientation or the semantically more appropriate term of wayfinding be defined as cognitive processes comprising three distinct abilities: a cognitive-mapping or information-generating ability that allows us to understand the world around us; a decision-making ability that allows us to plan actions and to structure them into an overall plan; and a decision-executing ability that transforms decisions into behavioral actions. Both decision making and decision execution are based on information generated by cognitive mapping.

These three abilities together constitute a spatial problem solving process. The South Sea navigators, the Australian aborigines, and indeed you and I have found ways to solve the problems of reaching spatial destinations, of establishing our position in space, of pointing out directions, and of completing all the tasks that necessitate an understanding of the spatial environment.

Wayfinding defined in terms of spatial problem solving is generic. It includes perceptual and cognitive phenomena and the various ways a person can relate to the spatial environment and to destinations; it involves memory and learning, all essential in explaining how people find their way. Furthermore, I believe this definition to be suited to design and planning. After all, information has to be extracted from the built environment; it has to be understood, organized, and remembered. To realize how these processes are affected by design interventions is basic to purposeful planning. Chapter 3 proposes a spatial problem-solving model for wayfinding. Chapter 4 will analyze the impact of various sources of information encountered in the environment on wayfinding.

NOTES

1. Contemporary research on migration and wayfinding actually shows that animals rely on environmental cues. In some ingenious experiments, Tinbergen (1958) succeeded in establishing that sand wasps not only depend on landmarks to find their nests but are actually able to learn new ones as a matter of course. They are even able to learn the configuration of such landmarks. Von Frisch (1954) demonstrated that the sun is a reference point for honeybees when communicating to other bees the location of interesting food supplies. The migration of birds, butterflies, and fish are more difficult to research. Birds have been shown to rely on the sun, the stars, and land masses when migrating. Homing experiments have led to the assumption that birds fly randomly until they perceive recognizable landmarks (Dorst, 1962; Griffin, 1964).

2. Romanes (1883), who is presenting Darwin's essay, interprets it to say that "savage men" show a sense of direction and that this sense is an instinct (see p. 287).

3. The original text from Wrangell does not actually contain the word "instinctively" but "practically." The citation reads "The native had always a perfect knowledge of it practically." (Wrangell, 1845, 141)

4. More recently, Kozlowski and Bryant (1977) tried to defend the notion of a "sense of direction" as a research topic worth investigating. They had people estimating their "sense of direction" which was then correlated with the ability to point to given directions. They found people with a "good sense of direction" performing better in familiar environments. In novel environments the two groups did not differ in accuracy. It is, of course, in the latter context that a sense of direction, as defined above, would have made a difference. The first test only relates self-evaluation to performance.

5. Downs (1981) warns that the "map control room" metaphor should be understood in its functional sense only. The brain is not a map control room, but it works as if it were one.

6. Although early writings in psychology justified the study of cognitive maps as a means to understand spatial orientation and wayfinding (Griffin, 1948), research progressed by focusing on the psychological construct and by de-emphasizing and finally ignoring its raison d'être.

7. Cognitive map, mental map, mental or spatial representation, and image are often seen as synonyms. When using the term "cognitive map," I want to emphasize that the representation is a product of a spatial integration of parts that were perceived independently, while "image" applies in a more generic sense to any visual as well as nonvisual representation. This distinction is not always possible. When visiting a city, for example, a person develops a cognitive map by integrating the different views he has experienced when walking along the streets, but he may also have seen a map of the city providing him with an already integrated image of the city layout.

8. Environmental characteristics facilitating the formation of clear images will be discussed further in Chapter 4.

9. For a summary description of all major buildings figuring in this text, the user is referred to Appendix A. The sketch maps chosen to illustrate image characteristics have been taken from a sample of first year students in architecture at the University of Montréal.

10. Appleyard (1970) proposed four levels of organization within each map type. They span from fragmented to netted for the route maps and from scattered to patterned for the survey map.

11. What and how much a child knows about his spatial environment depends to a large extent on his level of cognitive development, which, according to Jean Piaget, can be regrouped into four major stages. During infancy, approximately 0 to 2 years of age, the

child starts from simple reflexes to develop the first coordinated behavioral actions. These actions already involve images but not yet a spatial representation. After the first year, the child can usually evoke images of people and objects that persist in his mind, even though the person or the object may no longer be within perceptual grasp. During early childhood, from about 2 to 7 years of age, the child acquires the skill to represent in the form of images and symbols that which is not actually perceived. This allows the child to perform certain abstract operations although only in a limited and egocentric way. The mental representations of space remain essentially static. An imagined route may only be "seen" in one direction and not in the inversed sense. During that period, reference systems are first egocentric then fixed. Children frequently use their homes as a fixed point of reference. Cognitive maps are still organized on a sequential linear basis, reflecting the child's direct experience with the environment. During middle childhood, from approximately 7 to 12 years of age, logical thought is acquired. The child then becomes able to abandon a purely egocentric view of the world for a more nuanced integration of different point of views. In the early phase, a fixed reference system characterizes the child's relation to the geographic environment. In a later phase, the abstract system of reference makes its appearance. Cognitive maps can now also be organized in a spatial survey type manner. From adolescence on, that is after 11 to 15 years of age, the child reaches his full abstract thinking abilities. It is only then that he is able to operate extensively on spatial representations, such as are required for solving problems of descriptive geometry. The original sources on the child's developmental stages are Piaget (1955); Piaget and Inhelder (1967); Laurendeau and Pinard (1970). Hart and Moore (1973) provide a synthesis of Piaget's work and compare it to that of other developmental psychologists like Werner and Bruner. For an interesting discussion of various developmental theories see also Downs and Stea (1977). An account of recent research on the child's cognition of large-scale environments is given by Hart (1981), Piché (1981), Sadalla and Staplin (1980), and Siegel and White (1975).

12. Beck and Wood (1976) studied the short-term learning process of people exposed to unknown places. Their research was conducted in three different European cities: London, Paris, and Rome. Serving as guides to visiting high school students they were able to trace spatial learning in a natural and still controlled set-up. The acquisition of spatial knowledge and the confection of cognitive maps is highly dependent on movement through space. Certain distinctive environmental features (reference points) are selected, retained, and linked by routes. These reference points may also serve to subordinate secondary elements of the environment, thereby establishing a hierarchical order (Evans et al., 1981; Allan et al., 1978; Siegel and White, 1975).

13. Thorndyke (1981) suggests that the length of a route is estimated by performing an imaginary scanning of the path. The longer the path, the longer should be the time it takes to complete the scanning. Indeed, Thorndyke found a linear relation between the length of the path and the time needed to give an estimate (see also Allan, 1979, for similar results).

14. For a general review see Canter (1977) and Rapoport (1977).

15. The Gestalt principles considered in this study, which organize a stimulus field into figure and background, are: proximity (elements close together tend to be seen as a figure), similarity (elements resembling one another tend to be regrouped into a figure), closure (enclosed areas tend to be seen as a figure), symmetry (symmetrical dispositions of elements tend to be organized into figures more easily than asymmetrical dispositions), good continuation (a stimulus field is read for the simplest coherent form that is seen as a figure).

16. The blind tend to organize space through their perception of the time it takes to walk to places (see Cratty, 1971). Sommer (1967) also notes that travelers in monotonous environments, such as the praires of central Canada, will make greater use of temporal cues. Certain landmarks are singled out and the time-distance from and to these reference points is recorded. Sea voyages are perceived in similar ways.

17. Canter found higher correlations between distance estimates and actual distance than between time estimates and actual time. He obtained high correlations between estimated distance and estimated time but weak correlations between actual time and estimated distance as well as time. To what extent these observations are affected by the particular context of traveling on a subway is not known.

18. Canter and Tagg (1975), in a study of distance estimates and mapping of Tokyo, found that the ellipsoid form of the major railway lines tended to be reduced to the more simple form of a circle. Some of these transformations have recently been related to the basic Gestalt laws of perception. Characteristics of perceptual organization are assumed also to work at the level of memory organization. Distortions due to symmetry, to rotations toward the horizontal or vertical axes, and the tendency to align or group points into simple forms are commonly observed in spatial representations (Tversky, 1981; Byrne, 1979).

19. Systematic distortions are not only common for cognitive maps but for memory in general. Neisser (1981) compared John Dean's testimony with the released transcripts of the Watergate tapes to find that, although the testimony was essentially right about what happened, it was quite inaccurate concerning what precisely was said and when. Often the memory, even for the gist of the conversations Dean held with President Nixon, was poor when he believed he recalled part of the conversations integrally. Distortions went mostly in the sense of augmenting Dean's role.

20. Sketch maps are not to be equated with cognitive maps. They are only a particular expression thereof; they are environmental knowledge put into a specific form. One therefore has to take into account the information lost and the information transformed in the process of expressing that knowledge. The argument presented above is not based on subtleties. The poorness of the sketch maps is not due to the constraints imposed by the media of expression, that is, drawing, but to the nature of the spatial representation. This does not mean that the cognitive maps of the subjects were not adequate for wayfinding; in fact they were.

21. Downs and Siegel (1981) address the same problem in slightly different terms. They ask how to reconcile the apparent paradox between accurate spatial behavior during wayfinding and inaccurate cognitive maps. Accuracy they see as the notion to be contested. Accuracy should not be measured according to the metric standards of cartographic maps. Some authors have suggested that cognitive maps are essentially network maps or topological maps representing spatial relations such as connectivity and containment (Byrne, 1979). It has also been proposed that cognitive maps reflect several distinct spatial representations, some metric, some topological, and some process-oriented (Kuipers, 1982).

22. Here again I refer to metric accuracy, a prerequisite to spatial orientation if defined in the above terms. The anthropological literature contains evidence that some natives are able to reproduce accurate metric maps, although this is not the rule. Edmund Carpenter (1973) relates that Aivilik Eskimos provided George Sutten in his 1929 exploration of Southhampton Isles with sketch maps when cartographic maps of this vast stretch of land were not available. These sketches accord surprisingly well with today's cartographic maps, particularly in respect to the general form of the shore line.

23. The publications of Gladwin (1970) and Lewis (1975) have solved the South Sea navigation mystery, and they have also shed new light on the notion of cognitive mapping and wayfinding. For a discussion see Siegel and White (1975), Downs and Stea (1977), and Passini (1977).

24. Navigation of the Micronesians and Polynesians resembles the regular migration of the Australian aborigines. They also relied on the process involved in reaching a destination by remembering journeys of mythical figures, which they re-enacted when moving in the semi-desert landscape. For a description see Rapoport (1972) and Eliade (1957).

25. Downs and Stea (1977) describe being lost as a person's inability to make the link between his cognitive map and his perception of the environment. This description, although very

attractive in its simplicity and its precision, does, according to my position, address itself only to the static dimension of orientation. It further assumes people to have clear maps that can be meaningfully compared with the perceived environment.

REFERENCES

Akerbloom, K., 1968, *Astronomy and Navigation in Polynesia and Micronesia,* Ethological Museum Monograph Series, no. 14, Stockholm.

Allan, G. L., A. W. Siegel, and R. R. Rosinski, 1978, "The Role of Perceptual Context in Structuring Spatial Knowledge," *Journal of Experimental Psychology: Human Learning and Memory* **4**(6):617-630.

Allan, G. L., 1979, "The Perception of Time," *Perception and Psychophysics* **26**(5):340-354.

Appleyard, D., 1970, "Styles and Methods of Structuring a City," *Environment and Behavior* **2**(1):100-118.

Beck, R. J., and D. Wood, 1976, "Cognitive Transformation of Information from Urban Geographic Fields to Mental Maps," *Environment and Behavior* **8**(2):199-238.

Beck, R. J., and D. Wood, 1976, "Comparative Developmental Analysis and Aggregated Cognitive Maps of London," in *Environmental Knowing,* G. Moore and R. Golledge, eds., Dowden, Hutchinson & Ross, Stroudsburg, Pa., pp. 173-184.

Boulding, K., 1956, *The Image,* University of Michigan Press, Ann Arbor.

Briggs, R., 1973, "Urban Cognitive Distance," in R. Downs and D. Stea, eds., *Image and Environment,* Aldine, Chicago, pp. 361-388.

Byrne, R. W., 1979, "Memory for Urban Geography," *Quarterly Journal of Experimental Psychology* **31**(1):145-154.

Canter, D., and S. V. Tagg, 1975, "Distance Estimation in Cities," *Environment and Behavior* **7**(1):59-80.

Canter, D., 1977, *The Psychology of Place,* The Architectural Press, London.

Carpenter, E., 1973, *Eskimo Realities,* Holt, Rinehart and Winston, New York.

Coren, S., and J. S. Girgus, 1980, "Principles of Perceptual Organization and Spatial Distortions: The Gestalt Illusions," *Journal of Experimental Psychology: Human Perception and Performance* **6**(3):404-412.

Cratty, B. J., 1971, *Movement and Spatial Awareness in Blind Children and Youths,* Charles C. Thomas, Springfield, Ill.

Dorst, J., 1962, *The Migration of Birds,* Houghton Mifflin, Boston.

Downs, R., 1981, "Maps and Mappings as Metaphors for Spatial Representation," in *Spatial Representation and Behavior across the Life Span: Theory and Application,* L. S. Liben et al., eds., Academic Press, New York, pp. 143-166.

Downs, R., and D. Stea, 1973, *Image and the Environment: Cognitive Mapping and Spatial Behavior,* Chicago, Aldine.

Downs, R., and D. Stea, 1977, *Maps in Minds,* Harper and Row, New York.

Downs, R., and A. W. Siegel, 1981, "On Mapping Researchers Mapping Children Mapping Space," in *Spatial Representation and Behavior across the Life Span: Theory and Application,* L. S. Liben et al., eds., Academic Press, New York, pp. 237-248.

Eliade, M., 1957, *Mythes, Rêves et Mystères,* Gallimard, Paris.

Evans, G. W., 1980, "Environmental Cognition," *Psychological Bulletin,* **88**(2):259-287.

Evans, G. W., D. G. Marrero, and P. A. Butler, 1981, "Environmental Learning and Cognitive Mapping," *Environment and Behavior* **13**(1):83-104.

Frisch, K. von, 1954, *The Dancing Bees: an Account of the Life and Senses of the Honey Bee,* Methuen, London.

Gärling, T., 1980, *Environmental Orientation During Locomotion*, Swedish Council for Building Research, Stockholm.

Gladwin, T., 1970, *East Is a Big Bird: Navigation and Logic on Puluwat Atoll*, Harvard University Press, Cambridge, Mass.

Golledge, R., and G. Zannaras, 1973, "Cognitive Approaches to the Analysis of Human Spatial Behavior," in *Environment and Cognition*, W. H. Ittelson, ed., Seminar Press, New York, pp. 59-94.

Grey, G., 1841, *Journals of Two Expeditions of Discovery in North-West and Western Australia*, II, T. and W. Boone, London.

Griffin, D. R., 1964, *Bird Migration*, Doubleday, New York.

Griffin, P., 1948, "Topoligical Orientation," in *Foundation of Psychology*, E. G. Boring et al., eds., John Wiley and Sons, New York, pp. 380-386.

Hart, R., and G. Moore, 1971, *The Development of Spatial Cognition*, Place Perception Research Report no. 7, Clark University, Worcester, Mass.

Hart, R. A., 1981, "Children's Spatial Representation of the Landscape: Lessons and Questions from a Field Study," in *Spatial Representation and Behavior across the Life Span: Theory and Application*, L. S. Liben et al., eds., Academic Press, New York, pp. 195-233.

Hartley, A. A., 1977, "Mental Measurement in the Magnitude Estimation of Length," *Journal of Experimental Psychology: Human Perception and Performance* **3**(4):622-628.

Hebb, D. O., and K. Williams, 1946, "A Method of Rating Animal Intelligence," *Journal of General Psychology* **34**:59-65.

Honzik, C. H., 1933, "Maze Learning in Rats in the Absence of Specific Intra- and Extra-Maze Stimuli," *California University Publication of Psychology* **4**:307-318.

Howard, T. P., and W. B. Templeton, 1966, *Human Spatial Orientation*, John Wiley and Sons, New York.

Hull, C. L., 1932, "The Goal Gradient Hypothesis and Maze Learning," *Psychological Review* **39**:25-43.

Kozlowski, L. T., and K. J. Bryant, 1977, "Sense of Direction, Spatial Orientation and Cognitive Maps," *Journal of Experimental Psychology: Human Perception and Performance*, **3**(3):590-598.

Kuipers, B., 1982, "The 'Map in the Head' Metaphore," *Environment and Behavior* **14**(2):202-220.

Laurendeau, M., and A. Pinard, 1970, *The Development of the Concept of Space in the Child*, International University Press, New York.

Lewis, D., 1975, *We, the Navigators: The Ancient Art of Landfinding in the Pacific*, The University Press of Hawaii, Honolulu.

Lewis, D., 1976, "Observations on Route Finding and Spatial Orientation among the Aboriginal Peoples of the Western Desert Region of Central Australia," *Oceania*, **46**(4):249-282.

Lord, F. E., 1941, "A Study of Spatial Orientation of Children," *Journal of Educational Research* **34**(7):481-505.

Lynch, K., 1960, *The Image of the City*, MIT Press, Cambridge, Mass.

Miller, G. A., E. Galanter, and K. Pribram, 1960, *Plans and the Structure of Behavior*, Holt, Rinehart and Winston, New York.

Moore, G. T., 1979, "Knowing about Environmental Knowing: The Current State of Theory and Research on Environmental Cognition," *Environment and Behavior* **11**(1):33-70.

Neisser, U., 1981, "John Dean's Memory: A Case Study," *Cognition* **9**(1):1-22.

Orleans, P., 1973, "Differential Cognition of Urban Residents: Effect of Social Scale on Mapping," in *Image and Environments*, R. Downs and D. Stea, eds., Aldine, Chicago, pp. 115-130.

Passini, R., 1977, "Wayfinding: A Study of Spatial Problem Solving," Dissertation, Pennsylvania State University.

Piaget, J., and B. Inhelder, 1967, *The Child's Conception of Space,* Norton, New York.

Piaget, J., and B. Inhelder, 1969, *The Psychology of the Child,* Basic Books, New York.

Piaget, J., 1971, *The Construction of Reality in the Child,* Ballantine, New York.

Piché, D., 1981, "The Spontaneous Geography of the Urban Child," in *Geography and the Urban Environment,* D. T. Herbert and R. J. Johnston, eds., John Wiley, New York.

Rand, G., 1969, "Some Copernican Views of the City," *Architectural Forum* **132**(9):77-81.

Rapoport, A., 1972, "Australian Aborigines and the Definition of Place," in *Proceedings of the Third Annual Environmental Design and Research Association Meeting,* W. J. Mitchell, ed., University of California, Los Angeles, vol. 1, pp. 3.3.1-3.3.14.

Rapoport, A., 1977, *Human Aspects of Urban Form: Towards a Man-Environment Approach to Urban Form and Design,* Pergamon Press, Toronto.

Romanes, G. J., 1883, *Mental Evolution in Animals, With a Posthumous Essay on Instinct by Charles Darwin,* Kegan Paul, London.

Saarinen, T. F., 1976, *Environmental Planning: Perception and Behavior,* Houghton Mifflin, Boston.

Sadalla, E. K., and L. J. Staplin, 1980, "The Perception of Traversed Distance Intersections," *Environment and Behavior* **12**(2):167-182.

Sharp, A., 1964, *Ancient Voyages in Polynesia,* UCLA Press, Los Angeles.

Shemyakin, F. N., 1962, "Orientation in Space," in *Psychological Science in the USSR,* B. G. Ananyev et al., eds., Office of Technical Sciences, Report 62-11083, Washington, D.C., pp. 186-255.

Siegel, A. W., and S. H. White, 1975, "The Development of Spatial Representations of Large-Scale Environments," *Advances in Child Development and Behavior* **10**:9-55.

Small, W. S., 1900, "An Experimental Study of the Mental Processes of the Rat," *American Journal of Psychology* **11**(2):133-164.

Sommer, R., 1967, "Space-Time on Prairie Highways," *Journal of the American Institute of Planners* **33**(4):274-276.

Thorndyke, P. W., 1981, "Distance Estimation from Cognitive Maps," *Cognitive Psychology* **13**(4):526-550.

Tinbergen, N., 1958, *Curious Naturalists,* Basic Books, New York.

Tolman, E. C., 1948, "Cognitive Maps in Rats and Men," *Psychological Review* **55**(4):189-208.

Trowbridge, C. C., 1913, "On Fundamental Methods of Orientation and 'Imaginary Maps,'" *Science* **38**(990):888-897.

Tversky, B., 1981, "Distortions in Memory for Maps," *Cognitive Psychology* **13**(3):407-433.

Watson, J. B., 1914, *Behavior: An Introduction to Comparative Psychology,* Holt Rinehart and Winston, New York.

Woodworth, R. S., and H. Schlosberg, 1965, *Experimental Psychology,* Holt Rinehart and Winston, New York.

Wrangell, F., 1845, *Narrative of an Exhibition to the Polar Sea,* Harper and Brothers, New York.

3

Wayfinding: An Act of Solving Spatial Problems

To describe spatial orientation, or to use the more appropriate term "wayfinding," as spatial problem solving is to subsume a number of cognitive abilities responsible for information processing, decision making, and also for the transformation of decisions into behavioral actions. Any one of these cognitive abilities might be crucial to success or failure in reaching a destination. Compared to the more traditional static view of spatial orientation, spatial problem solving is more apt to describe the dynamics involved when people find their way. A person's ability to comprehend the surrounding environment and his position in it becomes only part of a much larger field of interest. By the same token, it is almost impossible to cover all the cognitive abilities in detail. To summarize the research on any one aspect of the process is a formidable task. In addition, our comprehension of these cognitive abilities is far from complete. Much research is in an early stage, and many of the explanatory links from one research field to the next have still to be established.[1] My own research effort has been descriptive and exploratory, aimed at gaining an overall view rather than at trying to test specific hypotheses. Its first purpose was to provide for a simple description that would permit a general understanding of the major wayfinding mechanisms. The second was to explore aspects of information processing responsible for the crucial relation between the environment, in particular, the designed features of the environment, and the wayfinding person.

This chapter introduces a general description of wayfinding as spatial problem solving.[2] The description addresses wayfinding in all its major components. The ensuing conceptualization is intended for comprehending wayfinding as well as for designing appropriate settings. The chapter comprises two semi-autonomous sections. The first introduces and defines the basic units and the structure of wayfinding. The second outlines the major processes of wayfinding, which are essential in giving the conceptualization its dynamic quality.[3] Observations of how people actually reach destinations are then needed to identify the rules underlying the process. If the units of wayfinding are seen as the equivalent of words in common language, the operational rules correspond to the syntax. The language analogy is not far-fetched. Such a conceptualization can indeed lead to a language of wayfinding, a language geared to describe and to research how people reach destinations and, maybe more interesting for the designer, a language aimed at simulating wayfinding behavior. We shall call this language a notation system. In the first application the notation system qualifies as a research tool, in the second as a design tool. The latter aspect is further developed in Chapter 5.

THE UNITS AND STRUCTURE OF WAYFINDING

The navigator in the South Seas, the client of an urban shopping complex like Bonaventure, the businessman traveling on the highway are all involved in wayfinding. Their common goal is to be at a destination at a particular time. We can say that "to reach a destination" represents a wayfinding task. The completion of the task depends on a variety of cues emanating from the spatial setting. These cues are extracted from signs, directories, maps; they may be obtained from what people do or say and they may also be taken directly from the natural or man-made environment. The cues can carry information about the nature and whereabouts of places. A person, in reaching a destination, not only picks up cues from the spatial setting, he also has some knowledge of the setting or of similar settings that can contribute to wayfinding. I will use the term "environmental information" to describe all relevant information available to a person when completing a wayfinding task. It should be noted that a task without any environmental information is meaningless. So, for example, "to go to *X*" in itself cannot be completed; it does not even represent a wayfinding problem. If, however, in addition to the stated task, the person is given some environmental information in the form of a map where *X* is indicated or if he is told that *X* stands for New York, he can try to complete the task or solve the problem. An identified wayfinding problem involves both a task and environmental information. We can say that a wayfinding problem is an interpretation of a task in the light of environmental information.

A person who successfully completes a wayfinding task by reaching a given destination has developed a wayfinding solution. This solution consists of the totality of behavioral actions leading the person in his movement from origin to destination. To each behavioral action corresponds a decision. To use an

𝕋
WAYFINDING
TASK

𝕀
ENVIRONMENTAL
INFORMATION

𝔹
BEHAVIORAL
ACTION

architectural metaphor, we can refer to decisions as being the blueprints for behavioral actions. The totality of decisions is therefore also a wayfinding solution, though it is of a cognitive rather than a behavioral nature. Among the introduced units, environmental information, decisions, and behavioral actions, which are the product of the three process components of wayfinding, are particularly important and require further clarification.

WAYFINDING
DECISION

Environmental Information

Environmental information includes a descriptive, a locational, and a time component. This composition has been proposed in essence by Downs and Stea (1977).[4] I will discuss each component and identify cultural and personal variations.

Content description

The descriptive component tells what something is. It can denote objects, people, places and give characteristics in more or less detail. In describing objects, people, and places two aspects can stand out: the particular, the unique, the distinctive or the general, the similar. The first aspect gives an identity, helps differentiate and separate one thing from another and renders it easily recognizable. The second establishes equivalences useful in classifying and grouping things together. Identity tends to emphasize one or a few characteristics and to ignore others. This simplifies the description, but it also distorts it and sometimes reduces it to the level of a stereotype. Historical Quebec, industrial Toronto, governmental Ottawa — the terms, although they designate a true characteristic of each city, cast them as historical, industrial and governmental to the detriment of the other characteristics of the cities. Stereotypes contain information particularly important in the original choice to go or not to go to a place. Who would want to spend a holiday in industrial Toronto or even in governmental Ottawa?[5]

Grouping things together in terms of likeness (equivalence) or difference (identity) is a basic taxonomic process. It classifies, orders, and thereby simplifies cognitively our complex surroundings. The ensuing categories, developed and adjusted over time, become basic cognitive building blocks used in perceiving, understanding, retaining, and communicating information. They are referred to as schemata. According to schema theory all knowledge gained from past experience is packaged into schema units. A schema is not specific to an object or an event in particular but encompasses that which is generally valid about a class of things. Schemata therefore have to be purposely vague and open-ended. An experienced mushroom hunter,

Historical Quebec. (*Cover of a tourist map published by the Information Office of the City of Québec*)

for example, will have a schema for various species. Although a *boletus edulis* may vary in size, in the form and the color of the hat, in the form of the stem, although that mushroom will look quite different when young or old, he will be able to distinguish it at a glance from related subspecies of *boleti*. Schemata change and evolve through experience. A novice may not see the difference between young specimen of the deadly *amanita verna* (destroying angel) and of the edible field mushroom *agaricus campestris*. Note that the collector of *agaricus* can not afford one single *amanita* for his dinner. Mushroom guides are dangerous because they are written by experts and used by novices, who do not share the experts' schemata.[6]

Most things people classify get a name or a label. Naming is a cognitive process that renders the world manageable. It is significant in this context that various cultures associate naming with religious and mythical ideas of original creation and of the transformation of chaos into order. Amos Rapoport brings our attention to the biblical conception of Genesis, in which creation is considered completed only after man has named its constituent parts (Rapoport, 1977). By the same token we often assume a phenomenon to be understood just because it has received a label.

Naming creates an order and also renders the unknown familiar. Early American immigrants often used names of places and cities of their countries of origin to designate the new habitats and this without concern for physical resemblance. David Lowenthal labeled this act of verbal appropriation "linguistic landscaping." Similarly, names are used to enhance and embellish. Pine Avenue in Montréal, for example, is suspiciously lacking pines or any other trees, just as the most common name for those high-rise instant slum dwellings is "Manoir" or "Chateau" something or other.

Although naming is no doubt fundamental in coping with the environment, a certain form of knowledge does not lend itself to labels. This knowledge may be retained as images that are not necessarily visual in nature. The memory of a good bottle of wine is an appropriate example. Wines have been described in flowery words, but inevitably one has to taste it to know what the description means.

The surrealist painter Magritte was interested in juxtaposing words and images, giving each its own autonomy. He noted: "An object encounters its image, an object encounters its name. It happens that the object's name and its image encounter each other" (Torczyner, 1977, 260).

Certain individuals operate essentially on a verbal mode of thinking, other rely more on images. Robert Sommer called them the verbalizers and the visualizers. Ontogenetically the visual preceeds the verbal. Young children think first in images. Only later do they acquire the use of words and abstract concepts. In adults a predominance of one or the other mode may remain (Sommer, 1978).

Location

Up to this point we have focused on the descriptive component of environmental information, which answers the question of what something is. The second component of environmental information is one of location. It answers the question of where something is. The "where" question leads to two basic responses, one using a process description, the other a state description of location. The process description indicates location by what one has to do to get there. If, in an unfamiliar city, you ask a policeman the location of downtown he will probably give you a process description of the genre: "Continue straight on until the third light, turn left, . . . you can't miss it." The "you can't miss it" should make you suspicious. Otherwise the policeman's reply has the advantage of getting you going immediately as it outlines the actions necessary to get there. It has its limitation in that it describes a particular route and is only relevant to the point of origin and the points on that route. If you make a mistake on the way, the process description does not allow for corrections. You will go on until you discover that the desired location is not where you thought it was.

The state description indicates location within some reference system. As seen in Chapter 2, reference systems can generally be of three types. The described location may be related to the location of the information-giving person. Based on such an egocentric system, a person may describe Québec City, for example, as being 300 miles east of his own position. The location may be related to other fixed locations. Within such a fixed system Québec City could be described as being on the St. Lawrence River. Finally, the location may be related to some abstract system such as the coordinates describing Québec City by latitude and longitude. The state description has the advantage of being valid independently of the person's location in the setting, but it does not necessarily tell him how to get there. It should also be noted that in a state description the system of reference has to be shared by the person giving and the person obtaining the information in order to be meaningful.

Time

In following daily activities we not only have to get places but we have to get there in time. The temporal component of environmental information answers the questions of when and how likely something is to occur. The information "an express bus leaves Montréal's central terminal for Quebec City at 14.00 every day" contains all the described components answering the question of what, where, when, and the likelihood of the event.

Time is fundamental in coordinating activities at all levels of contemporary society.[7] No arrangements, no appointments, no planning escapes a time specification. Yet people are notoriously bad at judging time. It is easy to fool innocent victims by modifying the speed of clocks. Experiments have shown that clocks can be made to go one and a half to two times normal speed before suspicion is aroused.[8] Estimated or subjective time is demonstratively affected by various factors. Motivation, especially in the form of liking and disliking, influences the perception of time, as does the density of notable events (Lynch, 1972). Finally variables related to a person's condition like health, age, levels of intoxication, all intervene in time estimates (Fraser, 1975).

We have already seen that time and distance (space) are associated notions. They are often used interchangeably to describe and measure each other. It is therefore not surprising to find similar confounding variables affecting judgments on space and time. Among the most important are motivation or valence, that is, the level of attraction emanating from a place or an event and the density of distinctive features or notable events respectively. Lynch (1972) has also noted that the further an episode lies in the past, the shorter it appears. Closer to the present, it will be perceived as longer in time. The same spatial distortions have already been described. Distances in one's own home territory generally appear longer than identical distances located further away.

Temporal estimates are essentially of two types. One, past oriented, measures the length of an episode that has occured; the other, future-oriented, estimates the time it will take to accomplish something or to get somewhere. Today we rely extensively on the clock to measure past episodes, but no clock will tell us how much time will be needed to do something. Whenever we plan, we have to rely on our subjective, inaccurate ability to estimate time. Inaccurate maybe, but we still function reasonably well in keeping our appointments, in turning up for work, in taking trains or planes.

People learn to be on time. In addition to estimating the time it takes to reach a destination, we rely on catching-up devices and allow for a certain safety margin. Most people working on regular schedules get to their work place with an astonishing precision, some on time and some always 10 minutes late. They may compensate for "running late" by walking or driving faster. The safety or error margin may be calculated in how many minutes one should arrive before the scheduled appointment or in the number of minutes one can afford to arrive late. In interactions with fellow citizens we rely on rather strict, culturally determined rules.[9] Hall describes different being-late periods, which shows how finely tuned our error margins are. In ascendant order, they are the "mumble something periods, the slight apology periods, the mildly insulting periods requiring full apology, rude periods, and downright insulting periods" (Hall, 1959, 24).

People used to given journeys have learned to estimate fairly precisely the time it will take them to reach a destination even in the light of small imponderables like traffic density, road conditions, and so on. It is also known that those who do not travel often are far less confident in their time-planning abilities and are seen waiting for hours at railway stations and at airports.

Perception and cognition

The source of environmental information is not only the directly perceived cues in the spatial setting but also a person's memory and knowledge of the setting, of other similar settings, and of past experience in general. It would be tempting to identify perception and cognition as two independent processes each responsible for coping with information from the setting and from memory, respectively. This interpretation is misconceived however. It is in fact extremely difficult to disentangle perception and cognition. Perception is strongly tinted by what a person knows and by what he wants to know. A magnificent illustration of the powerful effect images can have on what is perceived, even for artists who pride themselves on observing the "truth," is given by Gombrich (1960) in *Art and Illusion.* Dürer in 1515 completed a woodcut of a rhinoceros he presumably knew from second-hand evidence only. Associations with images of dragons of the Middle Ages were probably responsible for the armor-like shields in which the animal is clad.

Figure 3.1 compares Dürer's version of the rhinoceros on the left to an engraving on the right made by Heath more than 250 years later. Heath's rhinoceros is supposed to have been drawn *au vif* in Africa. It still shows an

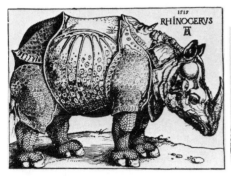

Figure 3.1
Images and perception; comparison by Gombrich of prints made by Dürer and Heath. *(From E. H. Gombrich, 1960,* Art and Illusion, *Princeton University Press, Princeton, N.J., p. 81)*

armor bearing little resemblance to the actual skin of the animal.[10] The eighteenth century engraver could not help seeing the unfamiliar rhinoceros through the familiar image created by Dürer.

The historical evolution of the visual arts conveys the images people associate with their everyday environment and the changes in these images over time. Of particular interest in this respect is the image of the natural environment as expressed in landscape paintings. Artists of most periods have tried and believed they succeeded in representing their surroundings objectively. In all probability, their images deviated only little from the popular images collectively held during a period. Gombrich believes that some painters, by creating new images, spearheaded the evolution of perception. We can indeed ask ourselves whether, without Monet or a Turner, we would see misty land and seascapes the way we do today?

Given this interrelation, it is not possible to make a clear conceptual distinction between perception and cognition. To refer to a specific moment in time, we can differentiate between environmental information that is dependent on direct sensory contact with a setting and environmental information evoked from past experience. I shall use the terms "sensory information" (Is) to account for the first case and "memory information" (Im) to account for the second case. It is understood that sensory information also involves memory and that memory information once went through the process of being directly perceived. The important criterion separating the two is that at a given moment memory information can be obtained without or independent of sensory inputs from the setting, while sensory information cannot.

Environmental information might further be obtained by inference. This may be achieved by any combination of sensory and memory information. An example taken from my research shows a subject who, during a wayfinding episode, infers that he is in a given corridor, because he finds the destination (sensory information) and he knew that the destination is in that corridor (memory information).

For wayfinding, all three classes of environmental information are important, although they are not assumed to play an equal role in all phases of the problem-solving process. Memory and inferred information (Ii) will be particularly important in the planning of spatial behavior, while sensory information is essential to the execution of that behavior. The differentiation between these classes of information is further justified when dealing with design issues. The sensory information relied upon has to be provided by the designed setting, while memory information, if shared by the population at large, is not necessarily required. Redundancy can be reduced by eliminating from the setting information that is shared by the population.

Is

SENSORY
INFORMATION

Im

MEMORY
INFORMATION

Ii

INFERRED
INFORMATION

Cultural and personal differences

I have argued that the image and through it the perception of the environment has changed through the ages. It is reasonable to assume perceptual differences from one culture to another, particularly if their development has been independent. The literature seems unanimous in pointing out such differences, although concrete evidence is not always strong. Lloyd (1972), in reviewing the cross-cultural literature on perception and cognition, blames this shortcoming on the imposition of values representing the culture of the researcher rather than on uniformity of the studied cultures. In spite of this shortcoming some striking examples have been reported. Amos Rapoport has compared the notion of space as it is experienced in different cultures. While for Western civilizations, he notes, space tends to be seen in physical terms, Australian aborigines conceive of space through meaning and symbols derived from their mythology. Elements of the landscape obtain their meaning from journeys of ancestral figures who have used or even transformed themselves into places, rocks, trees, and rivers. Mythology then provides the means to order and to name an environment that, at least for the outsider, is devoid of distinctive features (Rapoport, 1972). Like the Australian aborigines, American native groups visualize space as more fluid, having less sharp boundaries than we tend to see, but endowed with strong symbolic meaning. Moore (1979) describes the relation of American natives with the land as one of "identifying with" rather than owning it. This attitude manifests itself also in the architectural conception of housing and its relation to the natural landscape. A Mexican *municipio*, according to Rapoport (1977), typically contains the habitat of the Indians at the periphery of town, nestled among the vegetation, while the Ladinos choose to live as close as possible to the plaza in an essentially man-made environment.

The way a particular culture relates to the environment is often brought about by necessity and the population's ability to adapt. Eskimos, for example, have learned to survive in a very hostile climate and a very unstable one. Carpenter (1973) writes of a boat trip he experienced along a dangerous rocky coast in dense fog. His native navigator kept his distance by listening to the surf and the cries of the seabirds. Like Polynesians, Eskimos must rely on alternative cues perceived by different sensory modes. Their conception of space is therefore more explicitly multimodal.

People often tend to overlook the fact that environmental information is not only visual in nature. Much information can be perceived through nonvisual modes. Being blindfolded leads to "insightful" experiences. In a study of environmental perception subjects were guided through an unfamiliar shopping center. One group experienced the setting under normal conditions, one group without vision, and one group with neither vision nor hearing. The blindfolded subjects were able to identify major environmental features, and they drew sketch maps. The sketches were less accurate than those of the sighted group, but they showed a strong resemblance to the route taken.[11] The group deprived of vision and hearing, although little aware of environmental features, also produced maps. If one accounts for the very common inversions of direction, the sketched routes are again clearly recognizable (Passini, 1972).

Environmental information, we can conclude, describes events and objects and sets them in a time and space frame. From the perspective of the information-processing person it is possible, for a given moment in time, to differentiate between sensory information (Is), memory information (Im), and inferred information (Ii). Environmental information is the outcome of a person's understanding of the environment, and at the same time it is the unit upon which decisions are based. Being relatively simple and clear as a concept, it is easily operationalized (see Appendix B). This does not mean that we can do away with the notion of cognitive maps. These are important in the study of how people comprehend the spatial characteristics of the environment. In Chapter 4 we shall look at this aspect in more detail.

Although the basic cognitive processes are presumably universal in nature, it is important to keep in mind cultural as well as personal differences in the content of what is perceived, in the way this information is structured and retained, as well as in the importance given to the different sensory modes.

Decisions and Spatial Behavior

Cognitive and behavior solutions

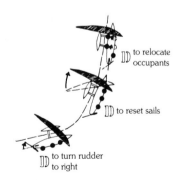

to relocate occupants

to reset sails

to turn rudder to right

Three behavioral actions and the corresponding decisions from a wayfinding episode.

A wayfinding task is completed when the person concerned reaches a desired destination. The solution to the wayfinding problem posed by the task is the sequence of behavioral actions leading from origin to destination. Behavioral actions could be observed and recorded, but they would not reveal much about the nature of the solution.

A fictive instance of South Sea navigation will serve as an illustration. By following a native craft, an observer might note that at a certain point in time, the navigator moves the rudder from left to right, that the sails are differently placed, that the occupants of the boat take on new positions, and that two of them are busying themselves with plaiting a cord. Given these observations, the three following questions might be asked in order to understand what happened: are these behavioral actions part of a wayfinding solution; if they are, why were they taken; and how do they fit together in a meaningful way.

The first question aims at separating what is part of the wayfinding solution and what is not. Plaiting the cord might indeed be necessary for catching turtles but not for wayfinding. The second question probes for the reason of the behavioral action. In this example, the action may have been taken to set the canoe on a new course, which in turn may have been necessary to follow a coral reef. The question of how the behavioral actions fit together probes for a common underlying cause. The three actions of turning the rudder, adjusting the sails, and relocating the occupants indeed form a package. Taken together and in that particular order, they set the canoe on a new course.

On the basis of the behavioral actions alone, it is not possible to answer the three questions probing the nature of the wayfinding solution. If the totality of decisions were on record, we would have data more amenable to analysis. "To turn the rudder," "to reset sail," "to relocate people," and "to plait a cord" would be the decisions corresponding to the behaviors observed. These would not be the only decisions on record, since "to catch turtles," "to set canoe on a new course," and "to follow coral reef" are also decisions. Although the decision "to set canoe on new course" did not lead directly to a behavioral action, it was responsible for the three decisions leading immediately to the behavioral actions. "To follow coral reef" is a decision that is even a step further removed from behavior, but it can still be seen as being a part of the wayfinding solution.

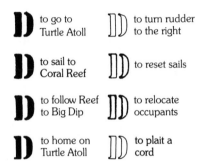

to go to
Turtle Atoll

to sail to
Coral Reef

to follow Reef
to Big Dip

to home on
Turtle Atoll

to turn rudder
to the right

to reset sails

to relocate
occupants

to plait a
cord

Two types of decision

We have now identified decisions that lead directly to behavior and decisions that lead to behavior via the mediation of other decisions. Let us focus on the latter. The intermediary decision becomes necessary because of some constraints emanating directly or indirectly from the setting. Such decisions can be described as tasks or subtasks. When viewed in the light of environmental information, a subtask is defined as a wayfinding problem that necessitates a solution if the subtask is to be completed.

Returning to the navigation example, we can say that the decision "to set canoe on new course" is a subtask and that the three decisions "to turn the rudder," "to reset sail," and "to relocate people" are the decisions describing the solution to the problem presented by the subtask. "To follow coral reef" is another subtask for which the decision "to set canoe on new course," even if not directly leading to behavior, can be seen as the solution or at least as part of the solution. If a record of the totality of decisions made for an original wayfinding task existed, which for the sake of illustration is "to go to Turtle Atoll," we could continue this process of identifying subtasks of a higher order until we reached the original task.

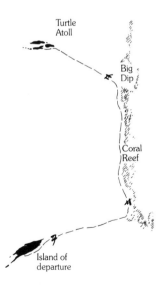

The fictive voyage to Turtle Atoll.

The Structural Framework

In introducing and discussing the basic units of wayfinding, we hinted at some links among decisions. These indeed are the structural backbone of wayfinding. A total set of decisions made to reach a destination can be seen to contain two structural characteristics. Each provides for an answer to one of the main questions raised above, that is, why is a behavioral action taken or a decision made and how do they fit together into meaningful sets.

Decision hierarchy

The first structural characteristic is the hierarchical linkage among decisions, as shown in Figure 3.2. Reading the decisions from left to right we can see that in order "to go to Turtle Atoll," it was decided among other things "to follow coral reef to Big Dip;" in order to follow the reef, it was decided "to set canoe on a new course" given by the reef's outline; in order to set the canoe on course, it was decided "to turn the rudder," "to reset the sails," and "to relocate the occupants." If the hierarchical decision structure is read in the opposite sense, we obtain the answer to why a particular decision was made. Indeed, the reason for any decision or behavioral action is found in the decision one step up the hierarchy, until the original task is reached.[12]

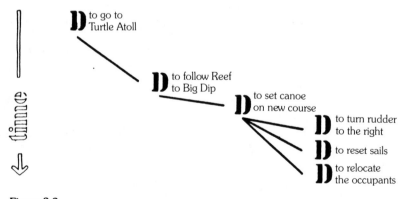

Figure 3.2
Decision hierarchies.

Decision plans

Figure 3.3 represents the same South Sea sailing scenario. In the second column from the left, we can see that "to sail to coral reef" is part of a set of general decisions that includes "to follow coral reef to Big Dip" and "to home on Turtle Atoll." This set indicates in the most general terms how the task "to go to Turtle Atoll" will be completed. The three decisions in the order given represent the decision plan for the task. Had the three decisions led directly to behavioral actions, the plan would have been executed and the problem solved. As can be appreciated from the diagram, the task could not be completed on the basis of the three decisions only. The decision "to follow reef to Big Dip," for example, could not lead directly to a behavioral action. It became a subtask in itself and required a plan to solve it. The plan this time consisted of two decisions: "to set canoe on new course" and "to sail according to reef outline." The decision "to set canoe on new course" required a plan composed of three decisions "to turn rudder," to "reset sail," and "to relocate people." These three decisions were finally executed, and the subtask "to set canoe on new course" was completed.[13]

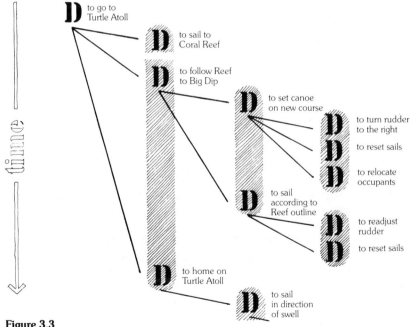

Figure 3.3
Decision plans.

A distinction should be made between the logical and the temporal organization of decisions. The hierarchical links, that is, the "in-order-to relation" represents the logical organization; the vertical axis in the diagram corresponds to the time sequence. A plan for a given subtask emphasizes the sequential order of decisions at that level of analysis. A proper sequence can be a prerequisite to the successful execution of a plan. Setting the canoe on a new course is only possible if the three actions composing its plan are effected in a given order.

The structural characteristics of decision plans provide for an insight into how decisions fit together into meaningful sets. An analogy to plans used in the design profession is possible to a certain point. The contract to build a house can be seen as the equivalent of the original decision and task to reach a destination. The general design plan may correspond to the general wayfinding plans of the intermediary decisions, while the working drawings correspond to the lowest plans in the hierarchy leading to the wayfinding behaviors.

THE PROCESS OF WAYFINDING

The conceptualization of wayfinding as spatial problem solving incorporates information processing, decision making or planning, and decision execution. In order to describe these cognitive abilities, if only in general terms, it is indispensable to analyze actual wayfinding, that is, to observe what people do to reach destinations. Therefore, we will have to move from the romantic but hypothetical South Sea navigation examples to more common wayfinding tasks. Less romantic, but by no means less intriguing are observations of how people find destinations in complex urban commercial settings. Given Montréal's rigorous winter, much downtown commerce is located in inside shopping malls rather than in the open street system. Many of these malls are further interconnected, thereby creating large indoor commercial complexes. The great number and variety of shops is only one of many factors rendering these centers intricate and often difficult for wayfinding. The density of directional and commercial signs, the movement of people, architectural and graphical extravagances, lighting effects and color, vast underground levels, indoor garages, all add up to provide for a perfect testing ground to observe wayfinding behavior, to identify the decision-making process underlying these behaviors, to look at signs and maps in use, to note instructions that people give or receive, and to study the images or cognitive maps people are able to build up to get around. The objective of this research relevant to this chapter was to obtain for a given wayfinding task a set of decisions that would be as complete as possible and an account of the environmental information relied upon. In a project undertaken in 1975, I identified tasks for reaching specific destinations in three commercial settings of downtown Montréal. Twelve subjects took part in the study. Each had to reach the prescribed destination in company of an observer. Unobtrusive microphones recorded their conversations. The subjects were asked to verbalize everything that went through their minds. Furthermore, they were asked to describe every behavioral action, such as turning right, going up stairs, so that a third person, by listening to the recording, would be able to follow their route. The observer had as a main function to stimulate the subject's verbalization by inquiring, if necessary, what the subject was doing or thinking and why he was doing the things he described. The first question aimed at recording the decisions; the second aimed at the environmental information used by the subject. The recordings were transcribed in their integral form and subjected to a content analysis to identify the decisions and the three types of environmental information introduced above. This account of spatial problem solving will be referred to as the wayfinding protocol. To assure an acceptable level of reliability, coding rules were established, first, to identify the units, that is, the decisions and environmental information and, second, to describe the links among them. The reader is referred to Appendix B for further detail on the research procedure.

Developing Decision Plans

General aspects of decision making

It is truly surprising how many decisions are involved even in a seemingly simple task. Some subjects accumulated more than 100 decisions to complete a task that did not last longer than 20 minutes. On the basis of the coding rules it was possible in each case to account for the decisions and to produce coherent decision diagrams where decisions leading directly to behavioral actions are linked to the original task over a set of intermediary decisions or subtasks.

These structural characteristics of decision diagrams tell about spatial problem solving. The development of decision plans is a solution-generating activity as well as a task-generating activity. The original complex task is broken down into subtasks. The subtasks lead to more manageable problems for which solutions involving a reasonable number of decisions can be found. Although a great number of individual decisions have been recorded for even relatively simple tasks, the single plan for a subtask never contains more than half a dozen, and more frequently, just three to four decisions.

To develop a decision plan is to develop a solution for a wayfinding problem. It could be assumed that for every wayfinding task a person confronts, a new decision plan is worked out, regardless of previous problem

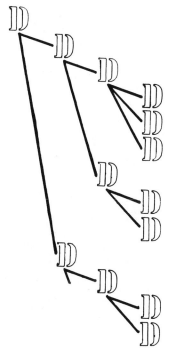

Breaking up a complex task into subtasks.

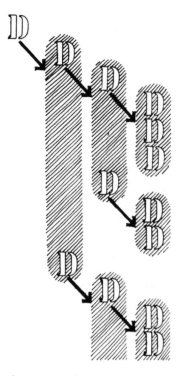

Composition of plans to solve subtasks.

solving. To keep solving problems for which solutions have already been found on previous occasions would contradict the parsimony and efficiency requirements essential to wayfinding. If the plan for a given task could be remembered, the development of a second identical decision plan would indeed appear as an unnecessary effort. At issue is the capacity to remember. If the decisions were just a series of unrelated commands to actions, it would indeed be impossible to keep track of them.[14] Given the structure that in effect packs decisions into coherent subsolutions, each containing a limited number of elements, it is possible to record very long decision plans.[15] Thus, plan making can be eliminated in part or completely if a decision plan has already been developed on a previous occasion.

The breaking down of the original complex task into subtasks implies a structured process that operates at different levels of generalities. This permits the treatment of individual subtasks or subproblems in semi-isolation while still taking into account the problem as a whole. To use once more the planning of a house as an illustrative analogy, we can refer to the subproblem of working out a roof detail as a semi-isolated subtask. In order to be successful, it will still have to take into account the overall layout and character of the house.

To summarize these general aspects of decision making, it can be stated that the development of a decision plan is characterized by a task-generating activity that breaks down complex problems into manageable subproblems to be solved in semi-isolation and the solution of which, that is, the decision plan, can be comfortably remembered.

Dynamics of decision making

It would be quite erroneous to assume that, for an unfamiliar task, a person works out a total plan and then executes it. Here the house-building analogy would not hold. The wayfinding protocol indicates people to have often only global and vague initial plans consisting merely of a few general decisions. These decisions at least allow for a start. The specific problems are then tackled as they present themselves.[16]

This approach makes good sense, given that not all environmental factors are known or predictable and, consequently, the problem cannot be fully assessed. Even starting off with a vague idea, the person can pick up new information that helps clarify the problem. The development of a decision plan has, therefore, to be seen as an ongoing process that is designed for dealing with unforeseen problems whenever they occur.[17]

In accounting for the chronological ordering of decisions, it is possible to arrive at some inferences about the dynamics of decision making. Plans analyzed within a time dimension reveal the order in which people tackle

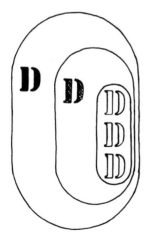

Plans within the larger context.

problems. Generally it is observed that a new plan is being formulated only after a previous plan has been executed. This is seen in a sequential ordering of plans and an avoidance of overlaps. The almost total absence of overlapping plans indicates the strong tendency to deal with one problem or subproblem at a time and not to solve problems in parallel or simultaneously.

Some attempts to execute decisions inevitably lead to failure. Although the tasks formulated in the research were representative of common wayfinding problems, many failures occurred. In such situations, two alternatives are observable. The first and more usual alternative is to devise a new plan to complete the same task. If one cannot go up to the offices by elevator, for example, one might choose to use the stairs. The second alternative is not to devise a new plan but actually to change the task. Tasks have indeed been reformulated or completely changed after plans did not lead to successful completion.

An alteration of a task within the decision structure implies the modification of a higher-order plan. The repercussions may move up through the whole system and even modify or nullify the original task. Giving up and going home is an illustrative example of just that situation.

Sometimes a wayfinding person behaves in a quasi-automatic fashion. These were the moments, in the research, when the observer had a hard time making the subject verbalize his plans, since the subject knew just what to do without paying any particular attention. Among the many examples illustrating this aspect of wayfinding is the use of elevators. Although each elevator is somewhat different in design and in the arrangement of the control board, there is a set of behaviors that is typical in the use of all elevators. On a slightly larger scale, food shopping in a supermarket falls in the same category. Although the layouts of supermarkets vary, there is nevertheless a set of typical behaviors and routes common to all.

It seems, therefore, reasonable to assume that the development of decision plans relies partly on a solution repertoire of a particular kind. While solving spatial problems, advantage is taken of type solutions that have already been established for type problems. The decision plans describing the type solutions must be open-ended and generally applicable regardless of the specificity of the setting. The assumption is functionally justifiable too. To rely on a solution repertoire whenever possible is easier than the actual process of solving problems. It requires less mental effort and is less time consuming.[18]

Environmental information, we have seen, may comprise a process or a state description of location. The process description of location is, in fact, the equivalent of a recorded decision plan. It tells what to do in order to reach a location. A solution repertoire takes on, therefore, the nature of environmental information.

Some of this information can be very precise, and some can be purposely vague, amounting to no more than some general rules of thumb to describe

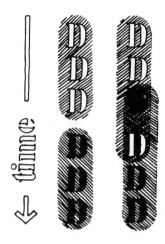

Sequential and overlapping plans.

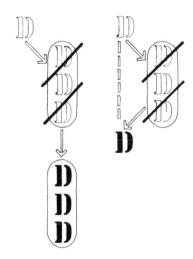

Two alternatives if a decision plan cannot be executed: to make a new plan; to alter the subtask.

where certain things, like stairs, toilets, information booths, tend to be and how they can be reached.

Strategies of decision making

The routes taken for identical tasks and the decisions involved may vary from one person to another. However, if the plans are compared on the basis of the environmental information used, a certain consistency becomes apparent. Indeed, for similar information used, plans are very much alike. What appears to create differences among wayfinding solutions is not different planning or problem solving but a reliance on different sensory and memory information. This leads one to view environmental information as being the important variable in determining wayfinding solutions. This statement does not imply an environmental determinism depriving the person of freedom of choice. It just means that if people have to solve a problem and they dispose of the same information to find a solution, the results have a good chance of being the same.

Consider now the three basic types of environmental information: sensory, memory, and inferred. To each corresponds a specific task situation, first, when sensory information is in itself sufficient to complete a task, second, when memory information is also required, and third, when information has to be manipulated to arrive at some inference. There is another task situation frequently encountered in wayfinding, that is, when no relevant information seems to be available.

We must differentiate between a task situation where relevant information is available and the one where no or only very little information is at hand. In the latter, the person can only hope to discover the desired destination or information leading to it by chance. Such a task requires a search strategy. The search can be random, or it can be systematic. In a given situation the chance of finding an object may even be calculated in function of the search tactic used. If the person can rely on available information to find a destination he will be using an access strategy. Three access tactics match the three previously introduced task situations. If a person relies on directly perceived sensory information only, he is employing a direct access tactic; if the person must include memory information about the setting or similar settings, he is employing an indirect access tactic; and finally, if he must derive the desired information by some mental manipulation, he is using an inference tactic.

The South Sea navigator will illustrate the differences between the various strategies and tactics. Let us imagine the canoe sailing the open sea after a night's navigation. If the captain does not see the expected reef that serves as a seamark, he might decide to cruise around randomly, or he might decide to follow the course of an opening spiral to hit the seamark. These are two examples of search tactics. If he sees the reef, he will decide to sail straight toward it; if he sees a colored patch of water, he may associate it with the reef and sail toward the colored patch; and if he does not see either but is able to figure out how much lateral drift he was exposed to, he may identify the course that will lead him to the reef. I have called these three examples of access tactics: direct, indirect, and inference tactics.

The degree of difficulty a wayfinding problem represents can be assessed on the basis of the task situations and the strategies and tactics available to complete them. A search strategy is usually less efficient than an access strategy. Only very few instances in the wayfinding protocol indicated the use of a search strategy when in fact information was available to rely on an access strategy. The reason for that exceptional choice was the perceived effort necessary to find the information. In observing a map a person may say that "it is probably there," but "it is too complicated to find." Increased levels of complexity characterize the three access tactics described above. Chances of error generally increase as processes become more complex. Naturally people choose direct access to indirect access and indirect access to access by inference. The reason of choice is to be found in increased reliability and in greater convenience. Access tactics are easier to handle than inference tactics.

Executing Decision Plans

Decisions have been presented as the main unit of analysis. We now have to consider the transformation of decisions into behavioral actions. The final result of spatial problem solving and wayfinding is, after all, the behavior leading to a destination.

General aspects of decision execution

The key to understanding the way decisions are executed lies in the composition of the decision itself. Wayfinding decisions such as "to go to office 809," "to take the metro," "to look for information," and so on, contain an action part, that is, "to go," "to take," "to look," and an object part, that is, "office 809," "the metro," and "information." The object part of a decision brings to mind a more or less clear image. This image creates an expectancy of finding, at the appropriate time, a corresponding counterpart in the physical environment. If at that moment the object corresponding to the image is perceived, the decision can be executed. The correspondence between the perceived and the expected image is again established on the basis of identity and equivalence, making it a natural extension of normal perceptual processes,

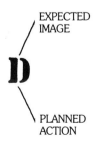

EXPECTED IMAGE

PLANNED ACTION

as discussed under schema theory. If no counterpart to the image can be found in the physical environment at the appropriate time, the decision cannot be executed. According to the previous definition, the decision becomes a task and a wayfinding problem.

The execution of decisions and of plans can be seen as a matching-feedback process.[19] Matching relates the expected object image to the perceived object. In case of a match, feedback sets the action part of the decision in motion; in case of a mismatch, it leads to further problem solving. Figure 3.4 illustrates the decision execution process in schematic form. The decision Dn on the left in the center is the starting point. The upper circuit corresponds to the successful execution of a decision, the lower circuit to an unsuccessful attempt resulting in the identification of a problem and the introduction of a new decision-making process.

Familiar routes taken to go to work, to return home, to do the weekly shopping are remembered. More specifically, it is the decision plans of such routes that are remembered. Although decision making in such situations is no longer necessary, the decisions still have to be executed and transformed into behavioral action. Decision making is a conscious process, while decision

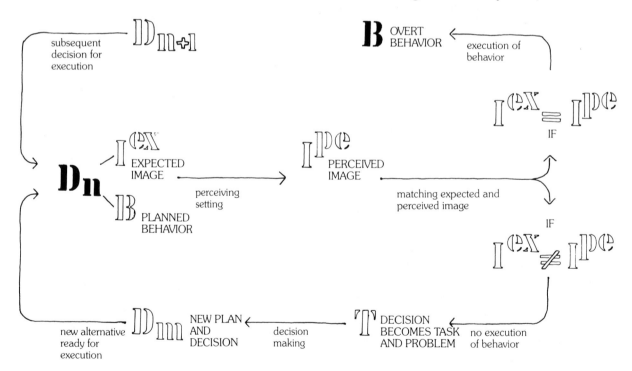

Figure 3.4
Decision execution as a matching feedback process.

execution is not. If a person who comes to a crossroad has to make a directional decision, it will absorb his thinking capacities, while if he knows the route and executes his decision plan, he can remain quite unaware of his actions and even be absorbed in other thoughts. It is not difficult to appreciate that plan execution is an unconscious process. Were this not so, every movement in space, which must be directed by decisions, would involve thought, which consumes energy and time. More importantly, it would monopolize our thinking capacities.

Memory plays a crucial role in recording decision plans of routes taken and in the actual execution of decisions. The image inherent in each decision has to be remembered so that the matching process can take place. A person can usually recall some general features along a familiar route, but he cannot remember the specific image of each decision. In order to understand decision execution it is important to differentiate between recall and recognition. The capacity to recognize, that is, to remember in the presence of the object, is far superior to recalling.[20] The process of executing decisions is largely based on recognition. Some recall, though, is necessary for the development of decisions in the first place.

In executing a plan, it is assumed that a person continuously matches expected decision images with perceived images. Sometimes a mismatch occurs. Maybe a tree is missing, maybe a house has been repainted. Typically, the person will react with surprise. A mismatch forces a shift from an unconscious decision execution to a conscious decision-making process. A mismatch has something of an alarm effect. In the end the person may have to develop a new plan for a decision that has become a task, or he may have to adjust the image expectancy attached to the decision.

Imaginary wayfinding

People also have the ability to mentally simulate wayfinding. It is, of course, possible to imagine the completion of a wayfinding task during which decision plans are elaborated and executed. The plan may or may not correspond to the plan actually developed if the task was being accomplished in a real setting. If the outlined model is also to hold for such simulations, the perceived object has to be substituted by an imagined one. So one ends up with an expectancy image from the decision and a mental representation of the setting (cognitive map) as a matching counterpart. This simulation is never as detailed as the real experience. In the simulation a person has to rely on recall rather than recognition. Figure 3.5 illustrates this simulation process.

The execution of decisions in simulated form might well be part of forming decision plans in the first place. This process can be seen as a means of evaluating the feasibility of plans.[21] It can serve to assess the possibility of a

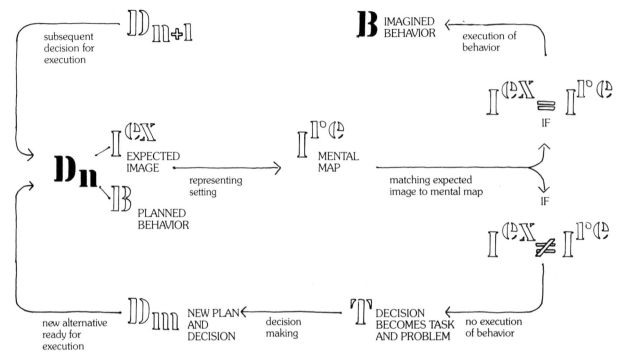

Figure 3.5
Decision execution in simulation: imagined behavior.

solution, and by mentally executing plans, some insight can be gained into the effort required for various options as well as their inherent interest. Decision execution in simulated form should, therefore, be seen as an integral part of heuristic problem solving.

Wayfinding, time, and effort

The same simulation procedure may be used to estimate the time needed to reach a destination. We have already seen that there is no experimental evidence suggesting that time estimates are based on distance estimates. Quite often, the time it takes to go somewhere has little to do with the distance traveled. Everyone who circulates in congested cities has had this experience. Time estimates are much more conveniently linked to behavioral episodes or activities. Going downtown to see a play involves me in: getting dressed—5 minutes (5 minutes longer in winter), walking to the bus stop—5 minutes, waiting for the bus—0 to 5 minutes, being driven downtown—10 minutes, and walking to the art center—5 minutes, a total of approximately 30 minutes. Furthermore, I know I have an error margin of 5 to 10 minutes; the play never starts on time. In this description I outlined a general decision plan to go to the art center, which broke my journey into five behavioral episodes. The estimation of each episode is then based on some previous experience or parts of such experience. These estimates are not necessarily done in hours and minutes but in much vaguer time units, which are then translated into measures that can be compared to a clock and communicated to others. Even if the individual estimate of episodes is imprecise, there is a good chance that errors will be cancelled out overall if the introduced bias is not systematic.

In estimating the time it takes to go somewhere we do in fact perform a simulation of plan execution. This simulation may be more or less refined depending on the need for precision. The feeling for time, it has been suggested, is linked to experiencing movement in space. Whatever the behavior, a time duration is associated with it, and we have a fairly good feeling of how long the duration should be. If, because of some unusual circumstance, a hammer suddenly took half a second longer to hit a nail than usual, we would be sure to react. It would also be interesting to observe how long people wait at a jammed traffic light before showing impatience and realizing the defect.

Time estimates, it would seem, are not directly based on distance estimates but on behavioral episodes experienced by the person. Repeated experience of the same episodes will eventually lead to an overall estimate, making the computation of individual episodes unnecessary. In such situations distances may be used as a substitute for a series of behavioral episodes, and distances may be linked to time estimates.

Deciding to go somewhere leaves open various options of routes and transportation means. A decision then has to be made to select the appropriate plan. The choice, as we have seen, is often based on a simulation of plan execution, that allows an estimate of the values of each plan. This simulation, which can be very general, leads to a form of means-end analysis, weighing the costs and the merits. Although the weighing is personal and subjective, there may be on the reward side factors of pleasantness and interest, and on the cost side factors of energy, finance, and also time.[22] Lynch (1972) wrote that in Western society, time is more and more seen as a commodity and as such is often in short supply.

Processing Environmental Information

The reader has been aware of the central role environmental information plays in the conceptualization of wayfinding. Indeed, environmental information is used in all phases of spatial problem solving; it contributes to the identification of a wayfinding problem and to the elaboration of the solution. Environmental information is fundamental in the making of decisions and decision plans as well as in their execution.

The provision of adequate environmental information is furthermore a crucial design issue. Signs, maps, verbal descriptions, as well as architectural and urban space can be seen as information support systems to wayfinding. Chapter 4 will focus on each of these support systems specifically. Here I shall introduce some general observations of information processing during wayfinding.

Little is known about perception and information processing in the complex environment where people live their normal lives and pursue their daily affairs.[23] As already indicated, a person is not passively exposed to the environment but plays an active role in the perceptual process.[24] Acquiring environmental information is a two-way process characterized by a direct impact of distinctive environmental features and also by an inverse action of search and selection in which the person looks for information. Given this fundamental position, some important questions emerge. What is the wayfinding person looking for? Are all people looking for more or less the same thing?

Wayfinding styles

In having people compare buildings in terms of wayfinding difficulties, I found strong opposing views among the sample of subjects. A compilation of assessments and their underlying reasons led to the identification of two independent groups, one stressing the problem of obtaining information from the sign system and the difficulties in understanding the meaning of the messages contained and the other group relating their problems to the understanding of the spatial properties of the setting and their position within it. Both groups were equally familiar with the buildings visited and generally agreed on the level of sign quality.

The assessments of the two groups can be seen to reflect the difficulty each group experienced in finding the information it was looking for. It can therefore be assumed that some people rely on linearly organized information as it is presented by directional signing, while other people tend to rely on spatially organized information that permits an understanding of the setting as a spatial ensemble. The tendency to rely on one type of information more than another marks two distinct wayfinding styles. The first we may call linear, the second spatial.

The idea of wayfinding styles is supported by the research on cognitive mapping reviewed in Chapter 2. Map typology, we have seen, reflects important differences in the representation of macro-spaces, one type being linearly organized, the route map, the other type being spatially organized, the survey map. While cognitive maps relate the organization and the structure of the environmental information retained, wayfinding styles specify the information a person seeks and uses when solving wayfinding problems. The link between the two is established if one remembers that people actively and selectively seek information. What is newly acquired has to make sense with what is already known. The selection criterion will be the relevance of that information to the body of knowledge already acquired, which, in terms of the physical environment, is characterized by the cognitive map. If, as I have suggested, wayfinding styles are indeed linked to a typology of cognitive maps, certain aspects of wayfinding behavior could be anticipated on the basis of a person's type of cognitive map.[25]

The identification of two wayfinding styles poses an interesting design question. In planning a building or any other setting, should the designer provide environmental information that corresponds to one style or to both styles? Does a person change style if the information suiting his normal style is not available?

People adhering to a spatial style may find a setting difficult although the signs are considered adequate. At the same time, it has also been observed that people who adhere to a linear style may find a setting difficult even if the spatial properties are readily accessible. Wayfinding is therefore facilitated if both types of information are accessible to the user. As a general rule, it is suggested that designers plan information systems of a spatial architectural nature as well as sign systems of a linear nature to facilitate both styles of wayfinding.

The wayfinding data show that a person can switch from a spatial to a linear style if the physical setting necessitates such a change. In the Montréal metro, where the spatial configuration of underground stations is often difficult to obtain, people rely on signs.[26] None of the subjects considered the metro system to be particularly difficult. It is therefore quite possible that, if a person understands clearly that he should rely on signs, he will adjust to the situation. A corresponding change from linear to spatial has not been observed. Even if a certain flexibility in styles is in use we should keep in mind that architectural and urban space as well as the various linear wayfinding supports are sources of information in their own right. In planning complex settings they should both appear as autonomous but complementary systems. I do not subcribe to the belief that signs are crutches designed to compensate for inadequate architectural solutions.

Receptiveness to information

Knowledge of the environment that may be expressed in verbal form or in images and cognitive maps directs a person's perception, his information processing. The perception of the environment is directed by what a person knows as well as by what he needs.[27]

In respect to a completed wayfinding task, the information a person needs is contained in the decision plans. If the information perceived and not perceived in the setting is analyzed with respect to these plans, an interesting correspondence emerges. While a person executes part of a decision plan, he tends to perceive information relevant to that part of the plan. Any information relevant to a more general task that does not apply to the immediate plan being executed has much less chance of being seen.

This aspect of information processing is illustrated in Figure 3.6. The diagram on the left shows, on the vertical time axes, the position of the environmental information Ix "passing in between" decision plans to reach the relevant decision Dx. On the right, the position of Ix coincides with the period of plan execution, when information relevant to that execution is sought. The plan, figuratively speaking, obstructs the passage of the information Ix to the appropriate decision Dx.

One of many examples occurred at the shopping center Alexis-Nihon. On the underground metro level, some subjects assumed that their destination, the offices, were generally higher up than the shops. They took the escalators to reach the upper floors. On the ground level they passed under a sign pointing to the offices without seeing it. They perceived only the information relevant to their plan to go higher. All subjects who at that time had not formulated a specific plan saw the sign. The subjects of the first group, when

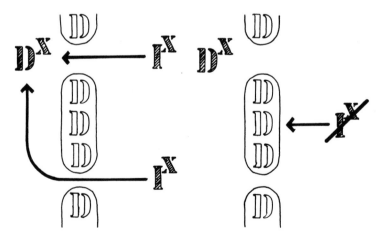

Figure 3.6
Optimal perception of environmental information in relation to decision plans.

returning to the ground floor after a fruitless search, perceived the sign without any difficulty.

This observation also has design implications. Signs, plans, and indeed all types of environmental information can be placed so that they are directly relevant to the wayfinding plan. If the information pertains to a higher-order decision, that is, to a task or subtask, it should occur once the previous part of the decision plan has been executed. This criterion is essential in determining the optimum location of environmental information in an existing or in a planned setting. The full application can only be discussed when the notation system in Chapter 5 has been introduced.

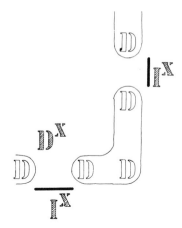

Optimal position of environmental information in relation to decisions in space.

Decision plans, a form of information

Environmental information has to be obtained, interpreted, understood, and used at a particular decision point, and it has to be retained for future use. As discussed in the section introducing decision plans, recall of verbal material from memory often shows an underlying hierarchical structure. It is generally accepted that hierarchies form an important basis for the retrieval and reconstruction of events.[28] Various authors have suggested that people also remember location hierarchically. Instead of recalling the exact position of a city, they may remember the position of a larger geographic unit, such as a state, in which that city is to be found (Stevens and Coupe, 1978). The same principle can apply to the architectural scale. A bed is remembered in a room that is in a house located in a given area, and so on.

Not only are place memories, that is, cognitive maps, often based on hierarchical structures, but they can be organized according to a decision plan. Memory tests have shown that people are extremely efficient in recalling the logical and temporal order of decisions if they are the result of an active involvement. We have also seen that each decision of a hierarchical structure is composed of an action part and an object part that incorporates any physical perceptual element. It stands to reason that the structure of a decision plan serves as a memory device to recall a decision as well as physical location. Such a recall technique would necessarily involve a person in reactivating the decisions and imagining the underlying trip. The resulting representation would have to be egocentric and sequential or linear, which in fact corresponds to route maps. Within this perspective it is not surprising that experiences in new, unfamiliar environments lead to route maps first.[29]

I have now introduced some general aspects of the three cognitive processes that characterize spatial problem solving.[30] In order to illustrate some of the scope of this conceptualization, I will conclude by interpreting some common and some less common wayfinding observations.

Interpreting Some Wayfinding Curiosities

When visiting a town for the first time, you may have the luck to be shown around by a friend, or you may have to explore by yourself. If your guide is well informed, you may learn a great deal about the town's historical and cultural highlights, but in terms of finding your way around it when you revisit, you are sure to do better after having explored by yourself. Also, it is common knowledge that a person who is merely a passenger will have more difficulty finding his way than the driver of the automobile. Although the perceived information is roughly the same for both, the active person gains a more coherent understanding of what is where. How can this difference be explained in the light of the previous discussion?

In exploring the city, the visitor will have to make wayfinding decisions. In order to reach downtown, for example, he may follow the main artery, look for the more densely built-up areas, and head for the streets where he sees advertising signs and many people. In other words, the exploring visitor is developing a structured decision plan. The hierarchical structure allows him to retain decisions in convenient packages. As each decision contains an action and an image component, the decision plans become the supportive structure for retaining images. Decisions can be seen as devices to store and to retrieve information.[30] The guided visitor and the driven passenger are not actively involved in making wayfinding decisions. Without the decision-making process, there is no supportive framework to organize the perceived information. If the person does not resort to some alternative structuring device, he will be left with a list of impressions not suited to being remembered and retrieved for later wayfinding.

Women often experience more difficulties with wayfinding than men.[32] This can be explained by the more passive role society has imposed on the woman. Compared to a generation ago, contemporary women are less bound to the house. For those who are, the range of travel tends to be limited to local friends and community services. If an important family trip is planned, is it not common for the man to assume his imposed role of decision maker?

For the moment, let us return to your visit of that unnamed city where, we will assume, you are asked to stay over night. Having enjoyed a good supper with your friends, plenty of talk, and a few drinks, you might wake up in the middle of the night debating whether you should or should not go to the bathroom. Having decided you should, you try to make your way to the bathroom in the dark. You do your best to figure out the layout of the flat that appeared so clear in the evening. You could try to find the light switch, but as you do not want to inconvenience your host, you keep on groping in the dark. Why does this task appear so difficult?

Having already been to the bathroom before going to bed, you will probably have recorded a reasonable plan of how to reach your destination, but in executing your decision plan the visual information that you want to match with your expected image is not forthcoming. So, there you would be, stuck with a decision plan that could not be executed because the matching-feedback mechanism of decision execution is not working. I said you would be stuck, because in the end you do make it to the bathroom. You had to replace the sensory information of a visual nature by touch, and to a lesser degree, sound. This requires ingenuity on two accounts. First, you have to interpret the sensations correctly, for example, you have to know that what you touch is the Chinese vase and, second, you have to locate the object in space. You have to know where the Chinese vase is or, if you are unlucky, where it was. In the latter case your host would almost certainly help you find the bathroom.

I cannot conclude this chapter without explaining wayfinding in labyrinths. The question to pose is rather simple. Why do people get lost in labyrinths? To start with, wayfinding in unicursal and multicursal labyrinths should be looked at independently. In a unicursal labyrinth one has no choice but to follow the only existing path or to retrace one's steps. The person is in the position of being led or guided. In terms of finding his way he has no option, he will find it, but to situate himself in space can be an almost impossible task. In a successful labyrinth, particularly if composed of open angles or curves, the person will soon lose track of his past movements. Taking no part in decision making, his behavioral actions are not structured into plans. He is essentially left with a linear sequence of behaviors. Again he is missing the supportive memory structure. He is, therefore, not able to describe his location, either in terms of a state description indicating his location in space or in terms of a process description recalling the behaviors needed to reach the entrance.

The situation is slightly different in a multicursal labyrinth. Here the person actually seems to make a decision whenever he reaches a cross-section or forking path. Why can he not recall his way back? One could blame the quantity of decisions as the cause of the difficulty, but this interpretation is not convincing if we consider that people often involve themselves in an equal number of decisions in everyday wayfinding tasks. The key difference between an everyday wayfinding situation and one in the labyrinth is that in the latter the choice between right, left, or straight ahead is arbitrary. The person does not really have any environmental information available upon which to base a decision. If the choice of decisions is arbitrary we cannot really talk about planning. So, the decisions remain unstructured and hence impossible to recall, if the person does not rely on some crafty strategy. He might perhaps associate a tone with each type of turn and recall his bi- or tri-tonal melody. Given the difficulty of reversing the melody, I would personally opt for Luis Borges' advice to always turn left. Even if I cannot find the central chamber, I can at least find my way out by always turning right on my return trip.

Unicursal labyrinth.

Multicursal labyrinth.

Assuming that you do come up with some mnemonic device that allows you to recall all behavioral actions taken to reach a certain point in the labyrinth, when retracing your steps, you would have to reverse the order of decisions. Depending on your mnemonic device, this may not be very difficult. After all we often have to reverse the order of decisions in everyday situations. Moreover, you would have to recognize where these choices were made. That is another difficulty a uniform labyrinth imposes on the user. To a specific decision, such as to turn left, there is no specific image attached. All crossroads and forking paths are identical. As already seen from the anthropological literature, inhabitants of uniform environments like deserts, snow-covered plains, and large water stretches are able to cope remarkably well. These inhabitants have developed a sensory acuity that allows them to observe features where most would see only sameness.

Conclusion

In the beginning of this chapter, the various terms necessary to describe wayfinding as a process of spatial problem solving were discussed. Decisions and the three forms of environmental information, sensory, memory, and inferential, are the major units of analysis and the key elements of wayfinding. Two structural components were then introduced: the decision hierarchy and the decision plan. On the basis of empirically observed wayfinding episodes it is proposed that the development of decision plans is not only a solution, but also a task-generating activity leading to simpler and more manageable subtasks, the solution of which can be remembered and reused if necessary. The development of decision plans is furthermore a continuous and flexible process that solves and adjusts according to the occurrence and the unforeseen nature of problems. Often the development of decision plans is based on a solution repertoire that also includes general type solutions for type problems. Environmental information available to the person is the important variable in determining the wayfinding solution. Two major strategies, the search and the access strategy, comprising various tactics defined in function of the environmental information necessary to complete the task, have been proposed.

I have then argued for a decision execution process based on a matching feedback mechanism in which expected environmental information in the form of images emanating from decisions is matched with perceived information. In case of a match, the action part of the decision is transformed into behavior. Otherwise the decision becomes a task, that is, a problem for which a plan has to be developed. All wayfinding problems can be defined as decisions that cannot be directly executed.

Some general observations on information processing stand out. Not everybody values the same information when completing a wayfinding task. Some emphasize the importance of information leading to a spatial understanding of the setting, to the location of the destination, and to their own location in the setting. Others emphasize the importance of information leading to a destination by sequential signing or linearly arranged information. I have described reliance on information of the more spatial nature to correspond to a spatial wayfinding style and reliance on information of a more linear nature to correspond to a linear wayfinding style. Although such reliance is not absolute, difficulties of wayfinding problems and of sites in general are assessed on that basis.

The chance of specific environmental information being perceived is affected by the immediate need for that information. Even information that can facilitate the completion of a general task tends to be ignored if it is encountered during the execution of a decision package, that is, during the moment when information relevant to that package is sought. The perception of information is directed by what people know and by what people need at a particular moment. I have used the verb directed and not determined, since information is also perceived thanks to its impact. This nondirected perception is, of course, fundamental to learning.

Chapter 4 aims at specific aspects of information processing in assessing the various wayfinding support systems. The object of the discussion is to identify the design characteristics rendering information processing difficult or, on the contrary, rendering it easy.

NOTES

1. Although the study of perception, for example, dates back to the early days of psychology, it is only very recently that researchers have become interested in the way complex environments are perceived. For a theoretical stand on this issue, see Ittelson (1973). The first published study of cognitive map formation during locomotion, to give another example, dates from 1980 (Gärling, 1980).
2. Some of the argumentation presented in this chapter has been published in *Man-Environment Systems* (Passini, 1980) and *Urban Ecology* (Passini, 1981).
3. The conceptualization emerged from empirically observed problem solving during concrete wayfinding episodes. Nevertheless, it owes its approach to the cognitive model proposed by Miller, Galanter, and Pribram (1960) and the process of cognitive mapping as proposed by Downs and Stea (1973).
4. Downs and Stea (1977) use the term "spatial information." I chose "environmental information" in order to avoid confusion with the meaning spatial as applied to cognitive maps, that is, spatial as opposed to linear.
5. Stereotypes can evolve, although generally they do so only slowly. Many Canadians today might disagree with the identification of Toronto with industrial, though they would have agreed ten years ago.
6. A schema has been described by Bartlett (1932) as an organization of past reactions and experiences. A major function of a schema is to facilitate the storage and retrieval of

information. Information is not usually retained in detail but only in its salient features. Schemata are assumed to be hierarchically structured and the retrieval of information to be based on schema activation, which can proceed from the general to the particular (concept-driven activation) or from the particular to the general (data-driven activation). See Rumelhart (1980) for more detail. Schemata are not only used for classifying, storing, and retrieving information but also to guide perception. Schemata lead to anticipating what ought to be there (Neisser, 1978). When going to a university library one would typically expect to find index catalogues, book stacks, check-out desks, people studying, and so on, but no car sales. Car sales are not part of a library schema. By anticipating what to expect, schemata facilitate perception. Experiments with various pictures showing scenes conforming to general schema and scenes not conforming to such schema indicated that looking time was longer for the latter (Friedman, 1979; Loftus and Mackworth, 1978). Schema theory extends its units to include information and knowledge about objects and events as well as about processes and behavior, such as how to use objects, what to do with given information, or how to behave in certain situations. For an excellent review article see Rumelhart (1980); for schemata and memory of places see Brewer and Treyens (1981).

7. Time and space are concepts we understand intuitively but have great trouble defining. For recent work on the time concept see Doob (1971), Fraser (1975), Von Franz (1978), Mellor (1981).

8. The experiment undertaken with US army personnel is described by Doob (1971). The author postulates two acts of judgment when estimating time: a primary judgment that is spontaneous and a secondary judgment that reevaluates the primary estimate. Looking at the manipulated clock may have let the secondary judgment override the first estimate. Even so, the experiment shows how little confidence people have in estimating time.

9. Permissible coming late rules vary strongly from one culture to another. For the Mormons one minute is a critical time, while in Quebec 15 minutes are still acceptable at university meetings. The Sioux Indians, apparently, have no word for "late" and no word for "waiting" (Doob, 1971). The rules also vary according to the event. You do not turn up late to an appointment when you look for a job, yet you do your best to arrive late when going to a party.

10. The African rhinoceros in contrast to the Asian species does not have the heavy folds that could be associated with armor plating. The African rhinoceros has two long horns. The only other species with two horns, which are very small, is from Sumatra. The Javan and the Indian rhinoceros have only one horn.

11. The blind, even those who never had vision, conceive of the environment in terms of a cognitive map, not fundamentally different from the sighted person (see Rosencranz and Suslick, 1976; Cratty, 1971; Stea and Blaut, 1970; Shemyakin, 1962). Representations are in the form of route maps, although some do achieve spatially organized survey maps. These astonishing performances should not detract from the fact that the perceptual horizon of a totally blind person is very limited and that their reliance on sonic cues is plagued by the instability of the sonic environment. Even the congenitally blind person goes through extensive training programs to achieve a reasonable level of independency. The most fundamental coordination of movement in space has to be learned (Cratty, 1971). In the city most blind use street blocks as major reference units; rarely do they explore new routes (Leonard and Newman, 1970).

12. Within the hierarchy I have defined the lowest level of decision as being that leading to a behavioral action. It is possible to identify smaller behavioral units such as moving an arm, turning a hand or even to consider individual muscle movements.

13. Lichtenstein and Brewer (1980) have analyzed the structure of goal-oriented activities when recalled from memory. They arrived at similar relations to those proposed here. It should be noted that our tasks and subtasks designate the same content as goals in the reported study. The authors identify two types of link among the units of a plan. The first is

an "in-order-to" relationship, which specifies the goal of an earlier act to be a precondition for a subsequent one. This relationship corresponds to the hierarchical links shown in Figure 3.2. The coding rule I used to identify these links among decisions was the set phrase "in-order-to" (see Appendix B). The second is the "enable" relationship, which applies when the outcome of a temporally prior action is a precondition for the execution of a subsequent one. This relation, although not fully identical to the plan idea outlined in Figure 3.3, still describes a link of sequential order, which tends to coincide with plans. In my definition plans retain their links to higher order decisions. Lichtenstein and Brewer classify actions as being either part of the actor's plan (goal or decision hierarchy) or as being nongoal oriented. If nongoal oriented they can be "irrelevant actions" or "side-effect actions." Side-effect actions serve to correct the nondesirable consequences of goal-oriented actions, such as an open door that has to be closed after entering a room.

14. Memory is known to be very limited in recording unstructured bits of information. The "magic number seven" proposed by Miller (1956) represents an upper limit not attained by the average person (Neisser, 1967). More representative is the limit of three to four elements for confortable recording. This order corresponds to the great majority of decisions observed within a single plan unit.

15. People can usually recall in some detail the occurrence and the order of goal-directed activities (see, for example, Lichtenstein and Brewer, 1980). Much work in cognitive psychology and modern linguistics has postulated hierarchical structures as a basis for memory organization. These structures manifest themselves when verbal material is recalled. Hierarchical patterns are evident when remembering stories (Mandler and Johnson, 1977; Reitman and Rueter, 1980). Recent research has shown that syntactic compositions and speech timing reflect tree structures (Cooper et al., 1978; Grosjean and Lane, 1977; Reitman and Rueter, 1980). Even the silent pauses between words correspond to the hierarchical syntactic structure of the sentence (Grosjean and Lane, 1977).

16. A comparison can be made between the characteristics of decision making in wayfinding and modes of thinking described as multiple, global versus linear, logical (see Neisser, 1967). The vague initial plans are an outcome of multiple global thinking, which often escapes verbalization, while linear rational thinking results in the formation of decision plans.

17. The hierarchical structure of decision diagrams does not, therefore, necessarily mean that decisions are taken in that order. For poorly understood problems, general plans may best be seen as open-ended and purposefully vague.

18. These decision plans, residues of past experience, resemble schemata in that they contain what was common (equivalence) among the solutions developed for a type of problem. Similar ideas of plan schemata have been proposed by Lichtenstein and Brewer (1980).

19. Miller, Galanter, and Pribram (1960) proposed a similar system based on four sequential phases: test, operate, test, exit. "Test" compares the perceived situation with a desired one, while "operate" represents the action planned to intervene.

20. In a study on recognition undertaken by Shepard (1967), subjects were exposed to 612 different pictures taken from various magazines. These pictures were then coupled with similar unfamiliar examples. The accuracy of recognition when choosing from a sample of 68 such pairs was as high as 98 percent on average; even a week later, accuracy was above 90 percent.

21. Kaplan (1976) notes that "selecting an appropriate action requires prediction of what is happening next" (p. 37). Some of this prediction is possible on the basis of stored sequential information taken from previous experiences. Decision execution in simulated form could be seen to activate prediction when such information is not readily available.

22. Lee (1969) calls this estimate a "profit and loss accounting with a very personal currency" (p. 12).

23. Ittelson (1973) in "Environmental Perception and Contemporary Perceptual Theory" calls

for the study of environmental perception, which, probably because of the methodological difficulties involved, has practically been ignored by psychologists. The difference between the perception of objects and the complex environment is not only one of scale. Environmental perception is more complex because it involves a multitude of objects surrounding a person as well as that person's movement through space. More important still is the contextual and motivational make-up of the perceiving person, his intentions and objectives.

24. Arnheim (1972) describes perception as a process of "visual thinking."

25. Given the small sample and the methodological difficulty of classifying sketch maps, which are often rudimentary, as being spatial or linear, I was not able to show strong correlations between wayfinding styles and maps.

26. Supportive are the protocol and the sketch maps of the metro station Berri-de-Montigny which is the major underground circulation node in Montréal. Certain types of building might be associated with a linear organization, made to process people through, others with a more spatial, centrifugal organization. It is possible that the expectation of a building's organization and function influences on the style adopted.

27. Appleyard (1969) identified three characteristics affecting environmental perception: form, visibility, and use, use being a reflection of the functional dimension, that is, of what is needed to do something.

28. Lichtenstein and Brewer (1980) have shown people to have much higher recall rates for goal-directed units (those being part of a hierarchy) than for similar nongoal-directed units.

29. The idea that cognitive maps, in particular, route maps are based on wayfinding behavior has recently been proposed by Kuipers (1982). According to the author, people make a link between each action taken along a route and the perceptual view at that point of action. Knowledge of the environment can therefore be based on knowledge of how to navigate from one place to another. This view agrees with mine. It explains why, for certain people and in particular for young children, representations of routes are not reversible (Piaget et al., 1969). If a person can rely on a spatial organization proper to a survey map, he can trace routes forward as easily as backward.

30. Problem solving is sometimes identified with work done in the field of artificial intelligence and computer simulation. The names of Herbert Simon and Allen Newell are intimately associated with this school of thinking. Wayfinding conceptualized in their terms, I believe, would in essence be a process that limits itself to a serial choice between alternatives at each decision point. It would not be a planning process involving complex cognitive abilities. Simon (1969, 1979) describes problems as being hierarchically structured and problem solving as being a search along the maze-like path leading from the original problem to the solution. This search, based on trial and error, has to be selective so as to reduce the options of trials to manageable proportions. Selectivity is guided by the feedback of trials and heuristics or general rules. It should be noted that, among problem solving heuristics, Simon refers to planning. In contrast to the cognitive school of thinking, Simon sees problem solving and cognition in general as being rather simple mechanistic processes. Some of the differences between the two schools of thought are illustrated in an exchange of opinions between Herbert Simon and the cognitive psychologist Ulric Neisser (Simon, 1979; Neisser, 1967).

31. The terms "stored" and "retrieved" are used for convenience. It is assumed by many researchers that memory is an act of reconstructing, based on traces of previous experience and a record of the act of construction. Memory is not just a simple filing system (see Bartlett, 1932; Neisser, 1967).

32. Sex differences in spatial skills are documented in the literature. See, for example, Lord (1941), Kaplan (1976), Downs and Stea (1977). Women perform generally more poorly in most wayfinding tasks. For a recent review and explanatory arguments see Harris (1981).

REFERENCES

Appleyard, D., 1969, "Why Buildings are Known," *Environment and Behavior* **1**(2):131-156.

Arnheim, R., 1972, *Visual Thinking,* University of California Press, Berkeley.

Bartlett, F. C., 1932, *Remembering,* Cambridge University Press, Cambridge, Eng.

Brewer, W. F., and J. C. Treyens, 1981, "Role of Schemata in Memory for Places," *Cognitive Psychology* **13**(2):207-230.

Carpenter, E., 1973, *Eskimo Realities,* Holt, Rinehart and Winston, New York.

Cooper, W. E., J. M. Paccia, and S. Lapointe, 1978, "Hierarchical Coding in Speech Timing," *Cognitive Psychology* **10**(2):154-177.

Cratty, B. J., 1971, *Movement and Spatial Awareness in Blind Children and Youths,* Charles C. Thomas, Springfield, Ill.

Doob, L. W., 1971, *Patterning of Time,* Yale University Press, New Haven.

Downs, R., and D. Stea, 1973, *Image and the Environment: Cognitive Mapping and Spatial Behavior,* Aldine, Chicago.

Downs, R., and D. Stea, 1977, *Maps in Minds,* Harper and Row, New York.

Fraser, J. T., 1975, *Of Time, Passion and Knowledge,* George Braziller, New York.

Friedman, A., 1979, "Framing Pictures: The Role of Knowledge in Automatized Encoding and Memory for Gist," *Journal of Experimental Psychology: General* **108**(3):316-355.

Gärling, T., 1980, *Environmental Orientation during Locomotion,* Swedish Council for Building Research, Stockholm.

Gombrich, E. H., 1960, *Art and Illusion,* Princeton University Press, Princeton, N.J.

Grosjean, F., and H. Lane, 1977, "Pauses and Syntax in American Sign Language," *Cognition* **5**(2):101-117.

Hall, E., 1959, *The Silent Language,* Faucett, Greenwich, Conn.

Harris, L. J., 1981, "Sex-Related Variations in Spatial Skill," in *Spatial Representation and Behavior across the Life Span: Theory and Application,* L. S. Liben et al., eds., Academic Press, New York, pp. 83-125.

Ittelson, W. H., 1973, "Environmental Perception and Contemporary Perceptual Theory," in *Environment and Cognition,* W. H. Ittelson, ed., Seminar Press, New York, pp. 1-19.

Kaplan, R., 1976, "Wayfinding in the Natural Environment," in *Environmental Knowing,* G. Moore and R. Golledge, eds., Dowden, Hutchinson & Ross, Stroudsburg, Pa., pp. 46-57.

Kaplan, S., 1976, "Adaptation, Structure and Knowledge," in *Environmental Knowing,* G. Moore and R. Golledge, eds., Dowden, Hutchinson & Ross, Stroudsburg, Pa., pp. 32-45.

Kuipers, B., 1982, "The 'Map in the Head' Metaphor," *Environment and Behavior* **14**(2):202-220.

Lee, T. R., 1969, "The Psychology of Spatial Orientation," *Architectural Association Quarterly* **1**(3):11-15.

Leonard, J. A., and R. C. Newman, 1970, "Three Types of Maps for Blind Travel," *Ergonomics* **13**(2):165-179.

Lichtenstein, E. H., and W. F. Brewer, 1980, "Memory for Goal-Directed Events," *Cognitive Psychology* **12**(3):412-445.

Lloyd, B. B., 1972, *Perception and Cognition: A Cross-Culture Perspective,* Penguin, Harmondsworth, Eng.

Loftus, G. R., and N. H. Mackworth, 1978, "Cognitive Determinants of Fixation Location during Picture Viewing," *Journal of Experimental Psychology: Human Perception and Performance* **4**(4):565-572.

Lord, F. E., 1941, "A Study of Spatial Orientation of Children," *Journal of Educational Research* **34**(7):481-505.

Lynch, K., 1972, *What Time Is this Place?* MIT Press, Cambridge, Mass.

Mandler, J. M., and N. S. Johnson, 1977, "Remembrance of Things Passed: Story Structure and Recall," *Cognitive Psychology* **9**(1):111-151.

Mellor, D. H., 1981, *Real Time*, Cambridge University Press, Cambridge, Eng.

Miller, G. A., 1956, "The Magical Number Seven, Plus or Minus Two: Some Limits on Our Capacity for Processing Information," *Psychological Review* **63**:81-97.

Miller, G. A., E. Galanter, and K. Pribram, 1960, *Plans and the Structure of Behavior*, Holt, Rinehart and Winston, New York.

Moore, G. T., 1979, "Knowing about Environmental Knowing: The Current State of Theory and Research on Environmental Cognition," *Environment and Behavior* **11**(1):33-70.

Neisser, U., 1967, *Cognitive Psychology*, Prentice Hall, Englewood Cliffs, N. J..

Neisser, U., 1978, "Anticipations, Images and Introspection," *Cognition* **6**(2):169-174.

Passini, R., 1972, *La perception de l'environnement sous differentes modalités sensorielles*, Faculté de l'Aménagement, University of Montréal, Montréal.

Passini, R., 1980, "Wayfinding in Complex Buildings: An Environmental Analysis," *Man-Environment Systems* **10**(1):31-40.

Passini, R., 1981, "Wayfinding: A Conceptual Framework," *Urban Ecology* **5**(1):17-31.

Piaget, J., and B. Inhelder, 1969, *The Psychology of the Child*, Basic Books, New York.

Rapoport, A., 1972, "Australian Aborigines and the Definition of Place," in *Proceedings of the Third Annual Environmental Design and Research Association Meeting*, W. J. Mitchell, ed., University of California, Los Angeles, vol. 1, 3.3.1-3.3.14.

Rapoport, A., 1977, *Human Aspects of Urban Form: Towards a Man-Environment Approach to Urban Form and Design*, Pergamon Press, Toronto.

Reitman, J. S., and H. H. Rueter, 1980, "Organization Revealed by Recall Orders and Confirmed by Pauses," *Cognitive Psychology*, **12**(4):554-581.

Rosencranz, D., and R. Suslick, 1976, "Cognitive Models for Spatial Representations in Congenitally Blind, Adventitiously Blind and Sighted Subjects," *New Outlook for the Blind* **70**(4):188-194.

Rumelhart, D. E., 1980, "Schemata: The Building Blocks of Cognition," in *Theoretical Issues in Reading Comprehension*, R. J. Spiro, et al., eds., Lawrence Erlbaum, Hillsdale, N. J., pp. 33-58.

Shemyakin, F. N., 1962, "Orientation in Space," in *Psychological Sciences in the USSR*, B. G. Anavigew et al., eds., Office of Technical Sciences, Report 62-11083.

Shepard, R. N., 1967, "Recognition Memory for Words, Sentences and Pictures," *Journal of Verbal Learning and Verbal Behavior* **6**:156-163.

Simon, H. A., 1969, *The Science of the Artificial*, MIT Press, Cambridge, Mass.

Simon, H. A., 1979, *Models of Thought*, Yale University Press, New Haven.

Sommer, R., 1978, *The Mind's Eye*, Delacorte Press, New York.

Stea, D., and J. M. Blaut, 1973, "Notes towards a Developmental Theory of Spatial Learning," in *Image and Environment*, R. Downs and D. Stea, eds., Aldine, Chicago, pp. 51-62.

Stevens, A., and P. Coupe, 1978, "Distortions in Judged Spatial Relations," *Cognitive Psychology* **10**(4):422-437.

Torczyner, H., 1977, *Margritte: Ideas and Images*, Harry N. Abrams, New York.

Von Franz, M. L., 1978, *Time: Rhythm and Repose*, Thames and Hudson, London.

4

Looking at the Built Environment

Architects and urbanists intervene in the environment to create settings capable of accommodating goal-directed as well as informal activities of inhabitants, to allow for desired levels of interaction, and to guarantee a certain balanced experience of an intellectual and emotional nature. Physical planning is in essence an act of conceptualizing and organizing spaces, of allocating functions, and of providing the necessary supportive equipment. By taking design decisions that bring about these interventions the planner determines, consciously or unconsciously, the wayfinding problems future users will have to solve.

Almost all the difficulties a person may experience in wayfinding have their source in some phase of information processing. The problems with finding relevant information in public settings like hospitals, shopping complexes, airports, schools, or housing developments at the urban scale are common impediments to efficient wayfinding. The information can be ambiguous or incomplete, requiring a particular effort of interpretation. Even if the information is obtained and the message understood the wayfinding person is not necessarily safe. Part of the information might be forgotten when it comes to be reused after a certain lapse of time. Furthermore, people may have difficulty relaying messages to one another or, especially when trying to comprehend the spatial characteristics of a setting, in organizing individual impressions into a global image or cognitive map. Finally, there may be trouble accumulating and assimilating information in an orderly fashion over short and long periods of time. These difficulties can be traced to inefficiencies in acquiring, interpreting, storing, and structuring information, that is, to the basic cognitive abilities necessary to process environmental information. In this chapter, I propose to identify some of these practical difficulties people have in processing environmental information while finding their way.

Information can be obtained from various wayfinding support systems, such as information booths, signs, maps, and also from the architectural and spatial characteristics of a setting. This chapter will look at each of these sources of environmental information separately; it will try to identify the difficulties generally encountered and the design characteristics leading to and, if possible, out of these difficulties.[1]

The data bank serving to identify wayfinding difficulties derives from three research projects undertaken in five of Montréal's most complex commercial centers. The sites are described in Appendix A, and the projects in Appendix B. In order to extend the discussion to other settings and in particular to the urban scale, I have felt free to include additional illustrations and examples.

SIGNS

A Classification

Signs communicate environmental information, they tell the viewer what is where and, when they refer to an event, signs may also specify when and how

likely it is to occur. Particular to wayfinding is the locational component which, as discussed in Chapter 3, may take the form of a process description or a state description.

Directional signs

Directional signs are the most common process description. They typically designate a place, an object, or an event in form of a name, a symbol, or a pictograph and an arrow. In the case of a corridor or a street, if the direction is spatially predetermined, the direction word "to" fulfills the function of the arrow. A process description is composed of a coherent ensemble of directional signs positioned on a path to a destination. Such a description of location is the equivalent of a decision plan spaced along a path, with each directional sign corresponding to a decision that leads directly or indirectly to a behavioral action.

Directional sign; example of a process description of location.

Identification signs

Identification signs are the most elementary state description of location. They identify an object, a place, or a person in space. The advertising sign above a creamery and the increasingly used letter *i*, which indicates an information booth, are examples of such state descriptions.

Identification signs are only one form of state description. Once they are perceived, the destination is usually reached. Other state descriptions provide the information necessary to develop decision plans. This information has to be read within some generally understood reference system, as described in Chapter 3. An example of a state description based on an abstract reference system is the now commonly accepted numbering of doors and floors in high-rise buildings, such as "Place Ville-Marie, suite 2108." A sign that reads "Office Building—Entrance Atwater" is also a state description, this time based on a fixed system of reference. It describes the office building lobby as being adjacent to the entrance of the shopping complex off Atwater Street. The two state descriptions are meaningful only if the reference system is shared by the information-receiving person. No decision plan can be developed if, in the first case, the numbering system is not understood and if, in the second case, the person does not know how to reach the place associated with destination.

Identification sign; example of a state description of location.

Reassurance signs

The key function of signs is to provide the environmental information needed to make wayfinding decisions. Some signs address themselves to the post-decision phase, when they act as checkpoints. These signs will be referred to as reassurance signs. They are frequently encountered on highways, where they reassure the traveler that he is still on the right road. The same sign can have different functions for different users. The traveler approaching an unfamiliar city may read a sign to decide that he should take an exit to go downtown, while the same sign may reassure a person who has already taken the route at a previous occasion.[2]

The form in which a message on a sign is being presented, that is, verbal, pictorial, or symbolic, is perhaps the most common method of classification. Given that our interest here is less in the graphic quality of signs than in their supportive function to wayfinding as information-giving devices, a classification according to content is more appropriate.

The following discussion will be organized around identified information processing difficulties. These are: first, difficulties in obtaining information, in particular, finding the signs in the setting and the message on the sign; second, difficulties in understanding the meaning of the message; and finally, difficulties related to the anticipation of information. Memory and learning, being an integral part of information processing, will be referred to throughout this section.

Signs in the Setting

Urban concentrations of commerce and entertainment often stand out by a profusion of signs and signals of all sorts trying to attract potential clients and to show off the superior value of goods and services offered. The density and intensity of stimulation in some indoor commercial complexes competes with displays found on many city main streets. Alexis-Nihon, which served as one of our wayfinding test grounds (Fig. 4.1), has a particular liveliness that is impossible to capture by photography. To compensate for the static black and white media, the reader has to imagine flashing lights of various colors and intensities, people, among them many teenagers, bustling around to the rhythm of rock and roll in competition with the eternal Muzak. Sometimes special entertainment features and promotion gags are performed in the central square. With every metro train, feeding directly into the center, a new lot of people visits the place or walks through it, hurrying to an adjacent city bus terminal.

Conditions of overload

Settings like Alexis-Nihon have a quality of their own that responds well to the diversionary needs of a certain population. To a wayfinding person who

Figure 4.1
Alexis-Nihon, information overload.

relies on signs, the center is a riddle. The difficulty of obtaining information and even of distinguishing relevant from unimportant signs is very common. The signs, as we shall see, are of poor quality. The signs in themselves and the combination with the quantity and intensity of stimulation from the setting reduce the reception of information.

The capacity to process information naturally has a limit that may vary according to the individual, to his disposition at a particular time, and to the peceptual channels involved. Conditions of stimulation exceeding processing capacities are referred to as stimulation overloads. Excessive stimulation can inhibit information processing. The analogy between overloaded information channels and city streets during peak hour traffic, even if not scientifically correct, is nevertheless illustrative. All the subjects who had to complete wayfinding tasks in Alexis-Nihon commented on being exposed to excessive amounts of stimulation and on the effect of the resulting overload on their ability to find relevant information. Some of their remarks, taken from the interview data, illustrate the problem and indicate the level of frustration experienced: "For me, everything was confused, . . . there was a lot of lettering, arrows, . . . there were a lot of shops, colors." "I don't like Alexis-Nihon, its commercial aspect with its flashes of light and colors, . . . it is impossible to get anything precise, . . . there is so much going on, that one sees nothing." "It is loaded with publicity. Every shop has its sign that shines in your eyes, so one does not know where to look anymore."

A differentiation of two types of overload has been proposed by some authors.[3] The first pertains to an excess of stimulation, the second to an excess of information. By stimulation is meant the sensory excitation provoked by the various forms of energy experienced as light, color, sound, odor, taste, texture, temperature, movement, and others. Information refers necessarily to an interpretation of that stimulus material and an attribution of meaning. This distinction is difficult to maintain in reality. Hardly anything perceived escapes a certain interpretation. A red light is not just stimulation but carries overtones of danger and excitation. The crucial distinction for overload conditions, I propose, lies in the nature of the information. It is possible to give information an essentially nominal value, but it can also have a functional use and an emotional impact. If an environment is merely read in terms of identifying its components, overload conditions are not common, even for very dense and complex displays. Looking down into Manhattan from the Empire State Building is no doubt a dense visual experience, but it does not lead to overload conditions. If information is to be extracted and used in problem solving, just a few simultaneous sources may evoke overload. In the extreme case, unique information, if it has, for example, a deep emotional impact, can lead to momentarily impaired information processing resembling overload conditions. A visitor to a hospital related his experience of immense confusion and undermined wayfinding after he had accidently seen a corpse on a stretcher.

Sign type and placement

If information overload is one of the main reasons rendering access to existing information difficult, the design and placement of signs need also be included in this discussion. Public settings typically exhibit a variety of signs for different functions. The wayfinding person must extract from this display of information that relevant to his task. Above all he has to distinguish place identification and directional signs from commercial identification and advertising signs. Certain design features can facilitate this distinction.

A first possible differentiation between wayfinding and commercial signs can be achieved by giving each its graphic identity. At the complex Bonaventure, for example, all directional and place identification signs are in black lettering on a white ground, while the commercial signs make use of the opposite contrast, that is, white lettering on a black ground. I have evidence that this and other graphic consistencies are quickly picked up and applied by users in their search efforts.

A second factor facilitating the discovery of wayfinding information in a

Graphic identity of wayfinding and commercial signs.

complex setting is the consistent location of signs. At Bonaventure directional signs are always mounted on the ceiling, while at the nearby center Place Ville-Marie directional signs are not differentiated from the commercial signs by typography but only by location. Wayfinding signs at Place Ville-Marie are always placed hanging from the ceiling, in the center of the corridor. No one had difficulty in spotting the signs; moreover, the protocol shows a high frequency of reference. A certain predictability of the sign's location is an important factor in efficient information processing. I shall again use extracts from the interview data for illustrative purposes. The first example refers to one of Montréal's main commercial streets, Sainte-Catherine, the second to the center Bonaventure.

If you are at Sainte-Catherine where there are quite a lot of signs from shops, cinemas, restaurants, et cetera, and you look for the metro, you know it [the metro identification sign] is approximately 15 feet above ground and one does not have to look everywhere.

[At Bonaventure] the signs are on the ceiling. You know where to look for information. You are sure it will be above your head, there is something reassuring about it all.

Place identity of wayfinding and commercial signs.

Similar findings are reported by Carr (1973), who conducted a study of sign perception in Boston. Based on his observations, Carr suggested the creation of specific communication channels in cities reserved for the exclusive use of public wayfinding and traffic regulation signs.[4]

Sign identity

Sign perception is further improved if the person is familiar with its overall form and design. The Montréal metro symbol, composed of a circle enclosing an arrow, is well known by all users of public transportation. This metro symbol is picked up even if it is minute and even if the sign featuring the symbol contains far too many units of information to be read comfortably. The particularity of a symbol is recognized as well as the total form and even the features of the supporting mounts such as sign columns, sign boxes, and frames. The protocol shows that wayfinding signs were frequently referred to long before they could be read. Sometimes signs were recognized by form and position after just one earlier example.

The act of becoming familiar with a sign is an act of learning that occurs without effort if the same sign type is frequently encountered. During a recent train voyage in Europe, I realized how quickly and easily I personally relied on a set of standard pictographs used in all railway stations. Application and design standards are most important to get people to understand, use, and depend on signs. It is surprising to read that only in 1975 were standard transportation signs for airports, train, and bus stations proposed on this continent (Carpenter, 1979). Standardization of building signs is still far from

Métro

Information
Magasins/Shops
Le Passage, Restaurants
Hall d'Exposition
Exhibition Hall
Hôtel, Garage
Cinéma   Le Viaduc
Métro 🚇 C⌁ C.P.

Metro1 symbol; detection facilitated by knowing the sign.

being implemented.[5] The common confusion created by floor identifications of ground levels, split levels, and underground levels, as well as by the array of symbols used for buildings on slopes that have more than one "ground floor" is an indication for the urgent need to develop and implement a generally recognized nomenclature. It is astonishing how little can give away the identity of a sign. The sign in Figure 4.2 is a Moroccan version of a well-known sign in the Western world. The reader not versed in Arabic who is able to recognize the sign will have done so by the form of the underlining only.

To pick up existing wayfinding information in highly active and complex settings can mean considerable difficulty. The factors responsible are in summary: (1) a general overload of stimuli and information; (2) insufficient distinctiveness among signs that have different functions or that address different populations; (3) inconsistent placement of wayfinding signs; and (4) inconsistent use of recognizable design characteristics. Some of these observations can be clarified and explained by reconsidering basic aspects of information processing.

A most important part of understanding peoples' information-processing behavior is to conceptualize perception as an interactive relation between a person and his environment. The viewer not only receives but also looks for information. If a person knows what to look for, he will be able to proceed by a

Figure 4.2
A sign well-known in the West.

matching process similar to the one proposed for decision execution in Chapter 3. This will spare the person the effort of scrutinizing a multitude of potentially relevant signs. If a person knows where to look for the desired information, he will simply reduce his field of search in space. Instead of having to sample the whole setting, he will be able to focus on a particular area, such as the ceilings of corridors, or pick particular architectural elements, such as columns, panels or kiosks.

Difficulties of obtaining information due to information overload require a more nuanced explanation. The greater the density of information in a setting, the harder it is to find a particular information simply because the person has to select, identify, and retain it among many others. This difficulty is not the only one. Dense environments, by requiring more effort from the user, can be tiresome, and fatigue decreases perceptual efficiency. In some situations anxiety may be increased through excessive information density, which again inhibits information processing.

If a person has to cope with stimulation overload for a length of time, he may adapt to the situation. Adaptation leads to the introduction of coping mechanisms that reduce the impact of the environment. A common coping mechanism is to regroup individual units of information into larger and less numerous chunks (see, for example, Dewar, 1973; also Riemersma, 1979). Design and placement consistencies of signs act as a support to such a regroupment and thereby help reduce even further the danger of overload conditions. It is therefore quite possible to plan very complex environmental settings that have no overload effects. Complex environments, as discussed in Chapter 1, may increase curiosity and interest and thus lead to a state of mind that facilitates the obtaining of environmental information.

If regrouping information is not possible because of excessive sign pageantry and heterogeneous spatial displays, the person will have to resort to the ultimate coping mechanism, which is to reduce perceptual intake by ignoring what is going on around him. This perceptual blackout greatly reduces the obtaining of relevant environmental information and leads to many of the reviewed wayfinding difficulties.

A hint for non-Coke drinkers.

Information on Signs

The graphic conception of signs, the choice of lettering, the contrast created by black, white, and colored elements, the size of signs, their position and illumination, all these factors contribute to legibility and to the relative ease of finding information. Much research has gone into the study of sign legibility, especially for highway design, where the consequences of inadequate signs can be particularly serious.[6] An excellent review of those studies and related research on the psychological aspects of information processing is

If the fine is not bigger than the no-parking sign . . .

given by Dewar (1973). My own research was not intended to generate data on sign graphics; nevertheless, two related questions stood out. The first concerns the amount of information contained on a sign; the second addresses itself to the structure of that information.

Quantity of information

The literature on highway signs, in general, agrees that sign panels should not contain more than three to four units of information at a time, to assure easy reading. It has been argued that such a recommendation, applying to car traffic, has no value for pedestrians; people do not rush through buildings at 70 miles per hour. Nevertheless, wayfinding observations show quite clearly that similar specifications are needed for signs addressed to pedestrians.

Figure 4.3 compares two signs consulted during the wayfinding tests. The first sign, located at the center Bonaventure, lists nine units of information. The subjects had to find the reference "information," which features in third place. Everyone reading the sign either had to stop or slow down his pace considerably. The subjects scanned the description again and again until they finally found the relevant information. The second directional sign, located at Place Ville-Marie, contains approximately the same amount of information, but here the information is regrouped into smaller packages. In those cases the subjects were able to follow the signs while walking at a constant speed.

I have been told by designers that they see nothing wrong in people stopping and taking their time to read a sign. However, users see little virtue in

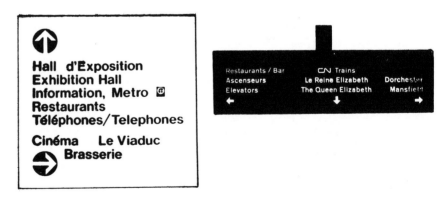

Figure 4.3
Comparison of two signs, containing approximately the same number of information units.

wasting their time for such a dull activity. One subject was explicit about this issue when referring to the signs at Bonaventure:

I believe it does not meet the needs of people to have so much written on the signs; in a commercial building people are moving fast, . . . one does the shopping and one does not want to lose any time, . . . when you are forced to stop to read, it breaks your rhythm. That I find annoying.

People are annoyed and frequently show bursts of impatience when they have to read through lists of names or study unstructured information on signs and maps. Often they give up looking even if they believe the required information to be there. Commenting on maps in Alexis-Nihon, a subject remarked: "It was not written to be picked up; they put down all the names of all the shops and then 'Office Building Lobby'; they write in the same size, so one would have to read everything . . . , that's very tiresome."

If signs are provided, the information they try to convey should surely be presented so as to facilitate easy detection. Gestalt psychologists have been interested in the perception patterns of form. They have shown that visual stimulation is organized into figures that are seen against a less differentiated ground. Furthermore, they identified five major principles by which these figures are organized.[7] One of these, the principle of proximity, states that elements in the visual field that are close together tend to be seen as a figure. Returning to our signs we can see three figures or three information packages for the Place Ville-Marie sign, while we have only one large package for the Bonaventure sign. That in itself does not explain why the Place Ville-Marie sign was easier to read, however.

Again and again I have been shown that the perception of signs in the real complex environment does not quite correspond to the perception of signs on the drawing board or indeed the reading of signs in photos. If you look again at the Bonaventure sign in Figure 4.3, you will probably find yourself reading down the list of items. In the real setting you would glance, you would then focus on something else, and then maybe return to the first object of attention. This observation is consistent not only in the reading of signs but also in the reading of maps.

Glances are of very short duration. Attached to a glance is a short-term visual memory. This memory, which is referred to as an iconic memory, may last from one to two seconds only.[8] For the information to be retained, it has to be coded into a memory of longer duration, and that is where the problems occur. In fact, people are only capable of coding three to four elements in that particular context. At a glance it is therefore not possible to retain the larger Bonaventure package, but it is within memory capacity to retain each of the three Place Ville-Marie packages. Perceiving the environment by glances is not just laziness on the part of the viewer. On the contrary, it is the only efficient way to take in complexity. Even the photos in Figure 4.3 may convince you that it is much faster to glance at the Place Ville-Marie sign than to read through the Bonaventure sign.

On a more general level, this example may serve the designer as an important warning: what looks good on the drawing board is not necessarily good when applied to the real setting. The perceptual processes are not the same when reading a text and when scanning an environment.

Structure of information

Information has to be visually structured so that in the setting the message can be picked up in glances. But there has to be yet another type of structure to make for good signing: a structure according to content. Some signs are general, others are more specific. The reader will remember that decisions made during wayfinding are also structured. The hierarchy of decisions also indicates levels of generality, the task decision being the most general, the decisions leading directly to behavioral actions being the most specific.

The notion of decision structure can serve as a means to organize information in the physical setting. At strategic points, when people have to make general decisions, they should have access to the appropriate general information; at other points, more specific decisions and information are requested. Knowing, as we have seen, creates an expectancy and facilitates finding the corresponding information. If the different levels of information are also distinct graphically and in design, people will at the appropriate time look for the specificity of the sign. It will be easier to find the sign in the setting if the sign corresponds to expectation.

Another aspect of this argument is just as important. A sign may also tell what kind of a decision is needed. The importance of a sign, that is, the level of generality in the hierarchy, may indeed urge the user to make a major wayfinding decision. Such signs are often experienced on highway travel through urban agglomerations. The design implications of these observations will be further examined in Chapter 5, when I will propose a method of conceptualizing environments and the wayfinding support systems. Let us now review the second major difficulty in processing environmental information: the difficulty of interpreting the message contained on a sign.

The Message

A common source of confusion while solving a wayfinding problem is introduced by the message a sign tries to convey. Three message-related obstacles can readily be identified: when it is not clear to whom a message is directed; when the content of the message is not fully understandable; and when an additional meaning, not intended by the sign, is evoked by the interpreting person.

The receiver

Underground garages are wayfinding riddles for many unaccustomed users. These garages are often difficult to understand as spatial entities, leading most people to rely heavily on wayfinding signs. Pedestrians and car drivers use the same space but not necessarily the same signs. An arrow that could be seen to address car drivers at the underground parking of Bonaventure, for example, points to a hidden stair. A directional sign to the elevators, in the same place, points to the left, while a directional sign to the exit points to the right. Elevators are a more appropriate means of getting out of the garage, especially if one has been driving downward for a while looking for a parking space. Still, there is no obvious cue that the exit sign refers to car traffic only. Not surprisingly, some of the subjects were misled by the sign.

Two signs for two populations: drivers and pedestrians.

The content

To devise a simple, clear sign understandable to all users is a deceptively difficult design task. The reduction of phrases to a few words that still have the ability to convey the message is a challenge not always met. Marks (1979), in an amusing article, shares some of her collected jewels of unintentional humor found on signs. Sometimes a word is ambiguous, sometimes a comma is missing and the sense of the message is drastically altered. A small sample reads as follows:

WAITING LIMITED TO 60 MINS. IN ANY HOUR
PARKING ALLOWED ON BOTH SIDES OF THIS ROAD ONLY
BEWARE – EXTREME DANGER – CHURCH ENTRANCE AHEAD
RHINOS PLEASE REMAIN IN YOUR VEHICLES
EAT HERE, GET GAS

Ambiguities of messages on signs are not always as evident as the humorous examples may suggest. We shall scrutinize some cases encountered during the wayfinding tests. In the underground parking at Bonaventure, the 14 different levels are referred to as sections, no doubt to differentiate them from floors above ground. The floor number appears on columns in the parking area and reads, for example, "section 13." Outside the elevator lobby, there is another sign reminding the user of the section on which he is parked. The

Floors or sections?

use of the term "section" for floors is in many cases not clearly understood and leads to wayfinding difficulties when the person tries to return to the parked car. Some of the subjects were indeed able to recall the number of the section but wondered on which floor that section was located. This misunderstanding is expressed in an interview extract: "The sign on the column saying section 14, well, I did not think it represented the floor where the car was; I thought it indicated only a section of that floor."

A similar confusion occurred on floor F of the same complex. The floors above ground are referred to by letters rather than by numbers, and the corridors on a particular floor have street names the first of which letter corresponds to the letter of the floor. Each corridor has an independent numbering system starting with one. On the way to destinations the subjects encountered the number of their address but in a different corridor. Some returned to the information booth, thinking they had the wrong number; others applied a search strategy based on chance and hoped to find the destination by just walking around: "I mainly relied on the numbers. As a matter of fact, I did not expect a duplication of numbers on the same floor." "I do find it a bit strange to use twice the same numbers on the floor."

Most large commercial settings are identified by a symbol they use everywhere, including their stationery and on wayfinding signs. The identification symbol of Bonaventure is a composition of four half circles arranged on a square that results in a rosette-like figure. This symbol is used on the keyboard of the elevator leading from the underground parking to the main shopping floor. No other description, inside or outside the elevator, associates the symbol with the main floor. The only other indications on the keyboard are the split levels of the parking area identified in paired numbers, that is, ½, ¾, . . . , ¹³/₁₄. The user is left to guess its meaning. The reaction to such a situation is typically divided. For the majority of the subjects the meaning of the sign, given its context was clear:

Keyboard in an elevator leading from underground parking to the main floor.

I understood that it was the right thing; it somehow looked public; . . . for me it was clear, immediately.

The numbers ½, ¾ . . . , I observed, related to the levels of the parking, so in any case one did not have a choice; . . . it was obvious to me, that symbol.

When you see that symbol, it's the only one. Everything else is numbers. I think that one can guess that it is the right floor.

The exact meaning of the symbol is not always understood, although it might still lead to the correct floor: "I told myself the flower [the symbol], that's for fashion so that's the level of the boutiques."

A minority, finally, did not select the Bonaventure symbol in their attempt to reach the main floor. They had to do a few test runs and explorations before arriving at the desired level. Later during the walk the symbol could again be seen on the identification sign of the information booth and also on the keyboard of the elevators going up from the main floor. The symbol was then perceived, and its meaning understood and remembered by everybody.

The examples of the underground parking sections and the elevator keyboard have in common the introduction of a new and unusual verbal and iconic code. Through the notation of the upper floors at Bonaventure a new and unusual naming and numbering system is being introduced. Each of the three innovations have led to information-processing difficulties. The conclusion is not that innovation in signs is not justified. Innovation can be necessary and desirable, but it requires particular consideration for the necessary learning process on the part of the user. This learning process can occur over a certain length of time when, for example, coding standards are adopted by the population through repeated experience, or it can occur in one single experience. In the latter case the designer not only has to provide a new code or sign system, but he has to ensure the necessary learning process.

Not all difficulties in understanding the precise meanings of signs are due to the introduction of new codes or sign systems. Some old codes are still and often used inadequately. One of the most common confusions occurs when directional signs are conceived as if they were identification signs and vice versa. In Bonaventure at level F a sign has the inscription "Frontenac" and contains an arrow. This sign is intended as an identification sign, while it was generally understood as a directional sign, pointing to the direction one had to take to reach corridor Frontenac. The situation gets even more confusing when different names are shown on a directional sign and the first one is to be understood as an identification.

Identification or directional sign?

[The signs to Fundy, Frontenac] told me that we were in none of these streets, but that one had to go there to find these streets.

I never knew that I was on corridor Frontenac; arrows were saying corridor Frontenac over there, but it could very well have said that I should go over here to find the corridor Frontenac.

In Figure 4.4 the reader can admire an identification sign for the corridor Fundy containing two arrows pointing in opposite directions. If all roads lead to Rome, opposing directions may conceivably lead to Fundy. If the sign simply contained the street name, it could only be understood for what it was meant to be, an identification sign.

At Alexis-Nihon, a sign reads "Cabot Square." That has to be a clear unambiguous identification sign. Not so; Cabot Square is located at least 300 meters from the sign and is only accessible after taking two escalators and passing under a main city street. The message should have been combined with an arrow or alternatively should read "to Cabot Square."

Realizing these inconsistencies of the most elementary nature, one may

Figure 4.4
A misconceived identification sign.

well wonder why people still rely on signs as much as they do. A final example at Bonaventure, level F, shows the absurdity of a situation that is by no means uncommon.

Getting out of the elevator we saw the sign, the arrow indicating that there was a right angle, and indeed there was one; it was written corridor "Frontenac," so it could well have been the corridor Frontenac. When I found 44 Haiti, I knew that was not so. Then later I saw the other arrow saying Frontenac [at the intersection]. I told myself they are not going to get me this time, they are trying the same trick on me; I have to go to the end there to go on Frontenac . . . , but when I saw 44 Swiss Tourist Office [the destination], I told myself, that's it, we have arrived, . . . they tricked me again.

The most important directional symbol is the arrow. It is easy to pick up and it is easy to understand. The inappropriate use of such symbols not only makes for inefficient signs but diffuses its meaning in a general sense. The power and the clarity of communication is compromised if the meaning of symbols in use is not consistent.

The content plus . . .

A third type of misunderstanding in interpreting a sign is caused by an additional meaning a person attributes to a sign or its message. This unintended meaning is usually derived from previous experience in which the sign was associated with a particular context. For an illustration of such a misunderstanding I shall return to the parking garage of Bonaventure. The first level of the garage situated under the main shopping floor is referred to as section 1, the next level down is section 2, and so on to section 14. The numbers on the elevator keyboard are indicated in a corresponding disposition. Although the numbers on the keyboard increase in a downwards sequence, higher numbers can take on the additional meaning of higher levels. In a couple of instances, the subjects chose to press higher numbers because they wanted to go up. "The levels in the elevator are confusing, . . . the levels [the numbers] went up while one was going down."

A sign in Alexis-Nihon contained the following state description: "Office Building—Exit Atwater." For a number of subjects the sign had the additional meaning: to get out of the building. This led to confusion as some of them knew that the office building was accessible from inside Alexis-Nihon:

Exit Atwater. Well, I said, that means taking the exit, going out. But then I thought, why go out when it is inside? Honestly it mixed me up because exit, that tells me to exit, to go out, but I wanted to go to the office building.

The metro system in Montréal reserves for each line a specific color that is used to differentiate directional signs and to identify routes on maps. This color code is applied systematically. Signs showing to the exits have a color apart, which I thought looked a bit faded. This color puzzled one of the subjects, who gave it a particular meaning, one certainly not intended by the designer.

The colors there [in the metro] are not very vivid and also I saw violet somewhere although there is no line of that color; there is only green, orange, and yellow. They must have made the sign afterwards, and they were not able to produce the same color.

Difficulties in interpreting sign messages, we have seen, are due to a number of factors, which can be summarized as: (1) insufficiently precise information on signs with respect to what they mean and whom they concern; (2) inconsistent application of sign type and symbol; (3) application of sign elements, generally understood in a familiar context, to new situations in which part of the original meaning is no longer relevant; and (4) introduction of new symbols, codes, and sign systems without accounting for the learning process necessary to efficiently use an innovation.

Anticipating Signs

Continuity and consistency

A person using a directional sign expects the sign system to continue until he reaches his destination. If at a decision point a sign in the system is missing, the person generally assumes that he is supposed to go straight on to pick up the next sign: "On the upper level there is a sign saying 'metro,' so I went down and there was no sign [at the bottom of the escalator], so I went straight on."

The subject ended up going toward Cabot Square and the bus terminal. Seeing his mistake, he had to return to find the metro. No means is as efficient to get people lost as to discontinue a directional sign system. To omit a directional sign is equivalent to introducing a wrong decision into a decision plan.

People anticipate a certain consistency in the provision and location of signs. If at an intersection a corridor is named, they expect the other corridor to be named too. If one floor is identified they expect other floors to be identified. This anticipation is not gratuitous; it stems from a need for information and from perceptual behavior geared at deciphering complex environments, as discussed earlier in this chapter.

Reassurance

Pedestrians do not often encounter reassurance signs. When they occur, they are generally welcome, especially after important decision points or after long stretches of walking. Reassurance signs reinforce decisions, but their function extends further to refresh the memory of information obtained at an earlier point. The form in which information is presented has a direct bearing upon the capacity of retention. Research has shown that pictorial representation is highly resistant to forgetting, while abstract information, if not rehearsed or reinforced, is more vulnerable to decay (see Haber, 1970). Application of these findings is common in large parking lots, fairs, and exhibition areas.

The anticipation of signs derives from a reliance on continuity, consistency, and a desire for reassurance. Anticipation results from a need for information in order to reach and execute decisions. In this respect, it is the decision diagrams of the wayfinding person that allow specification of when information is needed and anticipated. The diagrams indicate when signs of a general order or of a specific order are required. To predict the anticipation of environmental information for a given context is essential to the systematic planning of wayfinding supports. This question will be discussed further in Chapter 5.

Conclusion

I have identified three types of sign: directional, identification, and reassurance signs. Major difficulties in perceiving signs are due to a lack in design and placement consistency. The problem is accentuated in complex settings where conditions of overload can occur. The information on signs is read in glances. In order to be easily perceived and understood, information has to be divided into small information packages and structured hierarchically according to content. Difficulties in understanding a sign's message are manifold. Some major suggestions stand out: messages should be clear, nonambiguous in terms of content and in terms of whom that content is addressed to. Directional and identification signs should be clearly distinguished. Symbols should be used for one meaning only. If new symbols or new sign systems are introduced, a certain learning process has to be taken into account.

In this section we have looked at some general aspects of pedestrian signs in buildings. The problems and some of the solution criteria proposed apply not only to the building but also to the urban scale. From the various examples encountered, it appears that sign systems, even those designed by professionals, can contain shortcomings that create major difficulties in processing environmental information. Each trip, each completed wayfinding task, constitutes a learning experience. People learn to rely on signs if signs have proved successful; they also learn to distrust signs if they have been misled by them. High and consistent quality of sign systems is the necessary prerequisite of a trusted wayfinding support.

You do not have to be a cynic to distrust signs after an experience like the one illustrated in Figure 4.5. Having painfully deciphered the parking signs, all differently conceived, by the way, and having figured out when you are

Figure 4.5
Learning to distrust.

allowed to park from *lundi* to *samedi,* and having returned after the 30 minute deadline, you may find your car has been towed. Hidden by those half friendly signs is in fact an additional sign of a tow zone, bilingual, but still . . .

ARCHITECTURE AND SPACE

Piranesi's fantasies of prisons leave most veiwers with an uneasy feeling. A series of etchings entitled *Carceri* was conceived by the eighteenth-century architect and printmaker to evoke dimensions of physical and spiritual suffering. The means chosen by the artist to communicate the idea of

Carcere, with numerous wooden galleries and a drawbridge. *(From Giovanni Battista Piranesi,* Le Carceri, *1761).*

confinement inherent to prisons are of some interest to the topic of this chapter.

In the prison prints, Piranesi emphasizes spikes, heavy ropes, chains, and many other magnified objects of an ominous nature to contrast with the insignificance of people. A sense of powerless exposure emanates from the prints.

Most interesting to the discussion are the architecture and the space the etchings define. Stairs, ladders, a drawbridge and passages of all sorts lead to more passages and stairs that lead to nowhere discernible. They are the routes of aimless wanderings or the traces of fruitless attempts to escape. This is not all. Even by looking carefully at the print, one is not able to comprehend the place. True, there are many views that give a sense of space, but it is not really possible to figure out the prison, it is not possible to get an overall view and to organize the individual impressions into an all encompassing image. To be confined and unable to find a way out is skillfully expressed by the presentation of a confused space that denies the viewer-inmate a basic understanding of the place.

Of Images

A person in the act of finding his way continuously has to pick up information not only from signs but from the environment in general and from architectural elements and the space contained in particular. The information obtained serves different functions. As already indicated in Chapter 3, environmental information is necessary whenever a decision is executed. If a person wants to go up, for example, he will have to perceive the stairs or another means of vertical circulation to execute that decision. Sometimes, particular environmental information precedes a decision. Seeing an ice-cream stand on a warm summer day might entice a person to buy. In this case, the information creates a demand and prompts a decision.

Information has to be picked up; it also has to be interpreted. Seeing a door, for example, a person has to understand its basic function, that of communicating to another space, and he might also have to decide whether that particular door is intended for the public or only for private use. The interpretation is facilitated by a number of design cues the person has learned to associate with private or public doors. The act of interpreting the meaning as to accessibility also applies to space itself. Territories are spaces that individuals or groups claim as their own and over which they exercise control. In order not to intrude, a person has to pick up often subtle cues indicating the degree of personalization of the space. Private and semi-private territories not only limit access, they also prescribe behaviors, and a misinterpretation can easily lead to antagonistic exchanges.

Legibility

As discussed in the previous section on signs, it is possible to identify difficulties related to a person's information processing capacities concerning architectural elements and space, such as difficulties of obtaining and particularly of understanding information. Although the architecture and the spatial configuration of a building generate the wayfinding problems people have to solve, they are also a wayfinding support system in that they contain the information necessary to solve the problem. Quite apart from the difficulty of the wayfinding task, certain places lend themselves better to extracting and comprehending the relevant information. This quality will be referred to as a legibility factor. A place that facilitates the obtaining and understanding of environmental information will have a high legibility factor.

Imageability

Information extracted from space and architecture is used not only for decision making, decision execution, and the interpretation of environmental situations. That information may also be incorporated into an overall cognitive map that allows the person to understand the place he is in with regard to space. Cognitive mapping subsumes an additional information-processing capacity that is particular to the spatial representation of places not perceived at once.[9]

Again, we can assume that certain places lend themselves better to cognitive mapping than others. A rather awkward term, imageability, has been used to describe the ease with which a place can be mentally represented.[10] The prison space shown in Piranesi's print would be an example of low imageability.

Although the quality of legibility has to be a prerequisite of imageability, it does not in itself guarantee it. A uni-cursal or a multi-cursal labyrinth, such as discussed in Chapter 1, might be legible but not imageable. It would indeed be easy to obtain the simple, nonambiguous information of changes in direction and of intersections when encountered one by one but extremely difficult to put them all together in a map-like structure. Problems of architectural and spatial legibility resemble those covered in the section on signs, although, judging by the empirical data, they are much less evident. Predominant is the difficulty of spatially comprehending a place, that is, the problem of imageability.

Images of Cities and Buildings

Most places, be they cities, buildings, or regions, cannot be comprehended from one perspective only. Comprehension and representation in the form of a cognitive map or an overall image require the organization of bits and pieces of environmental information gathered at various points over an extended period of time. If cognitive maps require an organization or structuring of information, it can be assumed that not everything seen and heard is used but that a selection process takes place through which a certain type of information becomes more important and generally relied upon.

The Constituent Units

In a classic study of three American cities (Los Angeles, Jersey City, and Boston), Kevin Lynch (1960) was interested in the information people selected from complex urban environments to organize their cognitive maps. By having people describe their cities and draw sketch maps, Lynch was able to conclude that city images, at least for the North American culture, are based on five key elements he describes as paths, landmarks, nodes, edges, and districts. The study generated a number of corroborative inquiries in Latin American, European, and Islamic cities that confirmed the findings of Lynch.[11] The importance attributed to each of the elements might vary. In the Islamic city, for example, the element "landmark" is not as popular as the element "path" in comparison to American cities and culture.

Kevin Lynch has been criticized for overemphasizing the importance of physical features in his study of city images. Although the physical and spatial characteristics of an environment are foremost in clear image formation, the rather neglected dimension of environmental meaning has been recognized to be an important contributor to imageability (Appleyard, 1979; Moore, 1979; Rapoport, 1977). Certain places stand out in people's minds because of their meaning and not their architectural features. Meaning can be of a functional nature. A post office, a restaurant, a police station might be remembered for their use significance. Meaning can also be of a socio-symbolic nature.[12] A visitor to New York will probably know Harlem not for its functional meaning and even less for its design features but for its sociocultural particularities. Another form of meaning derives from a person's sensory experience of a place. An interesting setting is more imageable than a dull, monotonous one. Curiosity is more stimulating to the cognitive abilities than boredom.

The attribution of meaning to places and buildings, even when it leads to clearer cognitive maps, does not necessarily imply that people know what the place or building looks like. Experiments undertaken by Pezdeck and Evans (1979) have shown people to be less likely to recall the physical features of a building if they can associate it with a function or even just a label.

The inclusion of meaning does not invalidate the notion of basic building blocks in urban imagery; it does show that planning for increased image-ability is not only a question of creating legible objects and places but also of endowing them with meaning, of animating them, and of stimulating the active involvement of the participants.

Empirical studies of images have concentrated almost exclusively at the city and the larger regional geographic scale. Hardly any research has explored the images people have of buildings. In one of the Montréal studies (see Appendix B, study 1978), my collaborators and I were interested to know first whether the five basic elements identified by Lynch also applied to buildings. We had subjects complete wayfinding tasks in various commercial centers, but this time the emphasis was on the post-test investigation. We used two main response-eliciting techniques to externalize the information contained in the images the subject had formed of a building he had visited. Each individual had to construct a small-scale model of the building, and in a second phase he had to draw sketch maps of the internal layout. During both assignments the subjects were asked to enumerate and describe every aspect of the building they could recall. All comments were taped and coded to identify the environmental information contained. To facilitate the classification procedure, we started by regrouping the identified information according to the five categories defined by Lynch.

The analysis confirmed that much of the information mentioned at the building scale fitted into the five city categories, with only small adjustments to be made. Paths at the city scale are defined by Lynch as "the channels along which the observer customarily, occasionally, or potentially moves" (Lynch, 1960, 47). We found corridors, promenades, walks on galleries, and so on, to be the equivalent at the building scale (Fig. 4.6). Specific to buildings and of particular importance was vertical circulation: stairs, escalators, and elevators. Not only did they occur in just about all sketch maps, but they appeared very early in the composition of the map. Paths at the building level have to include the vertical as well as the horizontal circulation system, which would not seem to cause any conceptual difficulties.

Figure 4.6
Paths in cities and buildings.

Landmarks at the city scale are "a type of point-reference, . . . a rather simply defined physical object: building, sign, store or mountain" (Lynch, 1960, 48). Indoors we found much information that fitted the landmark definition as being at the same time a clearly remembered element and well localized in space. The high number of indoor reference points can be explained by the reduced visual accessibility of major landmarks. Examples of landmarks in buildings were: particular shops, bars, cinemas, information booths, sculptures, landscaping arrangements, and also structural and decorative elements, as shown in Figure 4.7. Sometimes it was not so much objects in space but the space itself that served as a reference point. The characteristic that would give a space landmark values was its distinctiveness from other spaces.

Nodes are "the strategic spots in a city into which an observer can enter, and which are the intensive foci to and from which he is travelling" (Lynch, 1960, 47). The equivalent points at the building scale were important circulation intersections, halls, and indoor squares (Fig. 4.8). Nodes in cities and buildings differ only in scale.

Figure 4.7
Landmarks in cities and buildings.

Figure 4.8
Nodes in cities and buildings.

Edges are "the linear elements not used or considered as paths by the observer. They are boundaries . . . edges may be barriers" (Lynch, 1960, 47). The building equivalents appear somewhat less evident, though walls have the impermeability of edges, in particular, the outside walls of a building (Fig. 4.9). An example of an edge at the city scale is a waterfront, let us say, a river. It could be argued that bridges for the city-limit river fulfill the same function as doors for the building-limit walls. They represent points where the barrier is broken and can take on the character of a landmark or a path.

The fifth element, the districts, is described as "medium to large sections of the city, conceived of as having a two dimensional extent . . . which are recognizable as having some common, identifying character"(Lynch, 1960, 47). Equivalent homogeneous areas were found in buildings. A public shopping zone, an office zone, or a residential zone are examples of uniform district-like areas, although "district" is semantically a poor descriptor. Within each district subzones may be found. The shopping area at Bonaventure has a large section arranged in stalls rather than traditional shops. This gives it a homogeneous bazaar-like atmosphere that was perceived as quite apart from the rest. In buildings changes in function and floor often coincide. In such cases district-like characteristics may be associated with floors.

Based on the described mapping exercise, it can be concluded that, after the necessary adjustments of scale and in respecting some specificities of buildings, the five elements proposed by Lynch do apply to buildings as well as to cities. The distinction between the elements, it has to be said, is not always easy; furthermore, certain features of the environment may take on more than one meaning. This difficulty is not specific to the building scale. A basic assumption underlies the application of these observations to urban and architectural planning. If indeed the five key elements are extracted from the environment and used to construct a cognitive map of a city or a building,

Figure 4.9
Edges in cities and buildings.

the planner should take care to emphasize them in his spatial conceptions. In doing so he would increase the quality of legibility and imageability of a place.

An application problem

The application of these findings to the planning of architectural and urban settings brings up two major questions: first, to what extent do these elements need emphasizing, and second, is the presence of these five elements in itself sufficient to guarantee imageability of a place? In partial answer to the first question De Jonge (1962) showed that even in rather uniform residential environments, where no major landmarks are apparent, people pick up small details, like the color of curtains, a particular design of doors, or trees, and use these as landmarks. As long as the environment has some distinct features, it is possible for the person to create his own landmarks. Concerning the other four elements, little is known, though it could again be assumed that if the environment is not excessively uniform the user will be able to select certain elements and give them the meaning necessary to construct his cognitive map. A well-articulated setting, such as discussed by Lynch, does facilitate image formation. I only suggest that a person's ability to select and relate elements should not be underestimated.[13] It is not so much the emphasis given to these five elements that is critical but, as Lynch concludes in the last chapter of *The Image of the City,* their articulation within a total setting.

In response to the second question, which concerns the prerequisite of high imageability, I shall argue that additional factors have to be considered in order to facilitate image formation. Of the wayfinding difficulties encountered by the subjects, hardly any related to the perception, understanding, or recording of the five elements. Nor was the absence of these elements remarked, with one noteworthy exception: landmarks. It was the lack of spatial landmarks or spatial distinctiveness that was deplored. Uniformity in the design of space and the architectural elements composing it led to comments like: "Things are all the same wherever you are; . . . you find yourself in a corner, and you ask yourself in which corner you are" "Everything resembles each other, you go around a corner, and the next corner is just the same."

Recent research in cognitive psychology has shown that key events, major goals, and landmarks are often used by people to retrieve secondary information from memory. Various studies have indicated that people rely on landmarks to identify the position of adjacent places.[14] Evans et al. (1981) suggested that landmarks are used as initial anchor points in the environment, followed by paths linking the landmarks into a network.[15]

Given that the subjects made few comments about the five basic elements described by Lynch, my collaborators and I were interested in exploring additional and alternative factors increasing imageability. First, we identified buildings or sections of buildings that led to very clear or very confused images and tried to find out what each group had in common. Second, we asked each subject to comment on the environmental characteristics they thought had facilitated image formation or rendered it more difficult. The reader might be skeptical as to the subject's ability to articulate the cause of varying image quality of different settings. It should be kept in mind that they all had directly experienced the settings and expressed the image of that setting in volumetric, sketch, and verbal form. Each subject was keen to reflect on the comparative difficulties. Although of an exploratory nature, the comparison of the two findings is revealing. I will even argue that the identified factors are also applicable at the city scale.

Spatial Organization

The master plan of the mind

Buildings containing a central open space are generally well understood and lead to clear sketch maps. The ease with which an image of such buildings is formed has also been remarked by all subjects interviewed. Such an opening, as shown in Figure 4.10, gives visual access to the different floors

Figure 4.10
Central square at complex Alexis-Nihon and Desjardins.

of the building and allows one to sense at least part of the building's volume. A single perspective of the space contains much information that in a closed floor arrangement has to be organized from a number of separate experiences at individual floors. Visual information is easily accessible, the legibility of the space is enhanced. In addition, much of the mental organization and map building becomes redundant. The person already perceives a spatially organized entity of at least a section of the building.

However, there is more to a central open space than increased legibility. This becomes apparent in the actual confection of a sketch map. By using a different color for every minute of sketching, we were able to keep a time record of the drawing sequence. Not only is the open space in such sketches typically exaggerated in size and centricity, but it becomes the focal point, drawn first, around which all the other elements of the building are ordered. What seems to be registered and used in making a sketch is not only the element "central open space," but an *organization principle,* that is, an order by which the spaces of the building are arranged. This observation is not specific to sketches. In verbal descriptions of a building one finds the same principle applied.

Whenever a subject drew a comprehensive map of a building and expressed a clear image, he would also be able to describe its organization principle. This principle can take on many forms, from the establishment of reference points to the geometry of the circulation system, to certain patterns and rhythms of spatial sequences, to any other order that establishes some lawful relations among spatial elements.

The importance of the organization principle in image formation can be illustrated by sketch maps of the main shopping level in Bonaventure. The layout in question can be described as ambiguous in its organization. By ambiguous is meant the possibility of multiple interpretations of the same spatial arrangement, such as Venturi (1966) has proposed. The layout indeed contains an inside square called Place de la Concorde. The square is not very open; it only links the main shopping floor to the underground metro level. The square, furthermore, is not very big, nor is it central. The layout also contains two major circulation axes intersecting in the center of the building. The important shops are generally located on that route. The circulation is further completed by peripheral corridors that break up the inner space into block-like shopping isles.

If the setting were mapped in terms of paths, landmarks, nodes, edges, and districts alone, one could expect to find a more or less loose arrangement of these elements, with emphasis given to those that were particularly important to the users. What appears from the sketch maps, though, is the predominance of the particular organization principle employed in the mapping process.

By far the largest group of subjects started their sketch maps with the Place

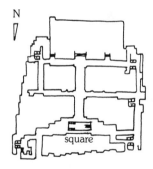

Bonaventure, true-to-scale map.

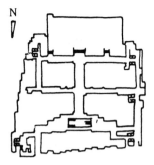

True-to-scale map of the Bonaventure shopping level.

de la Concorde and organized the building space around it. Figure 4.11 shows, on the left, such a sketch exaggerating the central square to the point where little else remains of the building. This organization is not the result of a first quick encounter with Bonaventure; the subject in question had visited the complex approximately ten times. To the right, a similar sketch also accentuates the central square. The position of the information booth, drawn as an octagon, is shown near the square, when in reality it has its place at the intersection of the central circulation.

A second group used the geometry of the central circulation system as their spatial organization principle. Here it is the cross of the circulation system that is exaggerated as can be seen in figure 4.12 on the sketch to the

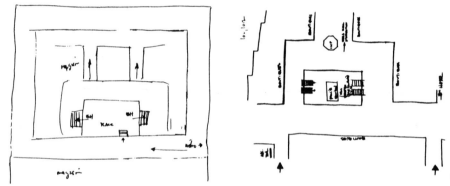

Figure 4.11
Sketch maps of the Bonaventure shopping level organized around the square.

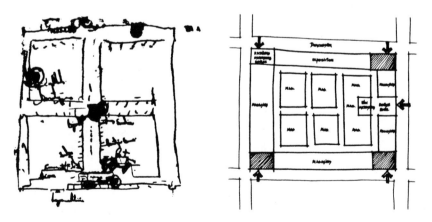

Figure 4.12
Sketch map of the Bonaventure shopping level referring to "cross-road" and "city blocks" as the organization principle.

left. The Place de la Concorde is shown in diminutive and more peripheral than in reality. Some described Bonaventure as an orthogonal city-like layout. An extreme sketch adhering to the "orthogonal city" organization principle is shown to the right. The subject has added more commercial isles and more streets, all, by the way, straight and meeting in rectangles. The Place de la Concorde has completely disappeared from the sketch.

If a layout can be interpreted in various ways, there is a good chance that the resulting image will be weak and disjointed or that it will contain gross distortions due to the impact of a chosen organization principle. Certain buildings provide the user with very little information to reveal an underlying organization. Maps emphasizing the spatial organization, or graphics and color applications in space, can often serve as a support improving communication. Built environments sometimes just do not have a clear organization, and no map, however cleverly done, can invent one. In such cases, some spatial organization can be imposed by allocating specific colors to parts of the setting.[16]

Cognitive economy

The sketch maps discussed bring out the important role of the organization principle in the construction of a cognitive map at the building scale. To establish such an organization principle is a means to come cognitively to grips with the quantity of information contained in the environment, to make sense of that information, and to retain what is needed.

The perception of an organization principle provides a person with the possibility of reducing the amount of information to be retained at a particular moment, and it establishes a rule by which to retrieve that information. We can look at this as being an economic measure of cognition. It is no doubt easier to retain the position of some key elements in conjunction with a rule by which other subordinate elements can be reached than to remember the position of each and every element individually.

In Chapter 3 I argued that decision diagrams are a means to record environmental information and to construct cognitive maps of a linear sequential type. The organization principle discussed here applies more generally to cognitive maps of the survey or spatial type.[17]

We may ask ourselves if and how the transfer from one type of map to the other is possible. Siegel and White (1975) have suggested that survey maps may be the result of dense, richly interconnected, and hierarchically organized route maps. It is important to realize that both types of map are organized. Survey maps are characterized by an abstract organization. The abstract organization may evolve through route maps, as Siegel and White described it, and it can also be transmitted directly from the spatial configuration of the setting.

Lynch (1960) has argued that the five elements, paths, landmarks, nodes, edges, and districts, are the basic building blocks in the process of image making at the city scale. As I have tried to demonstrate, there is no reason to assume that these elements do not apply to the architectural scale as well. If one inquires into the environmental characteristics that render image formation easy or difficult, one finds that the existence and articulation of these basic elements are important as well as the order that establishes a coherent relation among these elements.[18] This observation is significant to the architectural conception of complex places and to the design of way-finding support systems that can communicate this principle to the user, in particular through wayfinding maps.

From buildings to cities

It is tempting to extend the argument from the building to the city scale, even if only on a speculative basis. Try to imagine Manhattan. You will probably think of some major streets, Fifth Avenue, the Avenue of the Americas, and so on. They correspond to one of the five elements identified by Lynch, that is, paths. You may also think of some important buildings and monuments, the Empire State Building, the Statue of Liberty, which are landmarks. Then the major intersections and squares, Times Square, Columbus Circle, which are the nodes. Maybe you will think of the island's contour corresponding to edges and some homogeneous areas like Harlem, Chinatown, Little Italy, which are the districts. That is not all. You also know of an organization principle, the rectangular grid, with its avenues running north-south and its streets running east-west.[19] It is the knowledge of this grid that helps you organize your paths, landmarks, nodes, and so forth, into a coherent whole. This grid is so predominant that you will have no difficulty singling out exceptions like Broadway.

Other cities have different organization principles. Renaissance cities can be organized on a star pattern; medieval European cities often have circular layouts with the public piazza, the market place, and the church in the center.

The rectangular grid pattern is common to most North American cities. Washington, D.C., has a rather unique overlay of a rectangular and a radial street system, as shown in Figure 4.13. During my first day in Washington, that is, before understanding the underlying system, the city was quite a wayfinding puzzle. Once aware of the rectangular and radial overlay, I had no more problems there than in any other city.

I have already labeled the Islamic city a labyrinth in disguise. It is true that for the uninitiated the layout is often totally incomprehensible when experienced in the real setting. The old street layout of Cairo (Fig. 4.14), may serve as a convincing illustration. To the Islamic, however, there is an order.

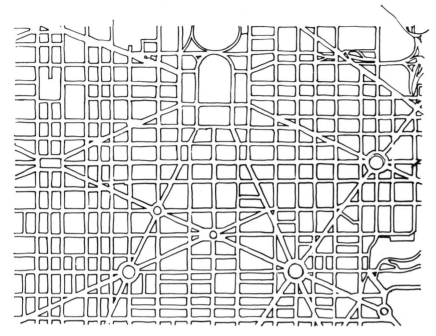

Figure 4.13
Washington, D.C., an overlay of a rectangular and a radial organization principle.

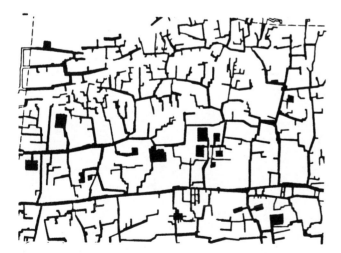

Figure 4.14
Cairo, Egypt, a hierarchical organization principle underlying the Islamic city layout.

The city is organized on a hierarchy of three types of streets each with its particular physical expression and its particular function. The main street, the Chari, is one of the few arteries to traverse the city. It represents the commercial and political establishments. The Chari also leads to the two most important Islamic institutions, the market and the mosque. Durub is a secondary road, often leading from the Chari to a dead end; it is semipublic in nature, giving access to shops and residences. Some of the Durub can be closed off at the junction with the Chari. Finally, the Zuqaq is the tertiary private road, starting at the Durub and also leading to a dead end.

The Islamic city layout has a quite clear hierarchical structure that organizes the city from the most public to the most private spaces. The level of privacy is physically expressed by the width of the street, its use, and its general atmosphere, for which a multitude of factors are responsible. To read the nature of the space, to extract the organization principle is done very naturally by the Islamic visitor, but it has to be learned by the uninitiated. This example illustrates that the imageability of a place is culture specific. Guidoni (1978) remarks that already in the thirteenth century the Christian conquerors of Spanish Islamic cities complained about the perceived disorder of the street system. Whenever possible the sinuosity of the streets was reduced, and dead ends of secondary and tertiary streets were connected, thereby adjusting an Islamic order to an occidental one.[20]

Spatial Enclosure

The comprehension of the principle by which spaces are organized appears as the single most important factor in facilitating image formation of a building. If the frequency of reference by the subjects serves as an indicator, the exterior form or envelope enclosing the space follows in rank. Settings, whose exterior form is not readily accessible, generally lead to poorer images.[21]

Form and volume

The commercial complex La Cité, located at the northeastern fringe of downtown Montréal, links four city blocks below street level. The shops are placed along the underground promenade, laid out essentially in the form of a rectangle (Figure 4.15). With fewer than fifty shops in use, the center is small compared to other urban shopping complexes, and the plan is relatively simple. Nevertheless, La Cité was judged to be difficult and led to confusing images.

Similar reactions were observed for other underground settings, such as underground parking areas and metro stations. These can only be experienced

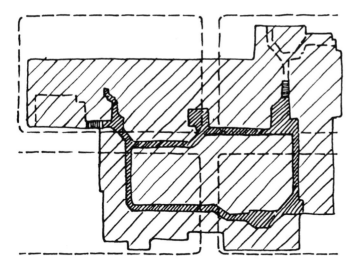

Figure 4.15
La Cité, underground shopping promenade; street system of the above
exterior shown in dotted lines.

from within as an extended space without a definite limit or edge. Spatial
enclosure allows the ensemble of a particular indoor setting to be viewed as a
building. It allows it to be seen as a form, a volume, and as an object.[22] This
representation is simple and easy to retain. It is this object-image that, after all,
comes to mind first in thinking about a particular three dimensional setting.

Spatial enclosure not only allows a setting to be circumscribed in a
retainable form, but it permits certain inferences about the inside. By looking
at a building most people can guess, most of the time, its content or function.
The exterior configuration can, therefore, serve to structure the inside. It is
generally not possible to extract the internal organization principle of a
particular layout but it is possible at least to allocate blocks of spaces
and functions in two or three dimensions.

A glance at the building form can, therefore, provide the viewer with a
general frame useful in allocating and structuring information obtained
inside. Some exteriors express the spaces and the functions contained more
clearly than others. In comparing various shopping complexes, all subjects
agreed that the spatial enclosure of Alexis-Nihon was characterized by a clear
volumetric composition that agreed with its major functions, that is, shopping,
offices, and residences. Each function, having its own architectural expression,
was helpful in gaining an overall image of the setting. Bonaventure, although
it has considerable aesthetic value, was considered to have a rather amorphous
building volume that did not communicate its content.

Spatial enclosure contributes to the object-like image people have of buildings. In addition, it allows one to predict the content of a building and provides for an overall structure. According to the architectural composition and expression of a building the predictions may vary in extent and accuracy. It is indeed possible that predictions will be erroneous, and the ensuing contradictions can lead to confusing images.

Organization versus enclosure

In Montréal the commercial complex Les Terrasses is considered as one of the most difficult indoor complexes for wayfinding. Some people refuse to shop there for fear of getting lost. The inside is composed of many split levels that make it difficult for the user to know what floor he is on. Probably more important is the internal organization principle and its relation to spatial enclosure. As can be appreciated from Figure 4.16, the complex is spatially organized around a triangular circulation system. The subjects who understood this quite simple organization principle did not have major wayfinding problems and their sketch maps were relatively clear. The majority failed to understand the triangular organization, and when asked to sketch the layout many would not venture to draw anything or at best produced a schematic rectangular circulation system or a symbolic circle, expressing their frustration at having continually moved in circles. Figure 4.16 shows that the spatial enclosure is essentially a rectangle, further reinforced by the rectangular city grid. Given that the internal organization principle was not strongly expressed, some people organized the inside according to the existing or even the

Les Terrasses, a sketch map telling it all.

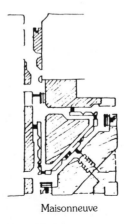

Maisonneuve

Figure 4.16
Les Terrasses, plan and view of building enclosure at Maisonneuve Street.

assumed outside enclosure.[23] The resulting contradictions tended to leave them utterly confused. Some have blamed the architect not only for getting them lost but of intentionally misleading them so that they would be exposed to more shops and would buy more.

Another urban hint

Cities, it could be argued, are not imagined in quite the same way. The modern city is generally seen as an extended space. However, when the opportunity presents itself, spatial enclosure is part of cognitive maps even at the city scale. Mapping the city of Montréal, for example, many people draw the contour of the island on which greater Montréal is located. Often the sketch is started by enclosing the isle.

Town walls of ancient cities also marked their spatial enclosure, which today is generally diffused by sprawling suburbs. Whenever such enclosures are unobstructed and visually accessible, as in the case of the small Italian city, Loco Rotondo (Fig. 4.17), the image of the city is greatly reinforced. Furthermore, the enclosing housing facade of Loco Rotondo corresponds perfectly to the concentric arrangement of the street system with, in its center, the imposing presence of the cathedral. It is, in fact, almost possible to predict the layout of the city, at least for the original section, by its enclosing form alone.

A circular street in Loco Rotondo.

Figure 4.17
Loco Rotondo, Italy, spatial enclosure at the city scale.

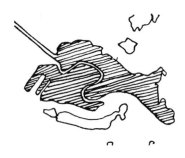

The clear spatial enclosure of Venice.

Contrary to Loco Rotondo, Venice has an internal organization that is hard to comprehend (Fig. 4.18). Two competing circulation systems, the land and the water ways, are superimposed, each being the obstacle to the other. Wayfinding in Venice is a challenge to the visitor and, I think, few Venetians would venture to draw a comprehensive sketch map of its canals and streets. Being encircled by water, the city has a clear unencumbered spatial enclosure. Venice can indeed be imagined in relatively simple forms, modulated by the lagoons and the Grand canal. Although it is very difficult to draw a map respecting the internal organization, it is quite possible to draw a map that specifies the general form of the city, that is, its spatial enclosure. Unfortunately, I did not have the opportunity to study wayfinding in Venice. Based on my own wayfinding experiences it appears that spatial enclosure can serve as a useful alternative to the complex internal organization. It allows one to structure the city mentally into zones to which one can try to relate, not always successfully it must be noted, while exploring the streets and canals.

The notion of spatial enclosure and of spatial organization, we may conclude, have a common characteristic: they are both instrumental in mentally structuring space, that is, in the confection of a cognitive map. Spatial organization establishes an order from within a setting, spatial enclosure from without. Spatial enclosure is furthermore responsible for that

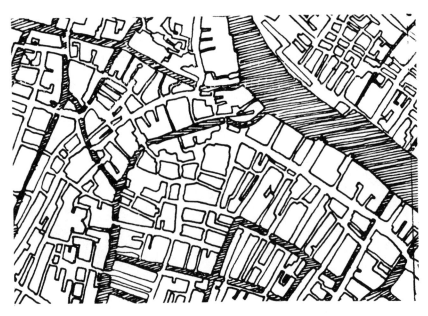

Figure 4.18
Venice, detail of complex internal organization.

simple, object-like representation people have of buildings and, to a certain extent, of cities.

Spatial Correspondence

Environmental information extracted from a cognitive map allows a person to develop decision plans in accordance to routes chosen. In order to be of maximum use, cognitive maps must represent a spatial ensemble in a continuous fashion. Frequently images do not exist as an integrated whole but as disparate, unrelated elements or partial maps.[24] Spatial correspondence summarizes the environmental characteristics that facilitate the development of comprehensive cognitive maps reflecting the continuity of space.

Ground and underground

In Figure 4.19 the reader is invited to return to the center of La Cité, which includes the underground shopping promenade as well as offices, a hotel,

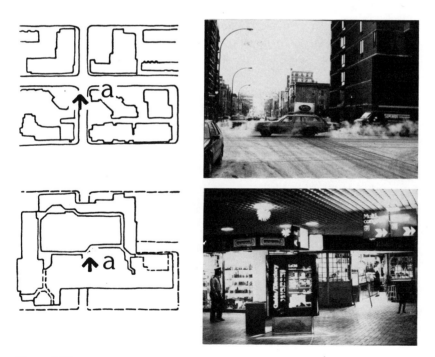

Figure 4.19
La Cité, layout and view of street level and the underground shopping level.

and residential buildings. The layout on the left contains, at street level, four building complexes, each occupying part of a standard city block. The shopping center, shown underneath, is accessible through these building complexes and links them below the street level. The two views on the right were taken from the same geographic position, facing the same direction at the street and the shopping levels. Two very different impressions emerge. As no visual relations exist between the two levels, people tend to develop two separate images. The split is so radical that most subjects expressed surprise when consulting the plan displayed on the directory at the shopping level.

Enclaves

Buildings that are accessible only in parts tend to leave disconnected images and a generally confused cognitive map. Examples encountered were partly excavated underground levels or private and semiprivate enclaves in otherwise public spaces. Even a strong barrier between two sections of a building can leave unincorporated images. The school of architecture at the University of Montréal is housed in an old convent. During a transition period, the school and the religious order shared the building. All links between the section occupied by the school and the one occupied by the order were walled in. When the school expanded and took over the whole of the building, the two sections remained separate. In order to go from the administration area to the studios located on the same floor, it is necessary to go up or down one level to make the link. After using the building for over five years, I still find colleagues thinking that they are actually "going up" or "going down" to the studios. Of course, after some reflection, they can figure out that both must be at the same level. Nevertheless, the initial reaction shows that their cognitive map of that floor is discontinuous.

Inside outside

A last aspect of spatial correspondence I would like to show is the relation between the inside of a building and the larger scale of the city. When asking subjects in a variety of buildings to point to destinations, my collaborators and I observed far greater accuracy for destinations within the building than for those outside. For many, space at the building level and at the city level exists as two nonrelated entities. Those subjects could only point correctly to destinations at the city scale once they passed through the doors or once they had some visual access to some prominent points of the city. The degree of error in pointing to destinations was often astonishing, and total inversions were not rare. Although performance varies greatly from one person to the next, buildings do seem to affect performance. The nature and the location of doors and windows is assumed to be a determining factor in allowing a person to set the image proper to a building within the image of a wider city context.

The complex Desjardins, for example, has large window fronts at both extremities of the central square. The main doors are part of the glass front. The space flows visually through the building (Fig. 4.20). City and building images in such a situation tend to be continuous.

The opposite is true at Bonaventure. Figure 4.21 gives an idea of the impermeability of the building envelope. Even the relatively small doors leave little visual access to the surrounding area. As could be expected, building and city images tend to be poorly connected in such conditions.

Figure 4.20
Desjardins, from outside in and inside out.

Figure 4.21
Bonaventure, from outside in and inside out.

Conclusion

The argument presented in this chapter has led from the five major elements of image formation as defined by Lynch to equivalent elements for buildings. Inquiries into the environmental characteristics facilitating image formation or rendering it more difficult have led to the identification of three information-structuring factors. The single most important one concerns spatial organization, the principle by which an order among various inside spaces and architectural elements is established. Spatial organization, it has been argued, applies to the city scale just as it applies to buildings. Spatial enclosure, permitting the appreciation of architectural and urban forms and volumes is assumed to be the second most important factor facilitating image formation. If spatial organization orders from within, spatial enclosure orders from without. Spatial correspondence, the third structuring factor, affects image continuity of spaces within a setting and among settings, in particular, the continuity between the inside of a building and the city at large. Each of these three factors is seen to complement the five elements of Lynch in their supportive function of structuring the basic elements into a coherent spatial whole.

According to the subjects' evaluation, the main problems encountered in forming a coherent image of a building are due to difficulties in grasping spatial organization, spatial enclosure, and spatial correspondence. Spatial uniformity, which manifests itself by a lack of landmarks, seems to be the only one of the five basic elements that was directly linked to problems of image formation. It can be assumed that the other four elements have been sufficiently accessible, at least for the places visited. It is therefore suggested that architects, and probably urban planners too, pay particular attention to the clear expression of the organizing factors if image formation and way-finding is to be facilitated.

MAPS

Maps We Encounter

Commercial centers, educational facilities, exhibition areas, fairs, urban agglomerations, in fact most large places giving access to the public, provide the user with some kind of wayfinding map. These maps can be found mounted on walls or displayed in showcases, they can be obtained in the form of pamphlets, pocket-size prints, or in those king-size sheets that can never be refolded the same way. Particular to each form are more or less sophisticated printing and mounting techniques, which cannot be covered within the frame of this book.[25] Although maps are mainly intended as a

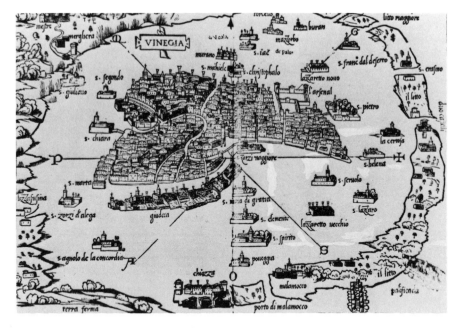

Venice and the lagoon; view of Benedetto Bordone, 1528.

support to wayfinding, promoters often include additional objectives. Shopping arcades, for example, may try to show how big, how interesting, how chic, and how much fun they are.

These additional objectives, which tend to compete with the original one, are common to commercial centers and are pursued by many institutions catering to the public on a competitive basis. Even the higher institutions of learning do their share in "showing off" their campuses.

Wayfinding signs have previously been classified according to their content, which led to the description of identification signs, directional signs, and reassurance signs. Maps provide the viewer with more than just one type of information. They can therefore not be classified on the same basis as signs. Common to all maps is a more or less abstract representation of space. The form this representation can take will serve as a general classification criterion.

Plans

True-to-scale plans (Fig. 4.22) are used to indicate the metric properties of an object or a place. They usually contain a set of standard planning symbols

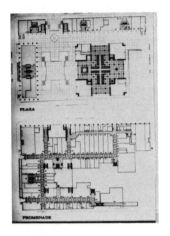

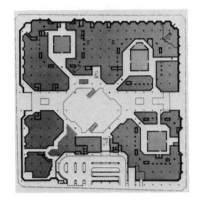

Figure 4.22
True-to-scale plans; map of Place Ville-Marie on public display and pamphlet of Place Desjardin.

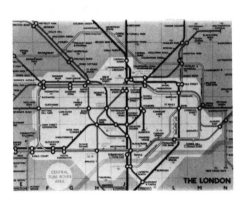

Figure 4.23
Schematic plans; maps of the London Underground and the Montréal Metro on public display.

representing walls, stairs, windows, roads, trees, parks, buildings, and so on. Equal emphasis is given to all parts of the space represented. No specific point of view (perspective) is assumed, no metric or spatial distortions are introduced.

Schematic plans can assume a variety of forms. The topological plan on the left of Figure 4.23 represents the spatial disposition of places without being metric.[26] This particular map of the London Underground was designed in 1932. It is still in use and has served as a prototype for most subways.[27] The illustration of the metro lines on the right, however, bears no resemblance to their geographic position. Schematic maps favor the communication of a particular aspect; they emphasize a feature and reduce others in order to facilitate communication.

Views

The axonometric view retains the true-to-scale plan, to which it adds the third dimension (Fig. 4.24). Although showing an object in three dimensions, it contains no metric distortions due to perspective. It does situate the viewer on one side of the building or the object shown, thereby creating a particular spatial emphasis. The higher the observation point, the more planlike the axonometric view becomes.

The perspective view has characteristics similar to the axonometric, but here perspective distortions are introduced by converging parallel lines to

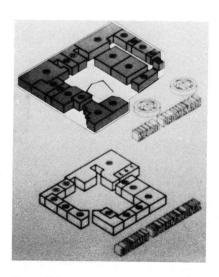

Figure 4.24
Axonometric plans; map of shopping center 2020 University on public display and of University of Montréal Campus.

focal points. Perspective views emphasize the three-dimensional impression as experienced from a particular point in space (Fig. 4.25). A perspective drawing may contain little pertinent information for the person viewing the setting from a different angle.

Many combinations of plans and views are possible. The tourist map of historical Québec, of which a small section is shown in Figure 4.26, combines a schematic plan, emphasizing the circulation routes, with elevations as well

Figure 4.25
Perspective views; poster advertising the highlights of Montréal and map of McGill University campus.

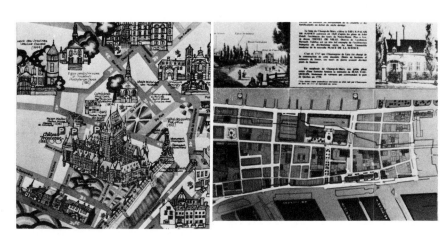

Figure 4.26
Plans combined with views; tourist map of the city of Québec and old Montréal.

as axonometric views. These are useful to point out and render recognizable the historical attractions of the city. The map of old Montréal, to the right, uses a true-to-scale plan and perspective views that are time-removed to the period of their historical importance.

Fantasy drawings

Fantasy drawings aim above all to attract and amuse the viewer, while giving him the essential information. The cross-country skiing area shown in Figure 4.27 communicates important information such as the existence of runs for beginners and intermediate and expert skiers, a parking lot, a bar, and so on. The University of Quebec in Montréal prints a fantasy plan that gives very little, and what is worse, erroneous information about the physical and geographic properties of its downtown campus.

Maps have been used to attract the viewer, to amuse him, to show him the various pretended or existing qualities of a place, but their most important objective is to assist in wayfinding. Concerning the latter I would now like to specify the nature of the information a map should contain to serve its supportive function. The notion of wayfinding styles, introduced in Chapter 3, hints at the ways users read maps, thereby defining the map's functions. Wayfinding styles also permit one to specify the information looked for by the map reader, thereby establishing the required information for a wayfinding map.

I have described a linear style of wayfinding as the tendency to emphasize the use of linearly organized environmental information, in particular, signs. A

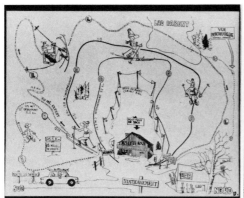

Figure 4.27
Fantasy drawings; leaflet for cross-country skiing and poster of the University of Québec campus in Montréal.

spatial style is characterized by the emphasis on information that can be spatially organized into an overall cognitive representation of a place. Given that both styles are in use, maps should present information that suits either, that does not privilege one group to the detriment of the other.

According to a linear wayfinding style, a map should be read in terms of "how to get somewhere," that is, in terms of the route to take, or more precisely, in terms of a decision plan linking a person's original position to a destination. It is the actual process of getting somewhere that is extracted. If a map is read in such a linear fashion, it is necessary for the user to memorize the decisions, their order, and the places where they are to be executed. According to a spatial wayfinding style, the main aim of map reading is to spatially comprehend a place as well as to locate a starting position and a destination. The physical map serves to complete the cognitive map. The spatial style of wayfinding does not necessarily require memorizing decision plans in detail. Alternative routes, made possible through the perception of new information, might indeed be developed while the person is actually engaged in finding his way. If a person adheres to a linear style, a single map reading or memorizing error would almost certainly get him lost. Given the possibilities to develop alternatives, errors tend to be less fatal for the spatial style.

Two key functions of wayfinding maps emerge: to provide information leading to the identification of a route that links a destination to the viewer's point of origin and to the development of a corresponding decision plan; to provide information leading to a spatial comprehension of a place. It may be added that maps are also used to reassure a person about a decision plan and to confirm his cognitive representation. The following discussion is structured according to the two usages or functions.

Maps for Decision Making

A map, if it is to be of any use, has to provide the viewer with specific indications about the setting it represents. Imagine, for example, a commercial setting and a person trying to reach a destination given by an address. Assume also that the person is slightly confused about his location, and that, seeing a map display, he decides to consult it. Probably his first intention is to localize his position on the map. That, in itself, does not help him if he cannot relate the space shown on the map to the physical reality he perceives. If he has been successful in establishing that relation, he will have to obtain additional information to transform the address of the destination into spatial indicators that have to be localized on the map. Finally, he has to find a convenient route linking origin and destination and memorize the decision plan necessary to follow that route. The three operations characterizing that type of map reading can be summarized as: to identify one's position on the map and to establish the spatial relation between the map and the physical reality of the setting; to find information leading to the location of destination on the map; to figure out a route and to memorize the decision plan necessary to its execution.

I will now identify some of the difficulties encountered in executing the three operations. Observations of map-reading behavior exhibited by the wayfinding subjects as well as their assessment of the maps encountered will again constitute the basic data for discussion.

Relation of maps to setting

The plan layout of horizontally displayed maps tends to correspond to the spatial layout of the setting. If a person identifies a location on the map, he can find the corresponding real location in the direction indicated by the map.

Maps displayed on walls reflect two different systems in use. The plan may be drawn on the basis of fixed cardinal directions, which traditionally locate north or a northerly direction on the top of the map. These maps will not take into account where the directions are positioned in the real setting. The other system is to draw the layout by respecting the plan's position in space. The top of the map corresponds to the direction the viewer faces when consulting the map, what is right and left on the map is also right and left, respectively, in the setting. If maps fulfill that condition, they can be considered to be aligned. The only mental operation necessary to obtain a spatial correspondence with the real setting is to flip the map down around its bottom edge.

Bonaventure, like many other centers, has a representation of both systems. The main wall maps located near major nodes are of the second type, taking into account the viewer's position when consulting the map. In each elevator lobby a map of the first type shows which of the four elevators is in use during the weekends. Two of these maps were mounted on the north wall and two on the south wall of the building. Although no cardinal directions are shown on the maps they are all drawn with north on the top. Thus, if the viewer faces the aligned maps at the north wall, a horizontal projection of the map corresponds to the real spatial layout, but if he faces the maps that are not aligned on the south wall of the building, such a simple projection does not work. The maps also have to be turned by 180° to be aligned.

The viewer, of course, may not know whether he has to make a rotation or

Bonaventure elevator map to be mentally rotated.

not. A number of subjects misread the maps that were not aligned. When I encountered those maps first, I thought them to be incorrectly drawn. It should be noted that the maps have since been relocated on walls facing north. A recent study by Levine (1982) indicates that people not only take longer to read a map that is not aligned, but they also make significantly more mistakes if confronted with such a map. In that particular study one person out of three walked away in a direction opposite to their destination.

The 1980 international Floralies exhibition in Montréal displayed a vertical map that had to be turned by 90° only. Here the visitor was faced with the additional problem of having to know which way to rotate. The site of the exhibition was a perfectly symmetrical island. In the shopping center Alexis-Nihon, a mounted map has to be turned approximately 150° to correspond to the real arrangement of the setting. The need to mentally rotate a map seems to be more evident and the rotation made easier if strong reference points (landmarks) that are visible in the setting are also shown on the map. This condition, found in Alexis-Nihon, allowed the majority of viewers to make the rotation.

In the metro train wagons, maps drawn with north at the top were originally displayed on both sides of the carriage, just above the doors. On the east-west line half the maps showed the directions corresponding to the real movement of the train, while the other half showed reversed directions. In the metro the subjects had their attention drawn to the contradiction between the direction of the moving train and the direction indicated on the map. These maps were clearly understood to be schematic and were not read in a spatial manner. Their function was limited to counting the stations.

We know from school geometry that the minimal information required to bring two congruent figures into a one-to-one relation is the presence of two corresponding points of references in both figures. Figures on maps do not necessarily have to be congruent with the respective configuration in the setting. Given the low level of required precision, the two-points rule can be seen to apply even if the maps are schematic or the correspondence is topological. Most fixed maps indicate the position of the user by the "you-are-here" sign. The minimal information needed to establish a one-to-one relation to the real setting is therefore one other reference in the form of a point or a direction. Levine (1982) discusses three means by which that additional reference can be given: by identifying and labeling an important element or landmark in the setting and on the map, such as a big supermarket in a shopping center; by choosing the map's location so as to accentuate the asymmetrical relation of the viewer's position ("you-are-here" symbol) and the surrounding spatial configuration; and by introducing a bi-part "you-are-here" symbol showing the positions of map and viewer. The author

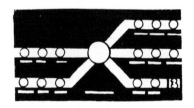

Montréal metro, map of stations mounted inside the trains.

A bi-part symbol.

suggests not relying on minimal information but introducing redundancy by combining various means to make certain that the correspondence is made.

I feel that the two systems of presenting wall maps can easily lead to confusion. The mental rotation of a map is considered to be very difficult by some. The choice of an aligned map is therefore suggested whenever this is possible. If maps are clearly understood to communicate nonspatial characteristics the problem would seem to be diverted.

Getting at the information

As with information processing from signs, people using maps can encounter problems of: finding the maps in the setting; finding the relevant messages if they exist on the map; and deciphering or understanding the message after it is found.

Although many maps in the setting were not consulted, the problem of finding maps when desired was not evident. The displays usually attract attention merely by their size. Furthermore, maps seem to have been strategically placed at points where people had to make major decisions and develop plans of actions. The problem of extracting the information from the map appears more frequent. We shall scrutinize two map displays, both found at Alexis-Nihon. The first is an indicator (Fig. 4.28) containing true-to-scale plans of the three commercial floors, placed vertically in ascending order and differentiated by three colors. Nearby, a second domelike structure

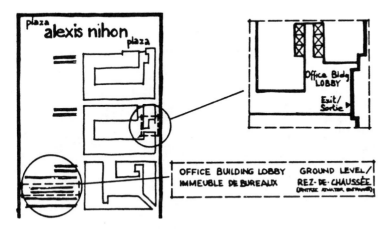

Figure 4.28
Drawing of indicator at Alexis-Nihon.

contains the plan specific to the floor. References to other floors are made on a vertical panel above the dome (Fig. 4.29). This display will be referred to as the kiosk. The task formulation gave the subject the following instructions: to find Montrad, the administrative office of Alexis-Nihon, in the office building of the complex. Some spend a long time looking and looking again at the maps of the indicator. The location of "Office Building Lobby," which is shown near the elevators on the ground floor plan (Fig. 4.28), was not spotted by anyone. The inscription "Office Building Lobby—Ground Floor" to the left of the metro-level plan was seen by half the subjects who consulted the map, and only half of them got the whole message, including "Entrance Atwater." The performance at the kiosk was just as poor. Some saw neither the reference to "Office Building" nor the reference to "Administration" (Fig. 4.29). The information at the kiosk is dispersed and all the features cannot be perceived at once. If a person looks at the map under the dome, he cannot see the message placed on the outside panel of the kiosk. Another instance of the same problem is the placement of different messages on different sides of the kiosk. Although the two examples chosen at Alexis-Nihon are particularly inadequate, the trend is not untypical of other maps encountered.

For many, maps appear too complex. They contain too much information, and too much is irrelevant to wayfinding. Not only are unnecessary details included, but all the information is shown as if it were equally important. One person confessed: ". . . really tiresome to search for something in there . . . , it was just an enumeration of names."

What is the important information to be emphasized? According to the discussion so far, we can already identify at least three elements that are important in reading a map. Reference points or, to use Lynch's term,

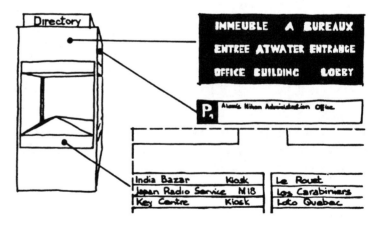

Figure 4.29
Drawing of kiosk at Alexis-Nihon.

"landmarks" are essential in situating the plan in the real physical context, and circulation systems composed of paths and nodes are important in locating points of interest (origin and destination) on the map. As the argument progresses I will add further elements to the list.

Frequent comments refer to the lack of structure that is observed in the presentation of the information. From observing map reading, it is evident that the subjects do not study maps in any systematic fashion. Information must be found within a short time and, most important, information must be presented so that it can be picked up in glances. The same reading behavior observed with signs applies also to maps. This important observation might be emphasized by further extracts from the interview data:

For somebody who really wants to find . . . , it is possible . . . , but to have quick information . . . , let's say, somebody who wants to shop or anything, he is not going to study that.

If I look for information, well, unconsciously I have a limited time at my disposal; I will look a bit here, and a bit there, in all directions. If after thirty seconds I have not found it, I say to myself it's not here and I try to find it somewhere else. If it takes more than thirty seconds, it is all missed. It has to come quickly.

For easy perception, the information has to be simplified and trimmed, and it has to be structured. The structuring principle that applies to signs also applies to maps. On a graphic basis, information can be presented in small packages, so that it is accessible in a glance. On a content basis, information can be structured by emphasizing the most important and regrouping hierarchically the necessary details. Graphics can also underline the different degrees of importance attributed to information, in the same way that a book has titles for chapters, subtitles for subchapters, and so on. A presentation of information can be achieved that fits perceptual behavior and that corresponds to cognitive decision-making behavior.

Not only must messages be picked up, they also have to be understood. I will draw the bad examples again from Alexis-Nihon, given that the context has already been introduced. This does not mean that only Alexis-Nihon had ambiguous messages. Over half the subjects who saw the message "Office Building—Entrance Atwater" did not understand its meaning. This is not surprising. The information needed by the user was something like: in order to go to the office building, go to the upper floor and walk toward the main entrance to Alexis-Nihon, situated on Atwater street; go to the elevator lobby, near the entrance, which gives access to the office building. The user may not need all that information, given that he will be able to extract some from the setting while he goes toward the lobby. Still, if he does not know of a street called Atwater or if he does not know that the entrance is located on the upper floor, the message is quite useless.

Moreover, the message at some kiosks referred to "Exit Atwater" and others to Entrance Atwater. This is an unnecessary variation of terms designating the same area that renders the message even more confusing. It is indeed difficult to recommend anything but the trivial. Messages have to be clear for those who know nothing about the setting; those who do, have no need for messages. The formulation of messages in few words or signs is a challenging task. As in signing, it might therefore be suggested that all major messages be pretested.

Developing a decision plan

Many messages, like the one in Alexis-Nihon, are state descriptions of location. If such a state description is given, one of two conditions has to be met. The user, given his experience, must be able to develop a decision plan based on the information alone, or if such is not the case, the necessary additional information has to be provided at the same place. If, for example, in an elevator lobby a person encounters the state description "Montrad—Suite 1209," he will probably decide to go to the twelfth floor. The decision plan is evident for anyone who has had some experience with high-rise buildings. The state description "Office Building—Entrance Atwater" does not lead to a decision plan for reaching the entrance Atwater if the person does not know its location. Additional information has to be provided to locate the entrance on the map. Often this additional information is incomplete or missing altogether. The kiosk on the metro level in Alexis-Nihon did not contain a plan where the entrance was shown, nor was any information provided that could lead to an intermediary point. In such a case the person has no choice but to look somewhere else or to reject the state description. It is therefore important that, if a message is formulated as a state description of locale, all supportive information necessary for the development of a decision plan be provided.

Supposing now that the person has identified on the map the position of his destination and his proper location, he can then link the two to establish the route to take. For this operation to occur without difficulty it is important that the circulation system be clearly indicated, showing the horizontal as well as the vertical links. Once a route is chosen, the person still has to remember the corresponding decision plan. We have already seen that each decision is composed of two parts, an action part (to turn, to go up) and an image part (major intersection, the end of the corridor). It is the image part that makes the link to the real environment; it is the matching of expected and perceived images that leads to the execution of the decision. It is therefore important that the image information obtained from the map be reflected in the environment. In other words, it is important that reference points or landmarks be clearly indicated on the maps. Distinctiveness of space and architectural features need emphasis in maps for wayfinding.

Maps to Comprehend a Place

Maps are used to work out a specific route to destination and also to spatially comprehend a setting. The two functions are not mutually exclusive. Nevertheless, the emphasis given to one or the other varies according to the wayfinding style in use. A geographic map or a building plan can provide the information necessary to form a cognitive map or, more often, to complete a partial map organized from direct experience of the setting. It is important not to equate a physical and a cognitive map. We have already seen in Chapter 2 that they are identical in function but not in form. We do not generally memorize a physical map, but we extract and remember information.

For buildings as for cities, I have argued, image formation is facilitated if the perception of certain architectural and spatial key elements as well as characteristics of spatial dispositions is guaranteed. It can be assumed that the same type of information is also extracted from a physical map, as the demand would seem to be the same. A prerequisite to all maps, therefore, is the use of the five basic elements or their equivalent at the building scale, that is, landmarks or reference points in terms of distinctiveness, paths and nodes representing the horizontal and vertical circulation systems in buildings, and the movement-confining edges.[28] Districts or functionally homogeneous areas in buildings might also be desirable for large diversified settings. In addition, a map should emphasize characteristics of spatial organization, spatial enclosure, and spatial correspondence. In this respect, the map has the important advantage of showing the ensemble of a place without the visual encumbrance experienced in the real setting.

Spatial organization on maps

A map cannot invent a clear organization principle if it does not already exist in the setting it represents. A map can emphasize spatial organization and thus communicate it to the viewer. It can also camouflage spatial organization and render it inaccessible even if the real layout is clearly organized. Figure 4.30 shows on the left a schematic plan of an office level at Bonaventure. The plan is greatly simplified, the circulation routes, both vertical and horizontal are slightly exaggerated in width and graphically emphasized. The viewer of that map has no difficulty in understanding that the interior office spaces are organized along a rectangular circulation system with extended arms. The true-to-scale plan on the right represents a shopping

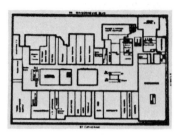

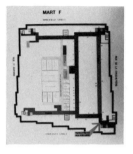

Figure 4.30
Spatial organization on maps; map of Bonaventure on public display and pamphlet of Alexis Nihon.

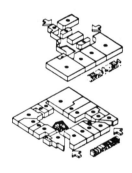

Figure 4.31
Spatial organization on maps; pamphlet of Les Terrasses and map of 2020 University on public display.

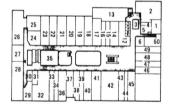

A more recent, improved version of the same floor of Alexis-Nihon as shown in Figure 4.30.

level at Alexis-Nihon. The shops are essentially organized around a central plaza characterized by an open well and an escalator. Although the spatial organization is no more complex, it is much less evident from the map. The vertical circulation and even the open well is not clearly indicated. Too much information is shown that has no relevance to wayfinding and, what is worse, that drowns the important information. A wayfinding map has to communicate wayfinding information and not be just a copy of an architectural layout.

The true-to-scale plan at Les Terrasses on the lower left of Figure 4.31 is not overloaded with details. Nevertheless, the spatial organization is not easily extracted. The spaces, as described in the previous section, are organized along a triangular circulation more evident at the upper levels. By emphasizing the configuration of the major route or by distinguishing the zone within the triangle according to its specific function, the triangular organization principle could have been strengthened. Finally, the right part of the figure is an axonometric view of a three-story shopping complex that is at the same time the entrance to a metro station. This center has a rather simple organization. All shops are regrouped around the central open staircase. The emphasis of the space, flanked by mirrors and enlivened by innumerable spotlights, is on this vertical volume, which is completely lost in the axonometric view. The drawing gives an impression of three closed-off floors. Not even the vertical circulation is clearly indicated.

Spatial enclosure on maps

Spatial organization, I have argued, provides a person with a means to structure space from within, spatial enclosure from without. Although the form of the University of Quebec in Montréal (UQAM) is complex, the simple map shown on the left of Figure 4.32 gives a clear idea of the spatial enclosure, at least for that level. The Bonaventure map to the right contains a little insert situating the floor in a section of the building. Although a modest attempt, it is nevertheless important in that it extends the image to the building and not just to the floor. An axonometric view might have given an idea of the true volumetric enclosure.

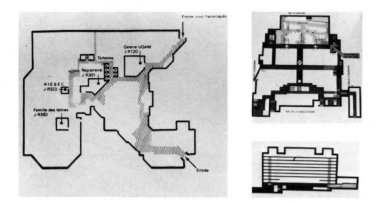

Figure 4.32
Spatial enclosure on maps; pamphlet of University of Québec in Montréal, and map of Bonaventure on public display.

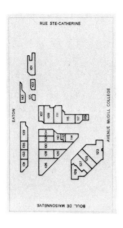
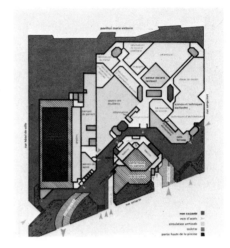

Figure 4.33
Spatial enclosure on maps; pamphlets of Les Terrasses and the CEGEP du Vieux
Montréal.

Two opposite examples are shown in Figure 4.33. The map of Les Terrasses
at the left has no enclosing walls. It is evident from the plan that an important
factor in the formation of a cognitive map is missing. On the right is a map of
the CEGEP du Vieux Montréal, the equivalent of a junior college. Here
everything is emphasized. The lawn, and the concrete pavement have the
same intensity of tone and color as the building. The original color print is
even more confusing than the black and white reproduction. In either case,
the form of the spatial enclosure, although shown, is hardly discernable.[29]

Spatial correspondence on maps

Different aspects of spatial correspondence have been outlined in the
previous section. Maps can show relationships that are not easily detected in
the real setting. Areas with restricted or no access to the public can be
outlined and localized, barriers separating parts of a building can be
emphasized and the parts clearly identified. Difficult relations among parts of
buildings, as encountered at La Cité (Fig. 4.19), can be rendered accessible
with small perspectives or axonometric views. One of the major problems I
would like to discuss in more detail is the correspondence between a building
and its larger urban context.

Maps designed for buildings tend to reach as far as the exterior walls.
Sometimes they name adjacent streets. The viewer generally has little
information to situate the building within the city. In consequence, people
often use the same door to enter or exit, even if it means a detour. Again, a

little insert locating the building in relation to some reference points will provide the information needed (Fig. 4.34).

The Sacré-Coeur hospital in Montréal (Fig. 4.35) inserted its building complex on a paler photo of the urban environment. The background is very pale and does not contain any particular landmarks. Nevertheless, the solution is remarkable in that it also satisfies the previous criteria of spatial enclosure.

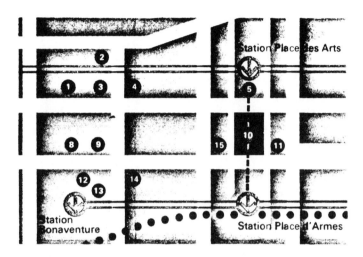

Figure 4.34
Buildings within the city context; pamphlet of Place Desjardins.

Figure 4.35
Spatial correspondence; leaflet of Sacré-Coeur Hospital.

Maps for the Blind

The visually handicapped person, whether congenitally or adventitiously blind, acquires spatial mobility and wayfinding skills only after an extensive learning and training period. The simplest aspects of body position and locomotion, like facing in a certain direction or walking straight, become difficult tasks (Cratty, 1971). The basic spatial notions of back-front, right-left are acquired only very slowly by the congenitally blind child. Distance perception without sight is greatly reduced. When the blind person finds his way, he is not only replacing visual by nonvisual information, but he has to organize that information accordingly. In psychology literature there is an ongoing discussion about the nature of spatial representation of the congenitally blind.[30] A blind person can certainly achieve a linear sequential representation based on his movement through space. He will typically recall decision plans. Various tests have shown that some are able to perform tasks that do require a survey-type map.

Tactile maps and models of environmental settings at the urban and the architectural scale can greatly facilitate spatial understanding for the blind and assist in wayfinding. Maps and models are often used in training programs; they have also been produced on an experimental basis for public transportation in big cities. In Montréal a tactile map of the metro system has recently been published.

Although the function of maps and the basic questions raised in this chapter apply to the sighted as well as the blind, major differences exist in terms of the information a map for the blind should contain, in terms of the amount and the form of tactile information that makes the map still readable, as well as in terms of the constraints placed on size and material.[31] In a particularly interesting experiment of map design, Kidwell and Greer (1972) developed a tactile map communicating open spaces, buildings, and routes with the major hazards on the front, and on the back the legend printed in inverse braille. The map, not extending the width of a hand's grasp, can be read with the thumb and the fingers simultaneously on both sides. The inverse braille necessitates a certain training period before the map can be used.

Conclusion

Maps are deceptively easy to draw. Yet the conception of a good wayfinding map is a complex design problem, not only in terms of how information should be presented but in terms of what information is important. Each of the six map types introduced exhibits certain advantages and disadvantages. Some emphasize metric properties, others communicate ideas in simplified form. Some give priority to the spatial dimension, others to humor and interest. These same maps might be difficult to read, they might distort information if not properly understood, they might bias information, or they might not contain much information at all. A well-chosen combination of these forms of presentation can often compensate for the inevitable weakness of a single choice.

Wayfinding maps have to serve two functions. They have to provide the user with information to develop and memorize decision plans to reach destinations; they also have to provide information for the user to spatially comprehend the place represented. The following summary requirements have to be met by an adequate wayfinding map. Maps should contain only information relevant to wayfinding. That information has to be structured according to content so that the user can pick out first the most important information. If he finds information pertinent to the problem, he can then obtain the necessary details. The information also has to be structured according to form so that the viewer can pick out the information in a glance. The disposition of the drawing on a map should take into consideration the direction the viewer faces when looking at the map. Whenever possible, maps should be aligned with the surrounding setting.

Maps can be composed on the basis of the five key elements or their equivalent at the building scale. Of particular importance are paths, nodes, and landmarks. These facilitate image formation, and they are essential to the development and the recording of a decision plan. In order to enhance image formation, maps should emphasize the communication of the underlying spatial organization of a place. Maps for buildings should also communicate spatial enclosure, if possible in three dimensions and with spatial correspondence, in particular the building's position in a geographic or urban context.

Even if a map is designed according to the outlined functions and the perceptual characteristics of map reading, it does not guarantee that the map will be understood by everyone. Map reading is a skill, and skills are learned. Maps always represent relatively complex bits of information simultaneously. The viewer has to attend selectively to the available information. Thorndyke and Stasz (1980) tried to identify the characteristics of a good and a poor map reader. A good map reader develops learning strategies. He typically regroups the information presented into subsets. He develops techniques for encoding spatial relationships and verbal labels. Finally, he evaluates his progress of coping with the information and revises his strategies in consequence. Map reading can probably be learned by everyone. If we consider how common maps are in our daily life it is surprising to observe how difficult it is for most people to read and to understand them. The problem lies with the design of maps and also with the neglect of map-reading skills. It is very rare indeed to find map reading in an elementary school curriculum, although the task would surely be worth the teacher's and the student's effort.

INFORMATION BOOTHS AND VERBAL INSTRUCTIONS

OK . . . you go down here, at the second . . . no . . . at the third intersection you turn left . . . follow the road to the petrol station . . . there you continue and turn left, one block further . . . go down to Kings road . . . follow it until you see a red brick building at your left . . . turn right . . . after crossing the railroad turn sharp left and drive for about two miles . . . you can't miss it . . .

Information Booths in Use

An account of the information a wayfinding person obtains from the environment would not be complete without the verbal instructions obtained at information booths or from other occupants of the setting. In fact, most commercial centers and large public places in general have information booths. If no information booth is provided, as at Alexis-Nihon, people tend to inquire at newspaper shops or other accessible shops or stands. Security personnel, if present, also seem to be the victims of the lost masses.

If an information booth is provided, it is usually heavily used. For example, at Place Ville-Marie during the lunch peak period, a person may give as many as 240 instructions an hour. At this rate, it is not surprising that the instructions are very short. The information booth at Bonaventure is usually occupied by two persons. At peak time, they average a somewhat lower turnover of approximately 180 people an hour.

From a small series of interviews with the personnel of information booths some insights were gained into their functioning. At Bonaventure the type of question asked varies a great deal with the time of the day and even with the yearly season, as they attract quite a different clientele. In each instance, the great majority of questions deal with wayfinding. The personnel usually visualize the setting as being composed of four quarters, with the elevators at the extreme corners of the building. Given an address by street name and number, they can immediately identify the level of the desired destination and direct the person to the closest elevator. The directions are given by verbal descriptions and pointing. No maps or drawings are used, as they seem to confuse people. Sometimes an address is written down if the client seems to have trouble remembering it. The training the personnel receive consists mainly of an initiation period in which they learn about the setting and visit its different areas. They sit in the booth with an experienced person and learn by listening.

The information booth and the verbal instructions make a considerable contribution in helping people solve wayfinding problems. No doubt some questions are asked just because there is an information booth available; this has been mentioned by the personnel and an administrative manager of Bonaventure. However, the overall function of the booth in the setting can hardly be disputed.

Wayfinding instructions

A wayfinding instruction describes the location of a destination. The instruction may again indicate "where something is" or "how to get there." The first, as previously discussed, is a state description of location, the second a process description of location. The process description is a decision plan containing the steps necessary to attain a destination. The state description may provide information that, combined with the user's knowledge and the environmental information perceived, may lead to a decision plan.[32]

A process description, if given verbally, cannot contain an unlimited number of decisions. Based on the interviews it appears that the number of decision units that can be grasped and retained is around three to five. We can easily see the limitation of a process description for getting people to a destination in a complex setting.

I will again refer to Bonaventure to illustrate verbal instructions. The wayfinding task given to the subjects was designed so that they had to consult the information booth to receive the address of destination, the Swiss National Tourist Office. The intention was to collect a sample of instructions for the same question given by different occupants of the booth.

All instructions contained a state description of destination (Frontenac 44), and a process description of how to get to the elevator and to floor F where the destination is located. The process description never exceeded five decisions. In no instance was a process description given that would have led to the destination directly. This is quite contrary to most instructions given by laymen, which the fictive instruction at the beginning of this section was meant to caricature.

Asking Passers-by

Asking other people is a popular way of obtaining information. During the experiment this became evident from the number of times the investigator had to discourage the subject from consulting other people. This restriction was imposed to get a better insight into the decision making process. I also observed that some subjects were very hesitant to ask for directions. One subject inquired only at information booths. To give proper information, he thought, exceeded the ability of most users. Another disliked asking to the point of not even consulting information booths. Even at Bonaventure he would have preferred to search for a directory.

There is another important question. What is the chance of obtaining a useful piece of information? I collected a number of instructions given by people in various places for similar destinations. The performance varied a great deal from one setting to the next. Generally, in asking for major shops in a commercial center one cannot expect more than a 50 percent chance of getting reliable information. If one considers that some of the answers are also misleading, one may well wonder why asking passers-by is as popular as it appears to be.[33]

In interviews with designers, it was occasionally mentioned that the user's dependence on others to obtain information was not a negative aspect of a setting. Indeed, it was argued that a certain dependence on others furthers social interaction. This sounds too convenient. The fact that the information is not very reliable, that it is often difficult to get, and that some people really dislike asking questions would seem to override all social interaction arguments.

Interestingly enough, during the experiment, the subjects and I were approached many times by other users who asked for wayfinding information. A subject, after a long fruitless search for the office building at the parking level of Alexis-Nihon, was asked when he came down the elevator: "Is there nothing up there, I am looking for the office building." Another subject, when asking a user in Place Ville-Marie, "I am looking for the underground passage to go to Bonaventure," was told coolly: "Me, too." Finally, I would like to apologize to that lady in Bonaventure who asked me during the trip: "Place Ville-Marie, is it here?" and all I was allowed to say was, "No madam, it is not here," and we left her standing in the breeze. How could she know that our unresponsive answer was all in the interests of improved wayfinding.

NOTES

1. Some of the data presented in this chapter has been published by *Man-Environment Systems* (Passini, 1980).
2. Reassurance signs can also serve as landmarks, particularly on highways, where there is a tendency to remove many of the distinctive features that naturally occur along a path (see Webb, 1956; McDonald, 1958).
3. See, for example, Wohlwill, 1970; Dewar, 1973.
4. Carr presents an opposing view to Venturi's *Learning from Las Vegas* (Venturi, 1972). Venturi sees a naturally occurring order between private and public signs; Carr insists on the necessity of protecting the public from an overemphasis of private signs.
5. The desired level of standardization is open to debate. The position defended here is not that all signs for all buildings and urban centers should be the same. Certain settings, like hospitals and airports, as well as certain users, like the elderly and children, will require

information adapted to their processing capacities. Furthermore, standardization should not interfere with the particular characteristics of a place. The sign to a cozy old-fashioned restaurant cannot be of the same idea as the one showing the way to a supermarket.

6. The first extensive research on traffic sign perception was done during the fifties, when sign systems for new highways were planned. For representative articles see Webb, 1956; McDonald, 1958.

7. See note 15 in Chapter 2 for a summary of the five major Gestalt principles. An interesting application of these perceptual rules to the conception of signs is discussed in Dewar (1973).

8. The iconic memory and its relation to visual perception is introduced and discussed in Neisser (1967).

9. We are generally little aware of this information processing. Some disabilities resulting from brain lesions appear almost unbelievable. Certain cases have been documented, for example, that show people to neglect the left half of the visual field and always turn to the right when a directional decision is to be made. Some people are incapable of remembering familiar landmarks, even their own homes when passing in front of them, and some are not able to relate visual impressions to a coherent pattern (Howard and Templeton, 1966).

10. Imageability and legibility are terms introduced by Lynch in *The Image of the City*. Lynch does not emphasize the distinction made here, which is more fully described by Appleyard(1979).

11. Cross-cultural studies of city imagery have shown the five elements described by Lynch to be applicable even if small variations in their relative importance were noticed. For studies of cross-cultural interest, see DeJonge (1962), mapping of Amsterdam, Rotterdam, The Hague; Gulick (1963), mapping of Tripoli in Lebanon; Klein (1967), mapping of Karlsruhe in the Federal Republic of Germany; Appleyard (1970), mapping for Ciudad Guayana in Venezuela; Stea and Wood (1974), mapping for Mexico City, Puebla, Guanajuato, San Cristobal, las Casas in Mexico.

12. Appleyard (1979) argues that design professionals as well as researchers are rarely aware of the symbolic and, in particular, the social content of the environment, although studies have indicated that social and functional meaning is significant in urban perception as well as behavior.

13. Heft (1979), interested in the way people learn routes, found that learning strategies varied according to the characteristics of the environment. People tend to rely on prominent environmental features if they are accessible, otherwise they distinguish secondary characteristics, even if they are not immediately apparent, and rely on those.

14. Allen et al. (1978), basing studies on simulations of routes by slides, concluded that people select distinctive environmental features and use these landmarks to organize other elements; Sadalla et al. (1980) also found that people refer to landmarks as an organization structure in large-scale environments.

15. The order of acquisition is still debated. Gärling et al. (1981) argues that paths are learned before landmarks.

16. In an experiment on wayfinding and cognitive mapping in an undifferentiated, institutional office building Evans et al. (1980) showed improved performance in both tasks after having introduced color coding.

17. Hart (1981), in describing the three systems of reference (egocentric, fixed, and coordinate or abstract), associates the organization of environmental information by key landmarks to the fixed system of reference. In the same line of thought it is possible to ascribe an organization of environmental information on the basis of decision plans emanating from direct experience of routes to an egocentric frame. Coordinate frames of reference are differentiated from fixed frames only by the nature of the organization principle applied.

18. Weisman (1981), in a study published after this chapter was written, assessed the ease with which certain plan configurations could be retained. Correlations were also shown to exist

between judged simplicity of plan configurations and wayfinding ease. Similarly, Zannaras (1976) showed a relation between urban form and cognitive mapping.

19. If New York leaves most inhabitants and even visitors with a relatively clear image, it is not only because of the rectangular grid. Other orthogonal city layouts can lead to poor images, particularly if the city covers large undifferentiated areas. The comparison of New York and Los Angeles is an illustration. It has been referred to by Lynch (1960).

20. Western authors have often stressed the physical formlessness of Islamic cities and the chaotic disposition of streets. Lapidus (1967), in criticizing this attitude, argues for the Islamic order, which has its origin in the family unit and the administrative structure of the community.

21. Sommer and Aitkens (1982) undertook a mapping study of supermarkets. The subjects had to complete two tasks: locate consumer items from a pre-established list on a map; and locate as many items of their own choice. The results showed than items in the peripheral aisles were recalled more frequently and more accurately than items in the central aisles. Memory tests generally indicate that elements at the beginning and at the end of lists have a better chance of being recalled. Sommer's observations may also be interpreted in the light of spatial cognition. If, as argued above, particular attention is given to contours or spatial enclosure, it stands to reason that items located in the peripheral aisles, which represent the contours of supermarket shelving, are recalled more accurately.

22. This form of Gestalt aspect of spatial enclosure is what differentiates it from edges as defined by Lynch. Spatial enclosure implies an order, an organization.

23. Les Terrasses have since introduced effective graphic displays to facilitate the identification of split levels and even the triangular circulation system. As shown in Appendix A the graphics are attractive and enhance the general appearance of the complex.

24. Support for the existence of disconnected cognitive maps is given by Lynch (1960), Appleyard (1970), Kosslyn et al. (1974).

25. For technical and practical design problems as well as implementation proceedings see Follis and Hammer (1979); for technical suggestion see *Environmental Graphics Source Book* (1978).

26. I would like to remind the reader of *Byrne's* suggestion that cognitive maps are not necessarily metric in nature but topological (*Byrne*, 1979). Such representations would be accurate in establishing general relations among spatial elements.

27. The plan was designed by Henry Beck; for an assessment see Doyle (1978). The New York subway system does not enjoy the same reputation for wayfinding as the London Underground. A study done by Bronzaft et al. (1976) showed the subway map, which is topological in nature, to be difficult to use and to lead to many errors.

28. The emphasis given to the elements used in cognitive mapping varies according to place characteristics. Francescato and Mebane (1973) have shown, for example, that paths are more frequent in Milan and landmarks in Rome. Similar variations have already been noted in respect to cultural variables (see Gulick, 1963). Maps that reflect these particularities could facilitate the comprehension of places by communicating the most pertinent information for constructing a cognitive map.

29. In addition to organizing space within its confines a clear enclosure creates a stronger figure, which, as we have seen, facilitates perception and memorization. Studies on map reading are rare; for an application of Gestalt principles to maps see Tversky (1981).

30. For a general review of cognitive maps in the blind see Shemyakin (1962); Rosencranz and Suslick (1976); Fletcher (1980, 1981).

31. Some of these questions are treated by Leonard and Newman (1970); Kidwell and Greer (1972, 1973); James and Swain (1975).

32. In one of the few studies on wayfinding communication, Riesbeck (1980) analyzed verbal instructions and the way they are used. The primary interest of the receiver is to judge

whether he can follow the instructions and not in constructing a cognitive map. The components of direction giving are motion (what to do); descriptions (where to do it); comments. In judging the clarity of a verbal instruction a person proceeds to identify motion units and description units and evaluates whether they are both clear and necessary. The instructions studied by Riesbeck are process descriptions; they therefore reflect decision plans. We have already seen that all wayfinding decisions contain an action part and an object part, which correspond to "motion" and "description" as used by Riesbeck.

33. Best (1970), in a study of wayfinding in a public building in Manchester (England), discovered that half the errors people made to reach a destination were due to faulty directions given by others.

REFERENCES

Allen, G. L., A. W. Siegel, and R. R. Rosinski, 1978, "The Role of Perceptual Context in Structuring Spatial Knowledge," *Journal of Experimental Psychology: Human Learning and Memory* **4**(6):617-630.

Appleyard, D., 1979, "The Environment as a Social Symbol: Within a Theory of Environmental Action and Perception," *Journal of the American Planning Association* **45**(2):143-153.

Appleyard, D., 1970, "Styles and Methods of Structuring a City," *Environment and Behavior* **2**(1):100-118.

Best, G., 1970, "Direction Finding in Large Buildings," in *Architectural Psychology,* D. Canter, ed., RIBA Publications, 73, London.

Bronzaft, A. L., et al., 1976, "Spatial Orientation in a Subway System," *Environment and Behavior* **8**(4):575-594.

Byrne, R. W., 1979, "Memory for Urban Geography," *Quarterly Journal of Experimental Psychology* **31**(1):145-154.

Carpenter, E., 1979, "Travelers' Aid: More DOT Symbol Signs," *Print* **33**(5):78-85.

Carr, S., 1973, *City Signs and Lights: A Policy Study,* MIT Press, Cambridge, Mass.

Cassini, G., 1971, *Piante e Vedute Prospettiche di Venezia, 1479-1855,* Stamperia di Venezia, Venice.

Cratty, B. J., 1971, *Movement and Spatial Awareness in Blind Children and Youths,* Charles C. Thomas, Springfield, Ill.

De Jonge, D., 1962, "Images of Urban Areas: Their Structures and Psychological Foundations," *Journal of the American Institute of Planners* **28**:266-276.

Dewar, R. E., 1973, *Psychological Factors in the Perception of Traffic Signs,* Road and Motor Vehicle Traffic Safety Branch, Department of Transport, Government of Canada.

Doyle, B., 1978, "Underground Maps: It's Hard to Improve on Beck," *Design* **349**:31.

Environmental Graphics Sourcebook: Materials and Techniques, 1978, Society of Environmental Graphics Designers, Chicago.

Evans, G. W., J. Fellows, M. Zorn, and K. Doty, 1980, "Cognitive Mapping and Architecture," *Journal of Applied Psychology* **65**:(4):474-478.

Evans, G. W., D. G. Marrero, and P. A. Butler, 1981, "Environmental Learning and Cognitive Mapping," *Environment and Behavior* **13**(1):83-104.

Fletcher, J. F., 1980, "Spatial Representation in Blind Children, 1: Development Compared to Sighted Children," *Journal of Visual Impairment and Blindness* **74**(10):381-385.

Fletcher, J. F., 1981, "Spatial Representation in Blind Children, 3: Effects of Individual Differences," *Journal of Visual Impairment and Blindness* **75**(2):46-49.

Follis, J., and D. Hammer, 1979, *Architectural Signing and Graphics,* Whitney Library of Design, New York.

Francescato, D., and W. Mebane, 1973, "How Citizens View Two Great Cities: Milan and Rome," in *Image and Environment*, R. D. Downs and D. Stea, eds., Aldine, Chicago, pp. 131-147.

Francescato, G., et al., 1976, "Impossible Dreams, Unrealizable Hopes?," in *The Behavioral Basis of Design*, P. Suedfeld and J. Russell, eds., Dowden, Hutchinson & Ross, Stroudsburg, Pa., pp. 5-8.

Gärling, T., et al., 1981, "Memory for the Spatial Layout of the Everyday Physical Environment: Factors affecting Rate of Acquisition," *Journal of Environmental Psychology* **1**(4):263-277.

Guidoni, E., 1978, *La Città Europea*, Electa, Milan.

Gulick, J., 1963, "Images of an Arab City," *Journal of the American Institute of Planners* **29**:179-198.

Haber, R. N., 1970, "How We Remember What We See," *Scientific American* **222**(5):104-112.

Hart, R. A., 1981, "Children's Spatial Representation of the Landscape: Lessons and Questions from a Field Study," in *Spatial Representation and Behavior across the Life Span: Theory and Application*, L. S. Liben et al., eds., Academic Press, New York, pp. 195-233.

Heft, H., 1979, "The Role of Environmental Features in Route Learning: Two Exploratory Studies of Wayfinding," *Environmental Psychology and Nonverbal Behavior,* **3**(3):172-185.

Howard, T. P., and W. B. Templeton, 1966, Human Spatial Orientation, John Wiley and Sons, New York.

James, G., and R. Swain, 1975, "Learning Bus Routes using a Tactual Map," New Outlook for the Blind, **69**(5):212-217.

Kidwell, A. M. and P. S. Greer, 1972, "The Environmental Perceptions of the Blind Person and Their Haptic Representation," *New Outlook for the Blind,* **66**(8):256-276.

Kidwell, A. M., and P. S. Greer, 1973, *Site Perception and the Non-visual Experience: Designing and Manufacturing Mobility Maps,* American Foundation for the Blind, New York.

Klein, H. J., 1967, "The Deliniation of the Town Center in the Image of Its Citizens," in *Urban Core and Inner City,* E. J. Brill, ed., Sociographical Department, University of Amsterdam, 286-306.

Kosslyn, S. M., H. L. Pick, and G. R. Fariello, 1974, "Cognitive Maps in Children and Men," *Child Development* **45**(3):707-716.

Lapidus, I. M., 1967, Muslim Cities in the Later Middle Ages, Harvard University Press, Cambridge, Mass.

Leonard, J. A., and R. C. Newman, 1970, "Three Types of Maps for Blind Travel," *Ergonomics* **13**(2):165-179.

Levine, M., 1982, "You-are-here Maps: Psychological Considerations," *Environment and Behavior* **14**(2):221-237.

Lynch, K., 1960, *The Image of the City,* MIT Press, Cambridge, Mass.

Marks, B. S., 1979," The Language of Signs," in D. Pollet and P. Haskell, eds., *Sign Systems for Libraries,* Bowker, New York, 89-98.

McDonald, J. W., 1958, "Directional Signing Must Come of Age," in *ITTE, Proceedings for Street and Highway Conference,* University of California.

Moore, G. T., 1979, "Knowing about Environmental Knowing: The Current State of Theory and Research on Environmental Cognition," *Environment and Behavior* **11**(1):33-70.

Neisser, U., 1967, *Cognitive Psychology,* Prentice Hall, Englewood Cliffs, N.J.

Passini, R., 1980, "Wayfinding in Complex Buildings: An Environmental Analysis," *Man-Environment Systems* **10**(1):31-40.

Pezdek, K., and G. W. Evans, 1979, "Visual and Verbal Memory for Objects and Their Spatial Location," *Journal of Experimental Psychology: Human Learning and Memory* **5**(4):360-373.

Rapoport, A., 1977, *Human Aspects of Urban Form: Towards a Man-Environment Approach to Urban Form and Design,* Pergamon Press, Toronto.

Riemersma, J. B., 1979, "Perception in Traffic," *Urban Ecology* **4**(2):139-149.

Riesbeck, C. K., 1980, "'You Can't Miss It': Judging the Clarity of Directions," *Cognitive Science* **4**(3):285-303.

Rosencranz, D., and R. Suslick, 1976, "Cognitive Models for Spatial Representations in Congenitally Blind, Adventitiously Blind and Sighted Subjects," *New Outlook for the Blind* **70**(4):188-194.

Sadalla, E. K., W. J. Burroughs, and L. J. Staplin, 1980, "Reference Points in Spatial Cognition," *Journal of Experimental Psychology: Human Learning and Memory* **6**(5):516-528.

Shemyakin, F. N., 1962, "Orientation in Space," in *Psychological Sciences in the USSR.* B. G. Anavigew et al., eds., Office of Technical Sciences, Report 62-1108 3

Siegel, A. W., and S. H. White, 1975, "The Development of Spatial Representations of Large-Scale Environments," *Advances in Child Development and Behavior* **10**:9-55.

Sommer, R., and S. Aitkens, 1982, "Mental Mapping of Two Supermarkets," *Journal of Consumer Research* **9**:211-215.

Stea, D., and D. Wood, 1974, *A Cognitive Atlas: The Psychological Geography of Four Mexican Cities,* Instituto Nacional de Bellas Artes, Cuadernos de Arquitectura, Mexico City.

Thorndyke, P. W., and C. Stasz, 1980, "Individual Differences in Procedures for Knowledge Acquisition from Maps," *Cognitive Psychology* **12**(1):137-175.

Tversky, B., 1981, "Distortions in Memory for Maps," *Cognitive Psychology* **13**(3):407-433.

Venturi, R., 1966, *Complexity and Contradiction in Architecture.* New York: Museum of Modern Art.

Venturi, R., D. S. Brown, and S. Izenour, 1972, *Learning from Las Vegas,* MIT Press, Cambridge, Mass.

Webb, J. M., 1956, *Correlation of Geometric Design and Directional Signing.* Report for the Department of Public Works, Division of Highways, University of California.

Weisman, G. D., 1981, "Evaluating Architectural Legibility," *Environment and Behavior* **13**(2):189-204.

Wohlwill, J., 1970, "The Concept of Sensory Overload," in *EDRA Two,* Proceedings of the Second Annual Environmental Design and Research Association Conference, J. Archea and C. Eastman, eds., Dowden, Hutchinson & Ross, Stroudsburg, Pa., pp. 340-344.

Zannaras, G., 1976, "The Relation between Cognitive Structure and Urban Form," in *Environmental Knowing.* G. Moore and R. Golledge, eds., Dowden, Hutchinson & Ross, Stroudsburg, Pa., 336-352.

5

Wayfinding Design

Not just a question of signs, and if signs not just any . . . anywhere.

Since the sixties the design profession has witnessed a growing disen-chantment with the creed of the modern "international style" as it was first proclaimed in 1928 by CIAM (Congrès Internationaux d'Architecture Moderne), the official organ of modern architecture. Such telling titles as *Form Follows Fiasco* (Blake, 1977) and *From Bauhaus to Our House* (Wolfe, 1981) manifest a final break with the most sacred beliefs and institutions of modern design and architecture. What came to be called the modernist movement is blamed above all for having overvalued the object of design to the detriment of its psychological, social, cultural and political content. What counted in the design we were taught and still counts for many planners today is form, in particular, the clarity, the simplicity, and the purity of form.[1]

The realization that the functional and aesthetic doctrines of such eminent architects as Mies van der Rohe, Le Corbusier, and Gropius had outlived their usefulness led to the search for new values and new approaches. It must be said that the modern movement of the early part of the century was socially and politically responsive but that only the formal language thereof has been retained. The recent evolution, which was experienced by many as a crisis, brought a shift from the preoccupation with form to a wider concern for what may be called, environmental quality and its impact on the individual and community life. The ensuing design task became more complicated and required new tools in the form of explicit design methods and reliable information on user behavior and their experience of the built environment.[2] The research undertaken in design related fields during the last two decades has to be seen within this trend.

Wayfinding is an important aspect of environmental quality. We can indeed identify two distinct dimensions. The first is of a functional nature; it corresponds to the reaching of destinations within acceptable limits of time and energy. The aim of wayfinding design in this respect is to provide the environmental information necessary for decision making and decision execution while respecting user ability to deal with basic perceptual and cognitive tasks. The second dimension is of an evaluative nature; it corresponds to the experience gained during wayfinding. We evaluate most things we do, and we like or dislike certain activities and situations, finding them more or less satisfying in retrospect. A wayfinding experience is somewhat different. It establishes a very strong relation with the environment and the spatial characteristics distinguishing it. I shall argue that wayfinding is a fundamental key to environmental appreciation, be it at the level of architecture or at the level of the urban and natural landscape.

This last chapter is devoted to design issues in wayfinding and to the development of guidelines. First, I shall review the role wayfinding plays in experiencing a setting and establish the relation between wayfinding satisfaction and environmental characteristics such as complexity. Returning to the more functional dimension of wayfinding, I shall propose a general design procedure aimed at determining the environmental support systems essential to efficient wayfinding. This is complemented by checklists summarizing the musts and must-nots of wayfinding design. The chapter concludes with an assessment of the design potential of labyrinth features that challenge and sometimes defy wayfinding abilities.

WAYFINDING EXPERIENCE

Wayfinding is an activity that, like few others, demands a complete involvement with the environment. Perceptual and cognitive processes are constantly in action when a person sets out to reach a destination. The environment is scrutinized in order to extract information selectively. The information describing the setting is not just passively retained. It is interpreted, structured, and integrated to the already existing body of knowledge. Sometimes information is extrapolated from inconclusive evidence and verified at a later stage. This is particularly true when trying to gain an overall representation of complex layouts. It is important to stress that the environment in this process is not just "seen" but dealt with, subjugated, and above all, experienced.

In his relation to the environment, the wayfinding person tries to understand the setting he is in, and he uses the information obtained; he makes decisions and structures these into an overall plan of action. He will predict the consequences of certain decisions and assess their merits. In executing the decisions he will formulate predictions about environmental features and compare them with the information he obtains. He will do all these things while moving through the environment and experiencing its character in an active, participatory and dynamic fashion.

The necessity to understand a physical setting and to act upon this knowledge attributes to wayfinding a capacity par excellence to assess the architectural and spatial qualities of a setting. If it is true that you only really know a place once you have visited it, it is also true that you only really appreciate a place once you have explored it.

Environmental Compexity

Wayfinding, because of the dynamic involvement, is an environmental experience of considerable depth. In order for this experience to be satisfying the environment has to offer something. Amos Rapoport (1977, 208), a protagonist of new design values, has made the following perspicacious observation: "The many environments in different areas, eras and cultures which are liked and preferred have one thing in common: they all seem to be perceptually interesting, complex and rich."

What makes an environment interesting, complex, and rich? A general answer to this question, however sketchy, would contribute to the design of settings in which satisfaction is gained from wayfinding experiences.

When one thinks about an interesting, complex environment, the first image to emerge is probably composed of an intricate arrangement of space, highlighted by unusual architectural features, executed with a tasteful use of material and color.

Figure 5.1 illustrates Paul Rudolf's futuristic proposal of a large urban renewal project for Manhattan, designed in the late 1960s. Various functions comprising office work, housing, recreation, and transportation are joined in a dense, multilevel spatial organization.[3] Although the project is surely complex in design, it is not certain that the user would experience it as such. The perspective drawing of the lower levels of a multifunctional building proves the contrary. Complexity of form does not necessarily guarantee an interesting and rich experience.

An additional component of environmental complexity, which is most important in experiencing a setting, is density and depth of meaning. Paul Rudolf's view of the project is complex in architectural form, but when we try to read its content, we realize that it is much of the same and really does not say very much. Meaning can take many forms. It can express a function, a social and cultural identity, a historical heritage; it can also communicate political, religious, and life-style values. Venturi (1966) has argued that

A down-to-earth view of the project. *(From P. Wolf,* The Evolving City, *Whitney Library of Design, New York, 1974, pp. 74 and 75; copyright © 1974 by the American Federation of Arts)*

Figure 5.1
Complexity of Mega-Projects. *(From P. Wolf,* The Evolving City, *Whitney Library of Design, New York, 1974, pp. 70 and 71; copyright © 1974 by the American Federation of Arts)*

ambiguity, which he defined as the multiple interpretation of architectural form, assures density of meaning and, through it, environmental complexity.

A place that is used and appropriated by its occupants is enriched by a meaning that represents the nature of the users as well as their activities. Environmental complexity, in its full sense, has to include people and all the signs that are associated with the relations they establish with a place over time.

New developments are often architecturally innovative and spatially diverse, but without human activity and involvement, they tend to be perceived as dead and sterile. An open-air market is interesting, complex, and diversified thanks to the participants who install their stands and the clients who stroll and interact (Fig. 5.2). The actual design is, if anything, simpler than that of the most common supermarket.

An explicit and more nuanced relationship can now be established between environmental complexity, satisfaction, and wayfinding than the mere fact of being in an interesting environment. The opportunity and the ability to solve problems, which are fundamental to wayfinding, are sources of satisfaction in themselves. The motivation derived from successful problem solving is evident in much of our working life. We are generous with the time we allocate to problem solving; the writing of a book is a good example. Family games with labyrinth puzzles and the Rubic cube also absorb people of all ages over

Figure 5.2
Complexity through participation.

extensive periods. Wayfinding is problem solving. The motivation to tread a labyrinth is at least partly derived from that very fact. In order to be rewarding the problem has to be of a certain interest. This interest is achieved if the setting reflects a certain architectural and spatial complexity, which explains a first link between complexity and the satisfaction derived from wayfinding.

Care should be taken in making the analogy between wayfinding and problem-solving games. An essential difference between the two should not be ignored by the designer. Once you have had enough, you can put the labyrinth puzzle or the colored cube away, but in wayfinding, you have to stick with it until a destination is reached. Wayfinding might be a game at times, but usually it is a means to get somewhere. If you had to solve puzzles in order to be fed, you might soon show signs of frustration and even despair. As I shall discuss at the end of this section, it would be irresponsible to advocate indiscriminate complexity without assuring proper design interventions and taking into account the conditions under which a person finds his way.

A second major source of satisfaction linking wayfinding to environmental complexity is exploration, which motivates much of our endeavors. We may explore in order to seek change and to break with the familiar. We may also explore in order to seek new information and to acquire knowledge. Berlyne (1966) called these two forms of exploration diversive and epistemic. The two often overlap. Walking in a setting can be specifically motivated by the pleasure of seeing new things, of encountering people, and of being exposed to unexpected situations. The diversionary aspect of this exploration is heightened if the setting is complex in terms of architectural space, in terms of meaning and people as well as their activities. Martina Franca and Palombara Sabina, the two "labyrinth cities" reviewed in Chapter 1, satisfy the explorer on all three accounts. Both cities are spatially diverse and architecturally interesting. They have a long and well-preserved history. Furthermore, the citizens have maintained their specific style of life and cultural expression, which are seen in countless traces throughout the city.

Palombara Sabina.

We also explore to acquire new information. Epistemic exploration in wayfinding depends on the particular interest of the explorer. Some will explore for historical information, others for alternative life styles, investment values, and so on. Of universal importance is the acquisition of information leading to an understanding of a setting as a spatial ensemble. The previously outlined perceptual and cognitive processes as well as the decision-making process are all part of this effort to come to grips with the spatial characteristics of a place. Again, we find that a certain level of complexity, reflecting the three discussed components, is necessary to make the exploration worthwhile.

The pleasure of solving problems, the pleasure of being entertained, and the pleasure of acquiring new knowledge are three major sources of satisfaction derived from wayfinding in complex environments. It is important to stress again that they are not just the result of a superficial aesthetic judgment but the consequence of a thorough environmental experience.

Being disoriented and being lost are issues to be discussed apart. It is true that they may heighten the sensations associated with wayfinding, but they also introduce new types of sensations. Labyrinth lore, as expressed through history, points to fear as well as to pleasure. The pleasurable dimension is easily explained if we think of the interest, the curiosity, and the distraction that the challenge of problem solving and exploration brings. Fear may be accounted for by the real danger incurred when being lost. The sensation remains even if the victim reasons that nothing can happen to him. The disappointment of not being able to comprehend a given setting or the possible frustration of not being able to solve a given wayfinding problem do not seem to account for the distress experienced by some in cases of disorientation. The reasons for the distress are poorly understood.

The history of labyrinths has shown that, despite the fear, some people not only welcome wayfinding challenges but at times even seek the sensation of being lost. Fear and pleasure, contradictions at first view, do not seem so far apart after all. Many forms of distraction that people value border on fear. To various degrees racing, mountain climbing, parachuting, skiing, as well as fun-fair entertainments like the roller coaster, contain a good dose of fear to season the sport. The thriller, the bone-chilling ghost story, Dracula and Frankenstein, and even the old-fashioned fairy tale, all use fear to fascinate.

The experience associated with wayfinding, we may conclude, is a deeply felt one. Satisfaction is derived from problem solving and from exploration. Environmental complexity, as reflected by spatial configuration, meaning, and user-related characteristics, is a necessary prerequisite. Without a certain level of complexity, problem solving is banal and exploration useless. Being lost or disoriented, although sought in certain circumstances, leads to contradictory sensations. I shall return to the design potential of labyrinth features at the end of the chapter.

Fun and fear.

How Complex?

To what extent should the planner design for environmental complexity? At what point can complexity become a negative force? Should he consciously create wayfinding challenges? It is extremely difficult to answer these questions in terms of specific design recommendations. We can only give an ordinal measure of complexity in relation to identified wayfinding conditions.

Under emergency conditions, such as a fire evacuation, the only thing that counts is reaching the destination as fast and as easily as possible. Lack of time, stress, and the possible impairment of information-processing and decision-making capacities, determine that nothing can be too simple or too "straightforward."

Most wayfinding does not take place under emergency conditions; even so, efficiency in reaching destinations is required. Meeting a person at a given address, finding a restaurant or a hotel, doing the shopping, in fact, most of our daily tasks can be regrouped into what may be called a resolute wayfinding condition. Although the functional aspect of wayfinding usually has priority, the experience of reaching a destination is also important. Environmental complexity, I would argue, is desirable as long as the design of the setting, including the wayfinding support systems, guarantees efficient information processing performances.

Finally, we may identify a recreational wayfinding condition in which experience takes priority over the functional aspect of wayfinding. Strolling, driving for pleasure are examples in which such recreational conditions prevail. People still have to reach destinations, but they are less in a hurry and efficiency is not all-important. In some contexts, such as the design of an amusement park or an exhibition, wayfinding may provide an opportunity to challenge basic information-processing and decision-making abilities with particularly complex and difficult spatial configurations. Again, the planner should be aware that the Minotaur fear can emerge and lead to quite unpredictable and irrational behavior.

I have discussed the functional and the evaluative aspects of wayfinding as two separate units. In reality they are related and affect each other. The functional requirement associated with wayfinding can determine what is being perceived as satisfying or as irritating. A setting that pleases under recreational conditions may well irritate if it is experienced under resolute or even emergency conditions. Having explored the intricate street system of Martina Franca, I expressed my enthusiasm to a traveling salesman I met there in a restaurant. After agreeing politely, he expressed his frustration with having to lose considerable time finding his clients. The assessment criteria used in his resolute and my recreational wayfinding conditions were obviously not the same.

The relation works in the other sense as well. The motivation gained from an enriching experience facilitates the wayfinding process. Thus, it is not necessarily the oversimplified, dull building that is most successful for efficient wayfinding. After all, interest and curiosity lead to heightened understanding and easy learning: boredom does not.

I have argued throughout the book, that it is possible to conceive of complex environments so that they can be understood and used in a challenging, satisfying way, without interfering with information processing and decision making. In our everyday environment, it is not complexity in itself that creates wayfinding difficulties but the combination with inadequate design, leading to featureless settings or conditions of overload.

Design for wayfinding should therefore be based on a method able to incorporate the observations about decision making and information processing. This it can do only if the method respects the dynamic temporal reality of wayfinding. I shall outline the logic of such a method. First, I will have to introduce a simple notation system useful in describing wayfinding episodes.

The reader who is only interested in the general idea of the design guide may turn to page **185** where he will find a synopsis.

A NOTATION SYSTEM

Notation systems as design aids are relatively recent and not very well known by planners. Philip Thiel (1961, 1970) was the first to introduce a detailed notation of the perceptual experience that users of a setting have while moving through it. The main contribution of his notation is the link of space and time through movement. Thiel got his inspiration from musical notation and choreography, both being characterized by the prime importance of time and movement.

Architecture and the environment in general are also experienced through movement. A notation system can provide the designer and the researcher with a tool respecting an order according to sequence or time. Architectural and urban planners as well as researchers all too often view the world through a static time-slice approach, which bears little resemblance with the way people interact with their environment.

Some designers, it is fair to say, do imagine themselves moving through space while they conceive a plan. Notation systems can then help to render this experience more precise, to verbalize it, and to communicate it to others. It is in this perspective that Appleyard et al. (1964) developed a notation system for highway design. This notation, which helps predict and evaluate the perceptual experience of highway drivers, is less complex than the one by Thiel. Still it requires a systematic approach to planning and a training period, which probably accounts for the relatively small impact it has had on the design profession.

A design method for wayfinding, more than any other, has to respect the time dimension. It is inconceivable, for example, to design an efficient sign system without taking into account the sequences of decision making or without knowing the moments during a journey when information is sought. The notation I propose contains two complementary parts, one reflecting the behavioral, the other the cognitive components of wayfinding.

The Behavioral Notation

I shall try to record in the simplest terms a wayfinding episode leading from a certain point of departure to a destination. Imagine the following scenario. A person finds himself on the ground floor of a shopping complex. He feels the need to urinate and looks for a toilet. He chooses to explore the basement and looks around until he finds a toilet at the end of a corridor.

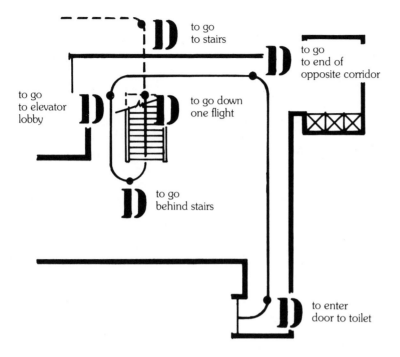

Wayfinding is spatial problem solving. The final solution to the problem is constituted of behaviors leading to a destination. The physical manifestation is the route chosen. I shall indicate routes with a simple line, the thickness of which may vary according to the frequency of use. If we look at the route, we can observe changes of directions. These correspond to the introduction of new behaviors. Each is based on a decision. So we may identify a series of decisions like "to go to stairs," "to go down one flight," and so on. These decisions can be inferred if we rely on the route as the only evidence.

The Cognitive Notation

The behavioral notation records movement and situates decisions in space. It is incomplete, as it only shows the decisions that led directly to a behavioral action and ignores the higher-order decision. These decisions are the prerequisite for the behavior we see. They also require environmental information. The cognitive notation is necessary in order to have an account of all decisions made. It is also responsible for showing the relations among decisions.

The reader has already been partly exposed to this notation in Chapter 3. It represents the structural characteristics among all decisions and their relation to environmental information. The vertical axis indicates the time sequence; the horizontal axis gives the order among decisions from the most general to those leading directly to behavioral actions. The first decision from the scenario, which is also the most general, is the task decision "to go to the toilet." "To enter the door of the toilet" is chronologically the last, and it also belongs to the decisions at the operational end of the hierarchy.

The lines among decisions refer to the in-order-to relation, specifying why a decision was made. In order "to go to the toilet" we "check places out of circulation." In order "to check places out of circulation" we "look behind stairs," we "look at elevator lobby," and so on. The hatched surfaces indicate plans at the execution level, specifying how the decisions fit together into meaningful sets.

When we use the notation system as a design tool, decision diagrams should be as simple as possible. Related decisions such as "to go" in order "to look" can be expressed as one. This suggestion does not apply to the coding of raw data from verbalized decision making. (See appendix B, pp. **211–218**).

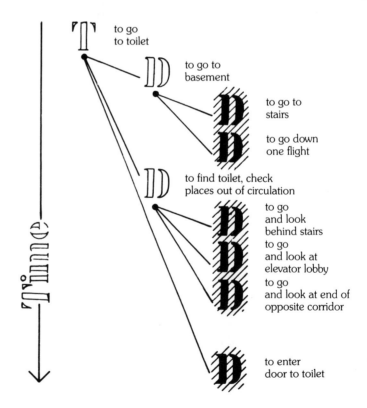

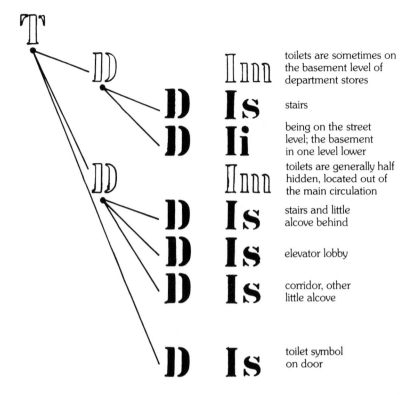

toilets are sometimes on the basement level of department stores

stairs

being on the street level; the basement in one level lower

toilets are generally half hidden, located out of the main circulation

stairs and little alcove behind

elevator lobby

corridor, other little alcove

toilet symbol on door

Each decision corresponds to at least one unit of information. The information may be directly perceived in the setting, like "the stairs," "the little alcove behind the stairs," and so on. I refer to this as sensory information (Is). We may also rely on information obtained during previous experiences, the memory information (Im), and information we infer (Ii).[4] In a second column of the cognitive notation we can indicate the information required to reach each decision of the diagram.

The cognitive notation now allows the behavioral notation to be completed by adding the higher-order decisions. In the scenario, these are "to go to the basement, to find the toilet" and "to check places out of circulation." We can also show on the plan the nature and the location of information corresponding to each decision. If a project consists of identifying environmental support systems, it is only the sensory information (Is) that will have a bearing on the design solution. The nature of the information is indicated by a set of symbols. Its content can be noted in the plan or in tables. It might also be of interest to distinguish visual from auditory information.

The behavioral and the cognitive notations constitute a complete short-hand description of a wayfinding episode both in terms of spatial and mental concerns. Such a notation has various application possibilities. It serves to

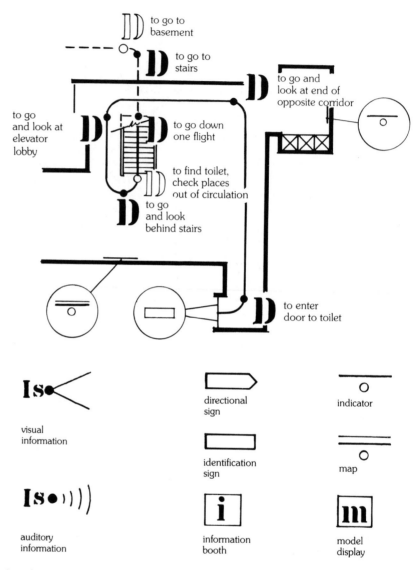

to go to
basement

to go to
stairs

to go and
look at end of
opposite corridor

to go
and look at
elevator
lobby

to go down
one flight

to find toilet,
check places
out of circulation

to go
and look
behind stairs

to enter
door to toilet

Is◄

visual
information

directional
sign

indicator

Is●)))

auditory
information

identification
sign

map

i

information
booth

m

model
display

identify and structure data in a form amenable to various analytical operations
when studying conceptual aspects of wayfinding. The content of Chapter 3
was essentially based on such data. It may also serve to assess existing
settings and support systems. Once a sample of representative wayfinding
episodes are thus recorded, the weak points can be identified where people
do not obtain the necessary information or where they are being misled. If
used as an assessment tool, it should be combined with additional methods
allowing the subject to communicate overall impressions, to make compari-

sons, and to express his understanding of the spatial characteristics, which is not usually described during wayfinding. The check lists on pages **187–191** do contain additional items of evaluation. Finally, the notation can be used to describe existing wayfinding and also to predict and to simulate wayfinding. In the latter application it becomes important as a design tool.

ARIADNE'S THREAD

Ariadne helped Theseus escape from the labyrinth after he had fought the awe-inspiring Minotaur. He was able to find his way out by following her wayfinding thread. Designers who specialize in signing must often see themselves in the role of Ariadne, helping the heroic users overcome the difficulties introduced by the master builders, that is, the architects and urban planners. The proposed design aid addresses itself to designers responsible for the planning of information systems containing signs, maps, information booths, and so on; it should also be of interest to architects and urban planners who build the settings.

The design aid is presented in two parts. First, I shall outline a guide aimed at determining the content of environmental information necessary to wayfinding as well as the optimal location of that information in the setting. Second, I shall propose a series of check lists summing up the most pertinent findings, described in Chapter 4, that have a direct bearing on the design of architectural and urban settings as well as signs and maps contained in wayfinding support systems.

Guideline to Wayfinding Design

The guideline presents the logic of a design method that has its roots in the conceptualization of wayfinding as a spatial problem-solving process. It is thought of as a basic guide, to be completed or adapted depending on the design problem at hand. The required details are evidently not the same if the method is used for designing an information system in an existing setting or for designing an altogether new setting. The underlying logic remains, whichever the application. Many designers will have developed their own methods. However, the outlined guide might complement parts of their approaches, or render certain operations more concise.

Design methods generally include a phase allocated to analysis that serves to clarify the design problem and a phase of synthesis that leads to a design solution. The first four steps of the guide are analytical. Steps five, six, and seven are intended to stimulate the necessary reflection to arrive at a design solution.

1. Identification of wayfinding tasks

The design of supportive information systems has to be based on clearly identified wayfinding tasks. In any setting there is an infinite number of tasks, as people may start anywhere and go anywhere. It is impossible to account for each task individually, and attention to so much detail would clutter the communication of the necessary information. It is clear that tasks and the corresponding destinations have to be regrouped somehow.

This regrouping, instead of being arbitrary, can agree with the user's own mental organization of a setting. Cognitive maps are a testimony of the way people organize space. The basic building blocks, known to be used in structuring the image of a city or a building, can therefore serve as criteria to regroup destinations and to identify the corresponding tasks. In particular, it would seem that the notion of districts would serve this purpose. Districts comprise homogeneous areas, distinguishing themselves from other areas. Landmarks, nodes, and key paths, although not clustering destinations to the same extent, may be included in what I will call *destination zones*. In any setting there are major entrances and exits that play a particular role in defining wayfinding tasks.

Having identified the destination zones of a setting and its major entrances and exits, three types of task can be formulated, to which all other tasks should be subordinated. These are: reaching the major zones from the key access to the setting, including the return route; reaching one zone from the other; and, finally, reaching places within the zone.

Each of the seven steps is illustrated by an example (Fig. 5.3) from a fictive

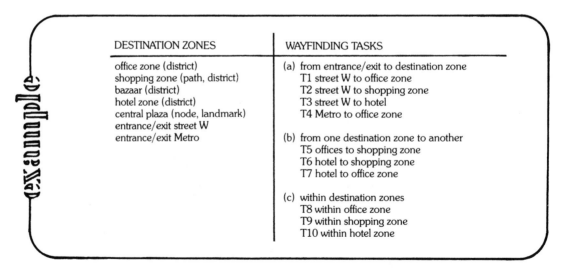

DESTINATION ZONES	WAYFINDING TASKS
office zone (district) shopping zone (path, district) bazaar (district) hotel zone (district) central plaza (node, landmark) entrance/exit street W entrance/exit Metro	(a) from entrance/exit to destination zone 　　T1 street W to office zone 　　T2 street W to shopping zone 　　T3 street W to hotel 　　T4 Metro to office zone (b) from one destination zone to another 　　T5 offices to shopping zone 　　T6 hotel to shopping zone 　　T7 hotel to office zone (c) within destination zones 　　T8 within office zone 　　T9 within shopping zone 　　T10 within hotel zone

Figure 5.3
Table used to determine major wayfinding tasks.

design project. In the first table are enumerated on the left the major destination zones and on the right the key wayfinding tasks according to the described typology.

Defining the tasks to respect the user's own collective imagery of a setting has the advantage of not introducing an additional structure and an alternative vocabulary. It has another advantage. Such a description becomes a direct aid to image formation. Even a sign system, if describing a setting in these terms, can contribute to improved imageability of a setting.

The first step can therefore be formulated in terms of two operations. First, identify destination zones as the homogeneous areas of a setting that stand out from other areas through their function, physical expression, or general atmosphere. Major landmarks, nodes, and paths can also be classified as destination zones. Second, define three types of wayfinding task as: going to the destination zones from the entrances/exits of the setting and back; going from one zone to another; and going from one place to another within a zone.

2. Identification of a user profile

The physical environment makes certain demands on the problem-solving individual. This demand can be mastered to various degrees depending on the information-processing abilities of the user and his previous experience with the setting or with similar settings.

Many user groups can be identified, among them, newcomers to a setting who experience difficulties, since they have not yet formed a coherent cognitive map. If the setting is completely unfamiliar, the user may not be able to rely on pre-established images in his search for information, nor will he be able to rely on plan schemata to guide his initial behavior. This may be true for foreign visitors, who in addition, often face language problems.

Certain user groups, such as the elderly, have specific information-processing difficulties, which can stem from reduced visual acuity, unfocused attention, and memory loss.[5] Children, at the other extreme of the age group, may pay little attention to conventional signs. Even when they try they may have difficulty understanding the verbal messages in particular. A sign language could be developed to take into account the child's developmental stage, but little work has been done in that area as yet.

In the last few years we have been sensitized to the problems of the physically handicapped. In terms of wayfinding much still has to be done. The handicapped are frequently confronted with architectural barriers that do not allow them to execute the decisions reached on the basis of the available information. Occupants of wheelchairs commonly have to find alternatives for which no information is provided. The blind are even worse off. They have generally no access to wayfinding support systems and are therefore incapable of making independent decisions. Adapted information systems of a nonvisual nature could conceivably be developed.

Having identified the potential user of a given setting, the designer has to decide which group to retain as a design basis. Various criteria intervene in the difficult choice. The size of the group, the knowledge the users have of the setting or of similar settings, particular information-processing difficulties, or problems of access are among the criteria. Depending on the type of setting and the available resources, the list of user groups might be more or less long.

Design is a problem-solving process, and as such, it has to respect constraints. Although it would be desirable to account for every user, it is generally beyond the capacity of a project. Whatever the limitation of choice, it should be clear and justified. In post-occupancy evaluation, these choices and their proposed justifications can be verified so that future decisions may respond to more adequately known user demands. Figure 5.4 gives a table describing a user profile for the design example introduced above.

A second step in planning for wayfinding, regardless of the nature of the product, is to establish a profile of the major user population as well as of user groups needing special attention. The profile should specify the level of knowledge the user group has of the setting or similar settings and particular problem solving difficulties. The choice of the retained user groups should be clearly stated and be justifiable.

USER GROUP	KNOWLEDGE OF SETTING	PROBLEM SOLVING DIFFICULTIES	TARGET POPULATION; JUSTIFICATION
General population			
U1 office worker	high	none	accounted for by U2
U2 clients	low	none	U2
U3 shopkeepers	high	none	accounted for by U4
U4 clients	low	none	U4
Special groups			
U5 elderly	low	acuity	insufficient number
U6 wheelchair users	low	access	U6
U7 children	low	understanding	in company of adults

Figure 5.4
Table used to identify user profiles.

3. *Identification of wayfinding conditions*

A differentiation between recreational, resolute, and emergency wayfinding conditions has been made earlier in this chapter. The three descriptors are best seen as characterizing sections on a continuum. The functional dimension of wayfinding, that is, reaching a destination, and the evaluative dimension, expressed through the experience wayfinding offers, vary inversely as one moves from one end of the continuum to the other. Strolling, for example, is a form of recreational wayfinding, where pleasure is gained from experiencing the setting. This evaluative dimension has clear priority over the pure fact of reaching a destination. In wayfinding under emergency conditions, all that counts is to reach a destination easily and in the shortest possible time. At this extreme of the continuum the functional aspect is all important.[6] In resolute wayfinding, the emphasis is on efficiency, but the evaluative aspect also enters the equation of an overall assessment.

The three descriptors are rather broad. The designer may require a more finely tuned measure to describe wayfinding conditions. He can do this by simply subdividing each condition into smaller units. The subunits may refer to the intensity of the condition as being strong, medium, or mild (Fig. 5.5). Particular wayfinding conditions prevail in certain types of setting and are important to their successful functioning. Recreational wayfinding has priority in fun fairs, resolute wayfinding in office buildings, and emergency wayfinding in hospital settings. These are not exclusive conditions. Most settings will

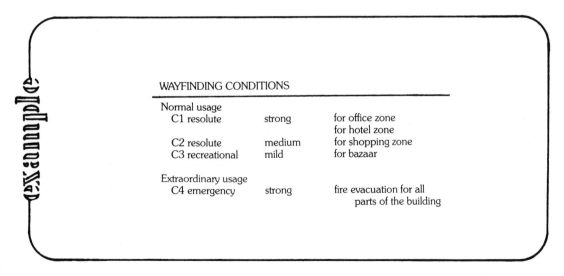

WAYFINDING CONDITIONS

Normal usage		
C1 resolute	strong	for office zone
		for hotel zone
C2 resolute	medium	for shopping zone
C3 recreational	mild	for bazaar
Extraordinary usage		
C4 emergency	strong	fire evacuation for all parts of the building

Figure 5.5
Table used to determine wayfinding conditions.

require some resolute wayfinding, and all have to cope with emergencies, for example, in a case of evacuation due to a fire.

The third step is to identify the appropriate wayfinding conditions for each major destination zone of the setting. It is advisable to differentiate between normal usage of a setting and extraordinary usage such as emergency evacuation.

4. Formulating the design requirements (design problem)

The design requirements are arrived at by combining the three previously discussed elements, that is, the basic wayfinding tasks (T1,T2,T3,...Tn) for a particular user group (U1,U2,U3, . . . Un) under particular conditions (C1,C2,C3,...Cn). Not all the combinations need to be retained. The design solution should take into consideration the least favored combinations, which generally satisfy the more favored ones too. Some user groups may require special means that are not necessarily appropriate to others. For example, elevators are essential for people in wheelchairs, but they are not efficient for great numbers of nonusers of wheelchairs moving up or down a few floors at a time.

The synthesis of the three previous figures leads to the design requirements outlined in Figure 5.6: (T1-U2-C1), (T1-U6-C1), (T9-U4-C2), and (T9-U4-C3). Each major wayfinding task (step 1) is linked to a target population using a destination zone (step 2) and the wayfinding condition appropriate to that zone (step 3).

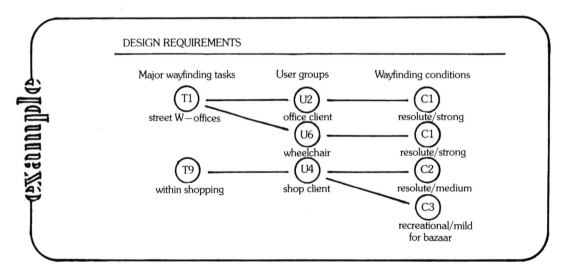

Figure 5.6
Table used to formulate the design requirements.

This fourth step can be described as the identification of critical Task-User-Condition combinations for the major traffic flow and combinations needing special attention due to particular user groups or emergency conditions.

5. Planning wayfinding solutions

Wayfinding design can be described as an act of conceiving information systems that allow the user in a setting to reach destinations within acceptable expenditures of time and energy. The required information is determined by the wayfinding solution the user develops.

In order to identify the information system, we need to have an idea about the wayfinding solution. In other words, we have to foresee wayfinding behavior, determine the corresponding decision plans the users will collectively reach, and design the information accordingly. Although not always explicitly stated, this process is common to all design interventions. In planning a kitchen, for example, we need to foresee activities like food preparation, cooking, and so on.[7]

Wayfinding design, whether in an already built or a planned setting, starts by choosing the routes the users ought to take to reach key destinations. Thus we establish a first version of the behavioral solution to the wayfinding problem presented by the task and the physical constraints particular to each project. In an existing setting routes will be determined to a large extent by the width of the circulation and the directness of access.

The choice of routes is still preliminary. The subsequent elaboration of information systems may bring about changes. The following three steps of the guide are, therefore, best seen as being cyclic, allowing for the gradual development of the design proposal.

Having chosen the routes, we can apply the notation system to indicate the decisions on the routes whenever a change of direction or a change of level is observable. We can also note decisions at intersections where the user has to decide to move straight on.

In Figure 5.7, a schematic layout of a commercial complex is shown with the route corresponding to the task "to go to office x from street W." On the right we have extracted the route and indicated the decision of each behavioral action.

The behavioral actions and the corresponding decisions, which are discernible from the route, are only an incomplete reflection of the cognitive solution to the wayfinding problem. The ignored higher-order decisions are also part of the solution, and they require information as well. The shortcoming of a design approach that simply provides signs at intersections is precisely the neglect of higher-order decisions.

Decision diagrams are for wayfinding design what functional diagrams are for architectural design. While functional diagrams represent the logic behind

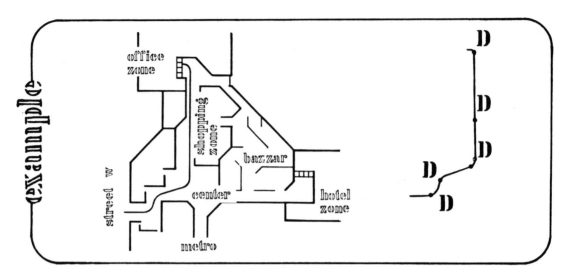

Figure 5.7
Schematic layout of a commercial complex showing a route and the corresponding decisions.

the organization of space, decision diagrams represent the logic behind people's actions and the required information. Decision diagrams lead to the planning of information systems rather than unconnected units of information.

Having identified a route, we now have to build up a corresponding decision diagram. Two basic approaches can be used. The first proceeds from the particular to the general, that is, from the decision leading directly to behavioral actions to the higher order decisions. Knowing that decisions are linked by an "in-order-to" relation, we can start with the lowest order decision, such as that extracted from the route, and by a simulation process probe for the next higher decision. This we do by applying the coding rule through the following set phrase: "I take decision D in order to . . . " until we reach the original task formulation.[8] This simulation has to take into account the task as well as the user characteristics and the wayfinding conditions, as established in step 4. In the example, we referred to the task "to go to office *x* from street *W*" for office clients, with no preknowledge of the setting, operating under strongly resolute wayfinding conditions. We know that in this case efficiency in wayfinding is important and that no knowledge about the particularities of the building can be assumed.

The first identified decision extracted from the route is "to take main route" in order to go to the center of the setting where further information would be found. "To go to center for information" we may note as a first formulation of a higher-order decision. We can see that the logic of the "in-order-to" relation is also maintained between this higher-order decision and the task formulation "to go to office *x*" (*see* left side of Fig. 5.8).

The decision "to follow route" is also linked to the higher-order decision "to go to center for information." The relation is nonsensical for the following decision "to follow shopping concourse"; at this point the center has already been passed. We therefore need a second higher order decision, which might be formulated as "to go to subcenter of office zone." Now we have a coherent "in-order-to" relation: "to follow shopping concourse" in order to "go to subcenter of office zone" in order to "go to office *x*."

The diagram is not quite complete. Having decided "to go to center for information" the user must pick up information once arrived there. This will lead him to consult existing displays. The decision "to read information displays" escaped our attention. It is not visible if we rely on the route as the only evidence.

The second approach to establishing decision diagrams proceeds from the general to the particular. It allows for filling the gaps left by the previous approach. Decision diagrams, like functional diagrams in architectural planning, are not completely neutral. If a designer, as in the described example, plans an information center from which all routes are distributed, reaching that central node will necessarily be part of the decision diagram. If, on the other hand, he wants to spread the information along a main route to single out the major destination zones, to follow that main route will be part of

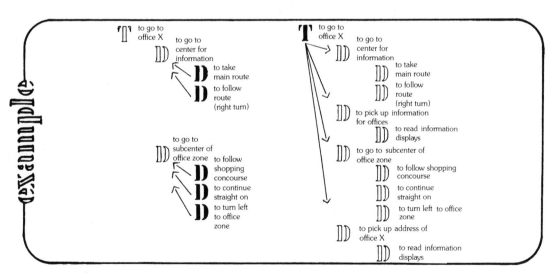

Figure 5.8
Procedure used to build up a decision diagram.

the decision plan. Such overall design ideas must be reflected in the most general plan people develop to solve a wayfinding problem, the most general plan being in fact the higher-order decisions of a diagram.

Returning to the illustration, we may determine that in order "to go to office *x*" we want the user "to go to center for information," and once arrived, "to pick up information for office zone," and having reached the office zone, "to pick up address of office *x*." As shown in the right side of the example, we now have all the decisions to build a complete, coherent diagram for which an information system can comfortably be planned.

The first approach may be referred to as being a behavior-driven simulation. We start with the identified behavior and ask ourselves which is the higher-order decision leading to that behavior. The second approach may be called concept-driven simulation. Here we start with a general idea, a "predesign" concept, and conclude from it the appropriate way for the user to go about solving wayfinding problems. The two are complementary. The probing of the behavior-driven simulation may lead to general design ideas. The concept-driven simulation, on the other hand, helps complete the design diagram.

Having developed a route and a decision diagram for the design requirement (T1-U2-C1), we can check all design requirements with the same task to see if any changes or compromise solutions are necessary. Given that the requirement (T1-U6-C1) represents a special case with access problems due to a wheelchair population, we have to verify whether the route contains architectural barriers. Should the route be barrier free, then the solution developed previously will also apply to this user group. If not, we have to overcome the barrier by changing the route or planning an additional route.

In order to proceed economically, we should start to solve the main routes for the general population first. Requirements for special groups will then necessitate a verification that the main routes are adequate.

The fifth step, in summary, is dedicated to the development of desirable wayfinding solutions in behavioral terms (the routes) and in cognitive terms (the decision diagrams). These constitute a basis for the planning of information systems outlined in the following steps.

6. Identifying environmental information

The aim of this sixth step is to plan the supportive environmental information that will allow the user of a setting to find the desired routes to a destination as specified above. The information can be presented with two distinct objectives in mind: to contain a complete decision plan spaced out along a route or to contain only the basic indications for the user to develop a decision plan on his own.

An ensemble of directional signs distributed at each decision point is the equivalent of a decision plan, each directional sign being in fact a decision. This is no doubt an information system that requires little effort on the part of the user. It has its place when speed and ease of wayfinding are of prime importance, such as in emergency wayfinding conditions. It becomes cumbersome, though, if many destinations on many routes have to be planned.

If only the basic information is provided, it will involve the user in an effort to understand and interpret that information, to complete it with his own knowledge and to make the necessary decision. These operations are not as demanding as they may appear. They are activated almost every time we visit an unfamiliar setting, and, as I have argued above, they contribute to experiencing a setting. For recreational and resolute wayfinding conditions, it would appear fully adequate to provide only the basic information supporting the decision-making process. That basic information also includes signs.

The information needed has to be formulated with respect to a wayfinding decision. If we are designing a directional sign system with the objective in mind of providing a full decision plan, we have to account for the lowest-order decisions in the diagram. To each change of direction and change of level corresponds a directional sign, with the exception of the "no-choice" situation, where only one prescribed movement is possible or reasonable.

The commonest case of providing basic information for decision making is slightly more complex. First, we have to account for all decisions of the diagram. Then we have to remember that information may be directly perceived (Is), that it may be part of a collective knowledge or memory (Im), or inferred (Ii). If we make abstractions of reassurance signs, it is only the sensory information (Is) that has to be provided by the designed setting, and only part of that is to be accounted for by a sign system.

In order to be able to describe the necessary information for each decision, I propose a table that differentiates among: (1) the no-choice situations, where no additional information has to be provided; (2) the information that can be assumed part of collective knowledge (Im) or that is easily inferred (Ii); (3) the sensory information (Is) contained in architectural elements and the spatial configuration; and (4) the sensory information accessible through signs, maps, models, information booths, and so on. According to the design project, it is columns 3 and 4, or only column 4 that contains the critical information (Fig. 5.9).

The actual process of identifying that information is also based on a form of simulation in which we ask ourselves what information would make the

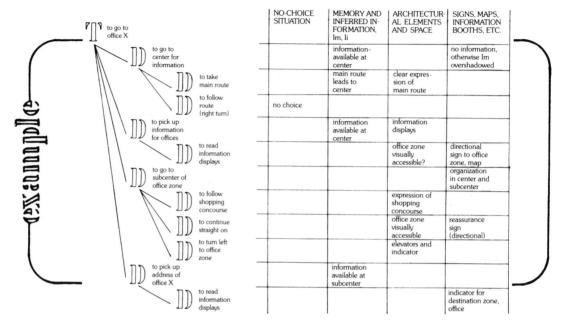

Figure 5.9
Table used to identify the required environmental information.

user make a given decision.[9] If the planner already has a preliminary idea of the information system to be designed he can draw from it to complete the table. The result will show whether the solution is adequate and what might be changed to complete the information needed. In the example, the decision diagram is shown on the left and the information table on the right. For the first higher-order decision "to go to the center for information," we can safely assume that if no other information is provided the person will refer to previous experiences with similar settings and go to the center (Im). He will decide "to take main route" if that route is clearly expressed in spatial terms (Is) because, again, he knows that the main route usually leads to the center. "To follow route" represents a no-choice situation; no other options are really open to the person. This process of identifying the supportive information for each decision has to be repeated on all major routes. Again, as in step 5, we could start with the general user and check the result for the special user afterwards.

When probing for the information needed to reach each of the decisions, we have to account for the two wayfinding styles described as linear and spatial. Those adhering to a linear style will have a tendency to rely on sequentially organized information, of which signs form an important part. At the same time we should allow those adhering to a spatial style to comprehend the spatial arrangement of the setting. Maps, models, and above all, the architectural and spatial expression will be of particular importance to the group.

The sixth step consists in identifying for each major decision diagram the supportive environmental information. A differentiation is made between the information to be provided by the design project and that which can be assumed to exist. Care should be taken to account for differences in information requirements due to wayfinding styles, special user needs, and wayfinding conditions.

7. Synthesis, information system, and optimal location

The sixth step resulted in specifications of information requirements, which are presented in listings specific to each route. Routes are not isolated spaces; they will cross each other or even overlap. In order to arrive at a design synthesis, we have to transform the lists into a spatial notation. It is only the overlay of all the information required that gives a total design picture. The overlay will show which information can be combined and what physical supports, such as signs, maps, information booths, and so on, best respond to the demand. The overlay may also show that routes could advantageously be altered to simplify the wayfinding supports. Such an operation could reactivate the procedure at step 5.

In order to transform the information lists into a spatial notation, we not only have to know what is needed but also where it is needed. A basic principle governs the choice for optimal location. Information relevant to a decision should be accessible at the point where the decision is made. The chances of perception are highest when the information is actually needed. Any information that is intended to bring about a higher-order decision should not occur at any point where a lower-order decision plan is being executed. Receptivity to that information, as discussed in Chapter 3, is optimal if it occurs in between the execution of decision plans. We can see, therefore, that decision diagrams are essential even for determining where information should be located for best results. Badly located information that has little chance of being perceived amounts to little more than no information at all.

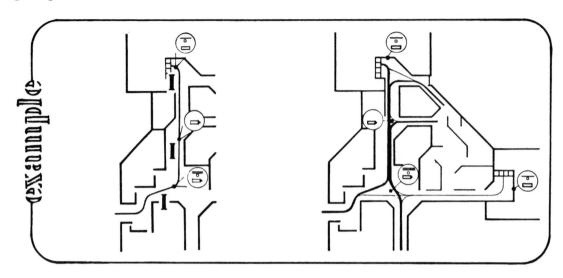

Figure 5.10
Schematic layout with spatial notation of the required environmental information.

The layout at the left in Figure 5.10 shows the previous route with the required information presented in schematic form. At the right, all major routes are superposed, including the information they require. Steps 5 to 7 have been presented as a successive approach toward a design solution. After having reached step 4, which specifies the design requirement, it is quite possible that the planner will emerge with a more or less clear image of a design solution. This being the case, the planner may move from step 4 to 7, express the solution in the form of spatial notation, and subsequently check whether the solution agrees with the projected decision diagrams (step 5) and the required information to make the decisions (step 6).

In this seventh step, the information listings are translated into a spatial notation that indicates the optimal location of individual units of information. From an overlay of these notations, the wayfinding support systems are finally extracted.

An overview of the design guide is given in Figure 5.11. The arrows indicate the suggested sequence. A feedback link from steps 7 to 5 is to show the cyclic nature of the design phase. The link from steps 4 to 7 is retained for

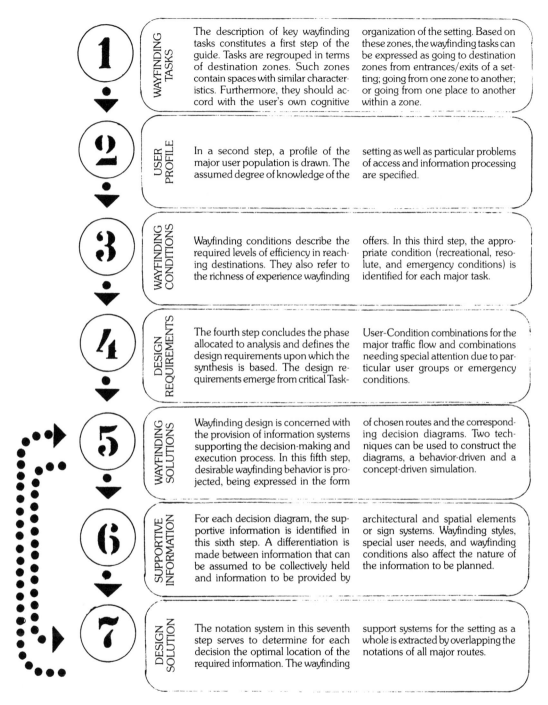

1 WAYFINDING TASKS
The description of key wayfinding tasks constitutes a first step of the guide. Tasks are regrouped in terms of destination zones. Such zones contain spaces with similar characteristics. Furthermore, they should accord with the user's own cognitive organization of the setting. Based on these zones, the wayfinding tasks can be expressed as going to destination zones from entrances/exits of a setting; going from one zone to another; or going from one place to another within a zone.

2 USER PROFILE
In a second step, a profile of the major user population is drawn. The assumed degree of knowledge of the setting as well as particular problems of access and information processing are specified.

3 WAYFINDING CONDITIONS
Wayfinding conditions describe the required levels of efficiency in reaching destinations. They also refer to the richness of experience wayfinding offers. In this third step, the appropriate condition (recreational, resolute, and emergency conditions) is identified for each major task.

4 DESIGN REQUIREMENTS
The fourth step concludes the phase allocated to analysis and defines the design requirements upon which the synthesis is based. The design requirements emerge from critical Task-User-Condition combinations for the major traffic flow and combinations needing special attention due to particular user groups or emergency conditions.

5 WAYFINDING SOLUTIONS
Wayfinding design is concerned with the provision of information systems supporting the decision-making and execution process. In this fifth step, desirable wayfinding behavior is projected, being expressed in the form of chosen routes and the corresponding decision diagrams. Two techniques can be used to construct the diagrams, a behavior-driven and a concept-driven simulation.

6 SUPPORTIVE INFORMATION
For each decision diagram, the supportive information is identified in this sixth step. A differentiation is made between information that can be assumed to be collectively held and information to be provided by architectural and spatial elements or sign systems. Wayfinding styles, special user needs, and wayfinding conditions also affect the nature of the information to be planned.

7 DESIGN SOLUTION
The notation system in this seventh step serves to determine for each decision the optimal location of the required information. The wayfinding support systems for the setting as a whole is extracted by overlapping the notations of all major routes.

Figure 5.11
Overview of design guide.

185

the introduction of a design solution to be subsequently checked against steps 5 and 6.

Check Lists

Having identified the required information, determined its location, and chosen the information support system, the actual design of information displays can be envisaged. In Chapter 4 I discussed some of the major difficulties people have when trying to obtain, comprehend and retain information from signs, maps, and also from architecture and the spatial configuration. The following check lists will sum up these observations.

Wayfinding and the architectural conception of a place

Les Terrasses, spaces reminiscent of visions by Piranesi.

Wayfinding considerations are not customarily included in the architectural conception of settings, though I do not know of any good reason why they should be ignored. Architectural elements like stairs, corridors, walls, the space defined, and the relationships among spaces provide the user with information just as signs and maps do. They are part of an information system used to solve wayfinding problems. Two aspects of information processing have been discussed in Chapter 4, legibility and imageability. Legibility I have defined as the ease with which environmental information is obtained and understood; imageability has been described as the ease with which a place is spatially comprehended and mentally represented.

Problems of legibility are essentially due to three factors, the ambiguity of the information presented, the inaccessibility of information, and the high density of information leading to overload conditions, which impair information processing. Legibility, I have noted, is a prerequisite to imageability, but it does not in itself guarantee a clear image.

In addition to obtaining and understanding the information presented, images of complex settings require a structuring process which is facilitated if: (1) the internal organization principle of a spatial arrangement is detectable; (2) the external organization principle given by the spatial enclosure or the building volume is accessible and expresses its content; (3) the relationships among spaces are articulated and visually accessible. Of particular interest for a building is the relation between the inside and the outside. Quite apart from the purely physical and spatial features of a place, imageability is increased if functional and social meaning enriches environmental experience and, not least of all, if the setting is able to stimulate the interest of the user.

Figure 5.12 serves to assess existing or planned settings.

obtaining information

overload

Are the major architectural elements pertaining to wayfinding, such as stairs, elevators, entrances, and exits, visually accessible from the key circulation routes? Watch for critical distance and the obstruction by structural and decorative elements.

Are the major architectural elements pertaining to wayfinding differentiated from the general background?

In complex settings, do architectural elements show consistent design features, allowing the user to learn what to look for?

In complex settings, are architectural elements placed in consistent and predictable locations?

understanding information

Do spaces clearly communicate who has access: the public, the private user, or officials only?

Do the circulation routes, both horizontal and vertical, communicate who has access?

representing information

images

Are major circulation routes articulated to be comprehended as paths and nodes?

Are spaces and architectural elements, as well as objects furnishing the space, articulated and distinctive in terms of form and meaning to serve as landmarks?

In complex settings, is it possible to regroup spaces into areas on the basis of function, use, or atmosphere, to distinguish them from other areas?

Does a general organization principle emerge from the spatial layout? Can the principle be comprehended in one way only?

Does spatial enclosure of building volume correspond and express the internal general organization?

Is the form of the enclosure visually accessible from the major approaches to the setting?

Does the articulation of space and visual accessibility allow for continuity between major parts of the setting and the setting in its wider environmental context?

Figure 5.12
Information processing and architectural conception.

New numbers, old numbers.

A one-way traffic sign.

Signs, what to watch for

The same factors affecting the legibility of a place are responsible for reduced information processing from signs: accessibility of information, ambiguity of messages, and conditions of overload. Information may be hidden; it may be too small to be perceived in the setting or drowned by the general decor. A frequent problem of obtaining information comes from overload conditions. Consistency in the design of signs, in their placement and their differentiation from signs having other functions, like advertising, provides a great help in finding information. After a short period of learning the person can reduce overload by clustering information, by knowing what to look for and where.

To facilitate finding information on signs, the designer should take into account information processing in the real setting. Information has to be visually structured into small packages, each of which can be picked up at a glance. Information should be further structured according to content. Some is general and refers to important overall decisions found in the upper levels of the decision diagrams; some is more specific to decisions leading directly to behavioral actions.

Ambiguity of signs can take many forms. It may not be clear to whom the message is directed, or maybe the message can be interpreted in more than one way. One of the commonest and most trivial confusions occurs in

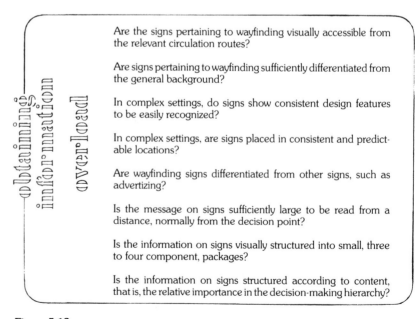

Are the signs pertaining to wayfinding visually accessible from the relevant circulation routes?

Are signs pertaining to wayfinding sufficiently differentiated from the general background?

In complex settings, do signs show consistent design features to be easily recognized?

In complex settings, are signs placed in consistent and predictable locations?

Are wayfinding signs differentiated from other signs, such as advertizing?

Is the message on signs sufficiently large to be read from a distance, normally from the decision point?

Is the information on signs visually structured into small, three to four component, packages?

Is the information on signs structured according to content, that is, the relative importance in the decision-making hierarchy?

Figure 5.13
Information processing and signs.

understanding information

Do signs clearly communicate for whom they are intended?

Can the message be understood and understood in one way only?

Are identification and directional signs used according to their meaning?

learning

If directional signs are used, is the system continuous until the indicated destination is reached?

Is a learning support provided for unaccustomed, innovative solutions?

Figure 5.13 *(Continued)*

the use of directional and identification signs. Signs are used by everybody, although they are especially important for those who adhere to a linear style of wayfinding.

Whenever an innovative sign or description is introduced, the designer should allow for a learning process and provide the context in which that process can take place. Figure 5.13 covers a series of points that have to be considered in any sign project.

Maps, what to watch for

Maps, the reader will remember, fulfill two functions. First, they provide information leading to identification of a route and a decision plan linking the viewer's point of origin to a desired destination. Second, maps provide information facilitating spatial comprehension of a place.

In its first function the map has to indicate the point of view ("you are here") in a space understood by the user. It is important that the relation between the map and the real setting be easily established by the map type

You are where?

and the graphics and by the elimination of any unnecessary mental rotation. The map has to facilitate the location of the destination and the extraction of an appropriate route. Maps in this respect must be simple and emphasize circulation routes, both horizontal and vertical. Information on maps again must be structured both visually and in terms of content. Map reading, like sign reading, occurs in glances when used in a real-life setting. The same problems of ambiguity found on signs should be avoided on maps.

In the second function, that of aiding the comprehension of a place, maps should emphasize the five basic elements introduced by Lynch (1960), which are: landmarks, paths, districts, edges, and nodes. In addition they have to communicate the internal spatial organization principle as well as spatial enclosure. Maps have the advantage of providing access to these organizing forms without the visual obstacles encountered in the real setting. They can also show the relations among the parts of the setting and situate them in their wider context, thereby guaranteeing image continuity.

Figure 5.14 presents checklists for maps.

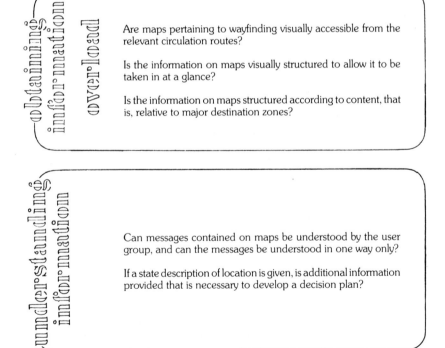

Figure 5.14
Information processing and maps.

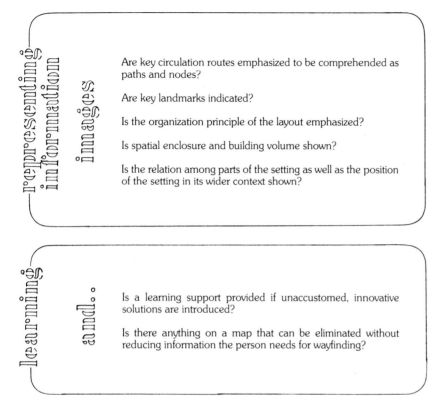

Figure 5.14 *(Continued)*

The design guide and the check lists are complementary. The guide is based mainly on observations of decision making and execution, the check lists on information processing. Thus the three basic processes of wayfinding can be respected. The reader might be struck by the complexity of wayfinding and wayfinding design. But is this not part of the fascination wayfinding has for the researcher, the designer, and the user alike?

DAEDALUS' CHALLENGE

Simple environments pose simple problems for wayfinding. This trivial observation can lead to serious pitfalls when research results are applied to design. For normal wayfinding conditions, that is, all conditions except emergencies, there is no justification for advocating simple environments. Simple problems tend to be banal, and simple environments dull. Wayfinding cannot be dissociated from experiencing space. We have seen that it is possible and indeed desirable to plan for interesting, complex, and diversified settings and still assure efficient wayfinding. Efficient, complex settings can be designed while respecting basic wayfinding processes.

When labyrinth features are introduced in design, wayfinding processes are challenged up to and beyond their capacities. The user may have difficulty understanding the spatial configuration and his position in that space. In addition, he may no longer know how to get out of it. The use of labyrinth features must be cautious and controlled, given the contradictory reactions of pleasure and excitement or fear and despair. It is in this perspective that I shall outline a few ideas of potential design effects of mildly disorienting settings.

Labyrinthine settings, if experienced in a stimulating sense, invite exploration, and they also heighten the pleasure of discovery. Think of the rambling castle with its underground network of passages leading to an inscription or a chamber of doubtful purpose. Think of the sinuous streets of a medieval city and the discovery of a particular architectural treasure. Think of the small attractive restaurant discovered in the same city. A certain state of mind brought about by labyrinth features seems to enhance the value of the discovery. The same inscription, the same building, and the same restaurant on Main Street do not have quite the same character. When people are out to explore, whether in nature, in cities, or in buildings, labyrinth features can have interesting design applications.

Labyrinthine arrangements may give the initiated inhabitants of a setting a feeling of security. The little private corner in a garden, for example, accessible only by an intricate path, provides a sense of safety and protection. The labyrinth then becomes a mechanism to reinforce a territorial claim. Furthermore, this claim assures the inhabitant a control over access and the desired social interaction. It is only a little step from this use to the labyrinth city and its intended defense protection as discussed in Chapter 1.

Related to the feeling of security is another effect of labyrinth design: the feeling and pleasure of being alone. Not many settings can measure up to the labyrinth in this respect. They provide the user who seeks solitude with a unique opportunity for recollection, contemplation, and meditation. The architecture of Islamic mosques as well as labyrinth gardens may be seen as examples of settings particularly suited for personal reflection.

Abraham Moles and his collaborators, who have written extensively on labyrinths, suggest such designs as a means to cope with high population densities (Moles et al., 1978).[10] Labyrinth arrangements guarantee privacy when space is relatively restricted. This economy of space has many possible applications. A garden, for example, gives the impression of being much larger if the paths are arranged in an intricate way and if the view over the total layout is limited.

Some of these ideas have found their way into contemporary planning. Figure 5.15 illustrates a labyrinthine housing project constructed in Givors, France.[11] The urban renewal development of high density, designed by Jean Renaudie, contains approximately 350 apartments. The conception is based on an intricate imbrication of triangular volumes, of which the organization is, if anything, disguised. Arranged on the slope of a small hill, the residences are equipped with many terraces, some for private and some for public use. Commercial facilities are located in galleries at street level. A Dutch architect, Aldo Van Eyck, also applied labyrinthine features in his very attractive exposition space, the Arnheim Pavillion in 1966. The setting is not actually disorienting; he wanted the space to unfold gradually as people move through it.

The application of labyrinth features to design is not necessarily an all-or-nothing proposal. The planner can, for example, conceive a setting in such a way that a person always knows where to go but cannot easily understand the space he is in. If labyrinth features were to be applied to a shopping arcade or a bazaar, we would still want the user to find his way. Furthermore, the intrigue may only be appropriate for a limited area. In settings like museums it might be desirable to organize space so that certain parts of the exhibition ground are labyrinthine, while others allow the visitor

Site plan. *(From "Les Étoiles de Renaudie Givors, 1975-1981,"* Architecture d' Aujourd'hui, **220**:11; *copyright © 1982 Architecture d' Aujourd'hui)*

Figure 5.15
Labyrinth housing project, Givors, France. *(From "Les Etoiles de Renaudie Givors, 1975-1981,"* Architecture d' Aujourd'hui **270**:14; *copyright © 1982 Arhitecture d' Aujourd'hui)*.

to resituate himself. Settings may also be designed to make the labyrinth experience optional.

The potential for application is vast, but the application has to be responsible. Unfortunately, little is known about the full effects of labyrinth features in design. Special care should be taken not to inconvenience user groups who may not be able to cope with the experience. The functional aspects of the various wayfinding conditions also have to be respected, as outlined in the design guide. Daring projects, like the reviewed housing development by Renaudie, should be subjected to post-occupancy evaluations in order to learn from these experiments.

If the reader should ever have the exciting task of designing a labyrinth for the purpose of getting people hopelessly lost, here at last is some advice: by all means avoid any arrangements that could be perceived as a pattern and understood as an organization principle. Try to conceive an enclosure that is as amorphous as possible. Avoid any distinct features; all parts should be uniform. Either no edges or an infinite number of edges should be provided. No path should stand out in any way from another, no zone be distinguished from another. By repeating uniformity and multiplying it to the utmost, you should do quite well. Of course, you can use more devious devices such as misinforming your victims or, what is worse, misinforming them once you have gained their confidence. You may confuse their senses by drowning them with irrelevant information; and if you aspire to the perfect labyrinth, jump the cultural barrier, follow Ts'ui Pen's example: don't let them find the labyrinth at all.

NOTES

1. Robert Venturi (1966), an outspoken critic of the modernist school, proclaimed his architectural credo in a controversial book *Complexity and Contradiction in Architecture:* "I like elements which are hybrid rather than 'pure,' compromising rather than 'clean,' distorted rather than 'straight-forward,' ambiguous rather than 'articulated,' . . . I am for messy vitality over obvious unity" (Venturi et al., 1966, 16). The questioning of the purist tendencies of the international style actually goes back to the fifties when an avant-garde linked to the Pop movement in Great Britain expressed a radical change of architectural values from the idealized design object to mass produced consumer goods and even to an architecture without buildings.

2. During the early sixties architects and designers were turning to the social sciences to look for this support. It was soon realized though, that the traditional disciplines, in particular psychology and sociology, were not able to provide information that could be translated into design criteria, nor were they equipped to cope with the new demand for such information. This led to the creation of the interdisciplinary field of environmental psychology or person-environment relations.

3. The project is fully described in a publication by Wolf (1974).

4. The detailed definition of each unit and the corresponding coding rules are described in Appendix B.

5. Weisman (1982) notes that the elderly experience wayfinding difficulties in their own nursing homes and long term care centers. The sample included alert and capable subjects. The author proposes interesting design directives specifically for care centers.

6. For recent findings and experiments in building evacuation see Hall (1980) and Pauls (1980).

7. Architectural and urban planning foresee activities and organize them in space. Often insufficient attention is given to the underlying behavioral solution "packaged" in the physical solution. The method proposed here is inspired by a design model developed by Studer (1969, 1971). Physical systems are planned to accommodate previously established behavior systems. The approach is furthermore justified by the observation that, given similar information to solve a wayfinding problem, the solutions do not deviate to any remarkable extent.

8. The decision diagrams accumulated during wayfinding research contain a considerable number of decisions. The diagrams developed for design can be much simpler for two reasons: first, there is no need and no basis for developing decisions to the same detail as we record them when following a person's real decision-making process; second, many of the decisions taken by the subjects were aimed at finding missing or inaccurate information. Long decision plans are partly due to faulty wayfinding design.

9. It might be more effective to pose the question in a negative form. We could, for example, follow the path on the plan and at each decision point ask ourselves what the user could do wrong and what information could put him back on the right track.

10. Moles and his students have undertaken various studies on labyrinths and their application to planning. In particular they have looked at labyrinth features in cities (Friederich, 1977) and museums (Cluet, 1975).

11. Published by *L'architecture d'aujourd'hui*, 220 (April 1982).

REFERENCES

Appleyard, D., K. Lynch, and R. Myer, 1964, *The View from the Road*, MIT Press, Cambridge, Mass.

Berlyne, D. E., 1966, "Curiosity and Exploration," *Science* **153**(3731):25-33.

Blake, P., 1977, *Form Follows Fiasco: Why Modern Architecture Hasn't Worked,* Little Brown, Toronto.

Cluet, I., 1975, *Plan d'un musée comme labyrinthe,* Travaux de l'Institut de Psychologie de Strasburg, Strasburg.

Friederich, P., 1977, *La ville comme labyrinthe,* Travaux de l'Institut de Psychologie de Strasburg, Strasburg.

Hall, J., 1980, "Patient Evacuation in Hospitals," in *Fires and Human Behavior,* D. Canter, ed., John Wiley and Sons, New York, pp.205-225.

Moles, A., and E. Rohmer, 1978, *Psychologie de l'espace,* Casterman, Paris.

Pauls, J. J., 1980, "Building Evacuation: Research Findings and Recommendations," in *Fires and Human Behavior,* D. Canter, ed., John Wiley and Sons, New York.

Piché, D., 1981, The Spontaneous Geography of the Urban child," in *Geography and the Urban Environment: Progress in Research and Applications,* IV, D.T. Herbert and R. J. Johnston, eds., John Wiley and Sons, New York.

Rapoport, A., 1977, *Human Aspects of Urban Form: Towards a Man-Environment Approach to Urban Form and Design,* Pergamon Press, Toronto.

Studer, R., 1969, "Some Aspects of the Man-Designed Environment Interface," in *Response to Environment,* G. J. Coates and K. M. Moffet, eds., North Carolina State University, Student Publication of the School of Design, Raleigh, vol. 18, pp.77-98.

Studer, R., 1971, "Human System Design and the Management of Change," *General Systems,* **16:**131-143.

Thiel, P., 1961, "A Sequence-Experience Notation," *Town Planning Review,* **32**(1):33-52.

Thiel, P., 1970, "Notes on the Description, Scaling, Notation, and Scoring of Some Perceptual and Cognitive Attributes of the Physical Environment," in *Environmental Psychology,* H. Proshansky et al., eds., Rinehart and Winston, New York, pp.593-619.

Venturi, R., 1966, *Complexity and Contradiction in Architecture,* Museum of Modern Art, New York.

Weisman, G. D., 1982, "Way-finding and Architectural Legibility: Considerations in Housing Environments for the Elderly," in *Housing for the Elderly: Satisfaction and Preferences,* V. Regnier and J. Pynoos, eds., Garland, New York.

Wolf, P., 1974, *The Evolving City,* The Whitney Library of Design, New York.

Wolfe, T., 1971, *From Bauhaus to Our House,* Farrar Straus Giroux, New York.

Appendix A:
Description of the Commercial Complexes Used in the Wayfinding Studies

Before presenting the reader with a short description of the major commercial settings studied, I would like to emphasize that any comments made in this book relating to the settings must not be seen as an assessment of the building nor of its architect or designer. The good and bad examples have been chosen to facilitate the reading and the writing of the argument and not to sample the quality of the setting. Illustrations taken from the same

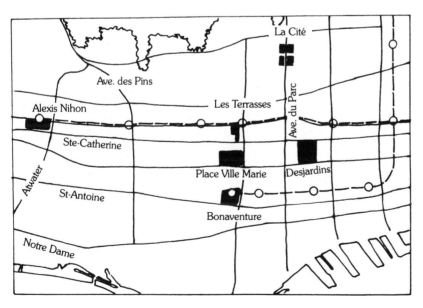

Figure A.1.
Downtown Montréal, location of reviewed commercial complexes.

Alexis-Nihon, viewed from Maison-neuve.

buildings were often used to spare the reader additional mental effort. Furthermore, examples showing faults were generally privileged, partly because they are easier to observe and partly because they assure greater impact. I am also perfectly aware that it is easier to detect specific weaknesses than to conceive an efficient wayfinding support system, whether in the form of signs, maps, or architectural space.

All five commercial centers referred to in this book are located in downtown Montréal. Four of them are directly linked to the metro system, saving the user a trip outside the system. Montréal is unique in its vast public underground resort; it has been described as the city of the twenty-first century or the "city below."

PLAZA ALEXIS-NIHON

A 16-story office building, a 33-story residential tower, and a 3-level shopping plaza constitute the complex Alexis-Nihon (Fig. A.2). Approxi-

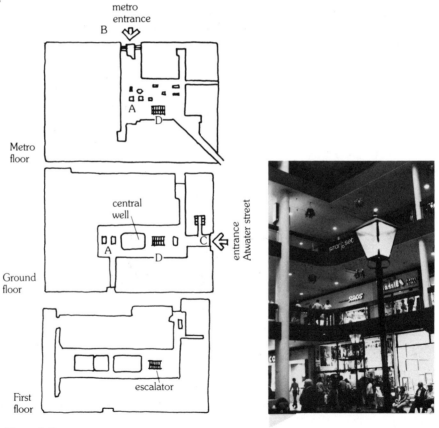

Figure A.2.
Alexis-Nihon, plan of the three shopping levels and view of central square.

mately 120 shops offer their goods and services in the plaza, which also features cinemas, bars, and restaurants. The central space is used for expositions, entertainment, and promotion. Three levels of parking are situated above the businesses.

Alexis-Nihon is located at the western fringe of downtown Montréal. It is directly accessible from the metro and serves as a link to a major city bus terminal. The center opened in 1967.

The shopping floors are organized around a central square (A); the lowest level communicates directly with the metro station Atwater (B). The access to the office building is on the ground floor near the entrance from Atwater Street (C). The vertical circulation in the plaza for the three shopping levels is assured by an escalator near the central well (D).

PLACE BONAVENTURE

This vast commercial complex contains on the main shopping concourse (ground floor) more than 150 shops, 80 boutiques, bars, restaurants, cinemas, and a vast exhibition hall designed for a capacity of up to 10,000 people (Fig. A.3). The five upper levels house wholesale commerces. On the sixth level is an international center and, on top, a first-class 400-room hotel, offering in a landscaped setting a number of business facilities, including major conference rooms that can cater to big international conventions. The parking, reaching seven levels underground, has a capacity for approximately 1,000 cars.

Figure A.3.
Place Bonaventure, view from La Gauchetière.

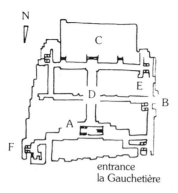

Figure A.4.
Bonaventure, plan of ground floor and view of central circulation system.

Bonaventure is located at the southern fringe of downtown Montréal. It is directly accessible from the metro; an indoor passage communicates with the central railway station and a second major commercial center, Place Ville-Marie. The complex was inaugurated in 1967.

The shopping floor is arranged as a street system (Fig. A.4) and is accessible from La Gauchetière, or by metro at Place de la Concorde (A). A special entrance gives access to the hotel (B). Of particular interest to this discussion is the open square, Place de la Concorde, the exhibition halls (C), the information booth (D), and the access to the underground parking (E). The elevators at (E) only link to the underground parking. The elevators for the upper floors are situated in the corners of the buildings (F).

LA CITÉ

La Cité combines a 26-story office and medical tower (A), a 500-room hotel (B) and three residential clusters totaling 1,350 dwellings (C) by an underground promenade (D), equipped with a potential of 100 retail shops (Fig. A.5). Fewer than 50 were actually in use during the time of the study. The underground garages can park up to 1,000 cars.

La Cité is located at the northeastern fringe of downtown Montréal. It is the only center discussed here that is not directly accessible from the metro system. The center opened in 1977. Of particular interest is the relation between the building structure above ground, occupying four city blocks and an underground promenade (Fig. A.6).

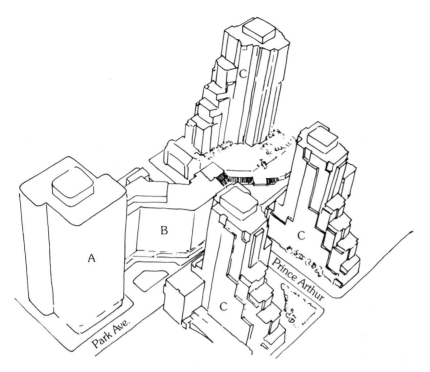

Figure A.5.
La Cité, birds-eye view.

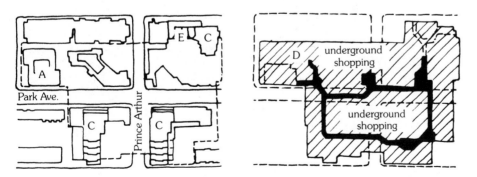

Figure A.6.
La Cité, plan of street level and underground promenade.

COMPLEX DESJARDINS

Three office towers, approximately 30 stories each and a 15-story hotel block are linked by a large central space (Fig. A.7). Artistic events and expositions are regularly featured in this central square. Approximately 120 shops are located on three levels of galleries bordering two sides of the square; they include restaurants, banks, cinemas and a government printing office. The hotel has a capacity of 1,000 convention guests. The indoor underground parking holds up to 1,150 cars. The center opened in 1976; an estimated 30,000 people visit the center daily.

Desjardins is located at the eastern fringe of downtown Montréal, opposite the cultural center Place des Arts, to which it is linked by an underground passage that also leads to the metro (Fig. A.8). Of particular interest is the vast open square with its glass fronts giving visual access to the cityscape.

Figure A.7.
Desjardins, view from the cultural center Place des Arts.

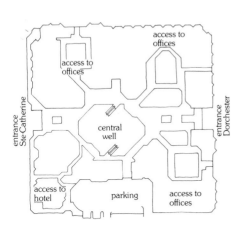

Figure A.8.
Desjardins, plan and view of central core.

LES TERRASSES

Four stories of shopping and eating places totaling approximately 120 establishments are inserted between two buildings, one a big department store, Eaton's (Fig. A.9). Three levels of underground parking and five office levels above the shopping area complete the complex. Les Terrasses, situated in the center of downtown, opened in 1976.

The internal circulation at the shopping levels is organized in triangular form. A number of split levels give the inside a terrace-like atmosphere. The outside view from St. Catherine (Fig. A.10) and from Maisonneuve (see Figure 4.16) have quite a different architectural expression, and neither indicates what is to be found inside. Also of interest is the recently introduced supergraphics (1979), which by a color code helps sort out the different split levels.

Graphic display.

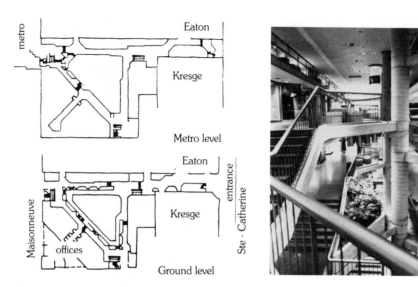

Figure A.9.
Les Terrasses, plan and view of the shopping zone.

Figure A.10.
Les Terrasses, view from St. Catherine.

Appendix B: Research Methodology and Coding Specifications of the Notation System

THE FIRST WAYFINDING STUDY, 1975

Given the poorly researched field of wayfinding, I started with a number of small inquiries aimed at gaining a general insight into the many aspects of the phenomenon. For this purpose a series of open-ended interviews were undertaken with designers who had been involved in the planning of sign systems for large architectural complexes. At the same time, the building managers of these complexes were interviewed in order to identify major wayfinding issues and the associated problems as well as the means employed to solve them. Another series of interviews was made with the personnel of information booths at Place Bonaventure and Place Ville-Marie. Here I was interested in drawing a profile of the user population, their questions, and the nature of the answers provided. These examinations also suggested wayfinding difficulties particular to those buildings. Additionally, over fifty sets of wayfinding instructions given by the general public were collected for each building of interest.

The overall objectives of the principal wayfinding study were twofold: to provide the basic data to elaborate a conceptualization of wayfinding in terms of spatial problem solving; and to identify the environmental characteristics that facilitate the wayfinding task or render it more difficult.

The study consisted of having subjects complete given wayfinding tasks in the commercial settings Bonaventure and Alexis-Nihon. The tasks were chosen to provide for a variety of typical wayfinding situations.

Two types of data were collected: a wayfinding protocol and a post-test interview evaluating the difficulties of the task and the setting. The wayfinding protocol consists of a verbalization of the subject's problem-solving process while completing the wayfinding task. The subjects were encouraged to describe freely what went through their minds at any time, to discuss the decisions they made, and to indicate what information they relied upon. The function of the investigator was to encourage this verbalization during the walk. The protocol contains an unedited version of the whole conversation pertinent to the topic as it was recorded on tape.

The post-test interview aimed at determining the subject's familiarity with the settings. Furthermore, it provided us with the subject's assessment of the various wayfinding tasks, an assessment of the settings independent of the task, an assessment of the signing system encountered, and a discussion of possible contamination of the data by the experimental set-up, particularly the equipment used. The interview was recorded and reproduced in an edited version.

Research Design

Each subject took the investigator over a route of the subject's own choice to the point of destination, predetermined by the task description. At no time did the investigator make any wayfinding decision for the subject. The investigator also had to guard against giving the subject any behavioral cues. The turning of the head or the lifting of the eyes, for example, was picked up by a pre-test subject. After a short training period it did not appear difficult to follow a subject passively in his choice of walking directions, walking speed, and so on, but it did prove difficult to refrain from behavioral reactions prompted by unexpected events.

The subject's wayfinding description as well as the investigator's comments were taped. Both carried a neck microphone under the clothing. The microphones were connected to a recorder carried by the investigator in a shoulder bag. The cord was hidden by the clothing, and only a length of one to two feet, connecting the subject to the shoulderbag, was exposed. This set-up allowed a recording to be made that minimized external noise, and yet at the same time it reduced obtrusiveness.

The research procedure specified a meeting with each subject at the University of Montréal, where he or she was given a written description of the project and his or her involvement in it. He was permitted to ask questions if he did not fully understand the description. He was then driven to the complex Bonaventure, where the car was parked underground. There he obtained the written instruction to the first wayfinding task. The instruction to the second task was handed to the subject only after he had reached the first destination. This destination was located in the same complex, while the second task led to Alexis-Nihon by the underground metro system. Having reached his second destination, the subject was given the instructions for the last task. This task brought him back to the car at Bonaventure by a different route. By specifying some intermediate destinations, the subject had to pass through a long underground shopping and passage system. After arriving at Bonaventure, he was driven back to the university, where the post-test interview took place immediately after his arrival. The whole experiment took approximately three hours per subject.

Description of Tasks

The tasks selected had to respond to a number of criteria. First, being an exploratory study, I was interested in tasks leading to a variety of wayfinding problems. This I hoped to achieve by formulating the task and choosing the spatial setting so that the subject had to rely on different environmental sources to obtain the necessary information. Diversity of wayfinding problems was further obtained by choosing settings that differed in spatial characteristics, in the quality of the environmental support system, and in the type and the density of activities.

Second, the task had to be fairly complex but still correspond to commonly experienced wayfinding situations. As I wanted the tasks to be representative of the wayfinding problems people encounter, only areas of buildings open to and generally used by the public were chosen. The first task led to a tourist office (Bonaventure). The second task led to the administration office (Alexis-Nihon), located in the same general area as the Canada Emigration Office; the last task led to the parking area. Each of the locations had to be accessible to people with various degrees of knowledge of the building.

Third, the tasks generally involved wayfinding problems in which the vertical spatial dimension was also of importance. This is a major criterion differentiating wayfinding at the architectural scale from wayfinding at the geographic scale. This criterion also led to the choice of tasks involving underground spaces.

The selection of tasks and settings was based on information obtained in the pre-tests. The interviews with the personnel of information booths and the building managers proved particularly relevant. Pre-test subjects who were given a number of wayfinding tasks helped me arrive at the final choice. The acceptable length of the wayfinding episodes was an important factor. I found that approximately an hour and a half could be endured without signs of fatigue.

The first task in Bonaventure consisted in finding the Swiss National Tourist Office. The subject started off on some level of the underground parking lot to reach level F (the sixth floor) of the trade center in the same building. In order to get the address of the office, he had to consult the information booth, which is situated on the ground floor. This wayfinding problem was chosen to include a task where the subjects had to execute verbal wayfinding instructions. At the same time, it provided a small sample of such instructions for the same destination.

The second task consisted in going from the Swiss National Tourist Office at Bonaventure to Alexis-Nihon. There the subject had to find the administrative office of the complex, situated on the eighth floor of the office building. In order to go to Alexis-Nihon, the subject had to take the metro to Atwater Station. Both metro stations, Atwater and Bonaventure, were located at the termini of two different lines, so that the task necessitated a change at Berri de Montigny.[1] The metro stations Atwater and Bonaventure are directly linked to the building complexes without any need for exterior travel.

In the third task, the subjects had to return to Bonaventure. The subjects were asked to travel to McGill station, which is the key station for Montréal's shopping district. The major department stores are accessible from there, and three of them, Eaton's, the Bay, and 2020 University, are directly accessible without going outside. From McGill station, the subjects had to go to Place Ville-Marie.

To reach the complex from the metro station McGill, there are a variety of possible routes. The one that goes through Eaton's department store is the shortest and also the one that is almost completely inside except for a short stretch before entering the complex Place Ville-Marie. The subjects were asked to enter the complex at the north entrance, so that the question of cardinal directions arose. From Place Ville-Marie, the subjects had to find the underground passage that links this complex to Bonaventure. This is one of the world's longest, and certainly Montréal's longest, inside promenade. The route leads through the Central station. The task was completed when the subjects located the car in the parking lot of Bonaventure.

The Subjects

A total of twelve subjects took part in the study on a voluntary basis. They had no previous knowledge of the nature of the experiment. All subjects were first-year students of the School of Architecture and Planning at the University of Montréal. They had been enrolled at the university for only a couple of weeks. Their knowledge of downtown Montréal varied a great deal, since they came from various areas of the province. The average age was 20.

In order to check and modify the application of the notation system an even smaller sample would have been sufficient, since there was no reason to expect that the units involved in spatial problem solving would differ from one person to the next. Differences in wayfinding behavior and differences in the ability to solve wayfinding problems were expected. However, I was less interested in showing these differences than in obtaining a rich and diversified record of problem-solving instances and the difficulties encountered. From this record the objectives of identifying characteristics of the spatial problem-solving process and of identifying environmental characteristics generating particular wayfinding problems could be achieved. Given these objectives, the sample provided me with a sufficiently rich collection of instances. It further allowed for some exploratory comparison between subjects, should the data invite such a comparison.

There were some limitations on the representativeness of the sample. These could not be eliminated because of the demanding nature of the study. The major limitations came from the fact that the subjects were volunteers, that they were from the same age group, and that they had chosen to study planning. Nonvolunteers and much older or much younger people would, if any differences are assumed, encounter even more difficulties than did the sample. The same could be assumed in respect to their professional interest. Students of design and planning may be more sensitized to the built environment and may have a greater facility in reading maps and signs. If these differences are real, the sample would have been better equipped to solve wayfinding tasks than the average user. The difficulties I was able to identify, therefore, can be assumed to be problems that would be shared by the general population.

Assessment

The research procedure in general appeared to work successfully. Although the subjects may not have expressed all their thoughts, the verbalization of decision making did not seem to be difficult. The first part of the route in the parking lot at Bonaventure served as a "warming up" period.

Whenever the investigator observed a behavioral action, he asked the subject what he was doing. This had to be answered by giving a description of the behavioral action or the underlying decision. If the subject did not indicate the information that led to the decision, the investigator would inquire why or on what basis the decision was taken. Once the subject got the feeling of what was required, the investigator's probing became less frequent. If other people were using the elevators, some subjects were observed to be inhibited in verbalizing their thoughts, but otherwise behavior and its description appeared spontaneous.

Subjects generally expressed decisions less easily if they were familiar with a given route, that is, if they were only executing known decision plans. Frustration was occasionally expressed at having to verbalize decisions or describe behavior that came to the subject without his having to think about it. When decisions were made, verbalization proved very natural.

The circumstances of not being alone and of having to partake in a study made some subjects pay more attention to signs and maps than they otherwise would have done. In the post-test interview half of the group also indicated that they would have asked passers-by for directions more frequently had they been alone. It should be noted that the subjects were discouraged from asking passers-by before other options of obtaining information were explored.

COMPLEMENTARY STUDIES, 1978 AND 1979

The previously described research provided rich and diversified data that permitted the collection of decisions and the environmental information necessary to develop the conceptual framework and to identify wayfinding problems created by environmental characteristics. If one views the coded data, one observes an abundance of environmental information of the directly perceived order. Statements about signs and physically present architectural elements tend to predominate. My collaborators and I suspected that while making decisions on site it was more difficult to tap the subjects' memory information, especially information implying a spatial representation of the site. We suspected that these representations, because they are often vague and not easily expressed in words, escape verbalization.

It should be noted that by having to justify his decisions the subject had to refer to memory information if it played a part. It could be only a poor out-cropping of the information actually available. The main objective of the two following studies was to obtain a more extensive coverage of all the environmental information involved.

The 1978 project comprised two distinct parts, the first identical to the previous study. Eight subjects were asked to reach destinations in two commercial complexes, this time Bonaventure and Desjardins. Once the test was completed, they were again interviewed to obtain an overall assessment of the site, the wayfinding problems encountered, and their causes. Most of all, we were interested in tapping the knowledge and understanding of the sites; in other words, we were interested in memory information. Taking into consideration the two distinct abilities, recalling and recognizing, we used two different means to reactivate that memory.

First, the subject was asked to model the exterior volume of the two sites and to enumerate anything he knew about the physical characteristics of the building. The same exercise was undertaken for the interior. The subject was asked to draw on transparencies the buildings layout and again to identify anything he possibly could. A series of questions comparing the two buildings was also intended to provide a stimulus for these information-probing sessions. The second means aimed at the ability to recognize an element. During this exercise, the subject had to respond to a series of slides showing various aspects of the two buildings. Forty slides were taken to show a variety of elements, from spatial ensembles to decorative details and finishes. The subject had to indicate whether he recognized the slide, and finally he had to locate from where approximately the picture was taken. All the subjects agreed that after this exercise there was little more they had to say about the places visited.

In the 1979 study, two new commercial centers, Les Terrasses and La Cité, were added to the building stock. Sixteen subjects participated in this research, each visiting two of the four buildings. The recognition exercise based on the slide show was abandoned; instead, additional tasks of pointing to visited destinations both inside and outside the buildings were incorporated into the first part of the research.

NOTATION SYSTEM

The protocol, containing the raw data of verbalized problem solving was first coded and then transcribed into decision diagrams showing the decision structure and the links between decisions and the environmental information used. The diagrams were analyzed for their structural and dynamic content. The protocol for the twelve subjects of the 1975 study alone contained close to 400 pages. Only part of that data could be transcribed in this way. The protocol was further cross-referenced to a photographic record of the environmental information used, such as signs, maps, and architectural features, which allowed us to compile the subjects' reactions to any item of interest.

The coding rules for the wayfinding protocol and the confection of decision diagrams had to be specifically developed for these studies. Given its potential application to further wayfinding research, I shall give a detailed account of the methodology used. The operational definition of the basic units and their coding rules are also necessary in the design application of the notation system, as discussed in Chapter 5. The following description will introduce the definitions and coding rules of the basic wayfinding units and the coding rules of relations among the units. As an illustration of the coding procedure, I will also present a small sample that has been worked through, from the raw data to the completed diagram.

Definition of the Basic Units and the Coding Rules

Decisions

To start with, I will define a decision as being the choice of a behavioral action. The outcome of some decisions is a behavioral action that can be executed immediately. In other instances, the outcome of a decision is a behavioral action that can only be executed after making further decisions. For example, the decision "to go to the lower floor" may only be capable of execution after the decision "to look for stairs" has been made. Furthermore, the decision "to go to the lower floor" may be preceded by the decision "to start again." The differentiation of these types of decision became important when dealing with decision structures. However, in terms of defining a decision, the differentiation is not important. Thus, we can describe a decision as being the choice of a behavioral action that might be executed with or without making further decisions.

The linguistic mode of expressing decisions allows us to determine the coding rules. Being a choice of a behavioral action, the decision is usually expressed as an intended action which takes on the infinitive form of a verb, such as "to walk (towards)," "to look (for), and so on. In reviewing verbalized wayfinding data, I realized that decisions were not always fully expressed but were often embedded in the description of the action itself. This may be explained as a manner of speech, or it may correspond to a situation where a person is already engaged in the action while he is still verbalizing the decision. So, for example, from the statement "I am going to the upper floor," we can identify the underlying decision as being "to go to the upper floor."

In summary, we arrive at the following rule: we code as a decision, statements about an intended behavorial action or the actual description of the behavioral action. In the transcription of the raw data, the decision is given in the infinitive form of the verb. The letter D is used to symbolize decisions. Decisions contained in a task description are symbolized by the letter T.

Sensory information

We define as sensory information any element provided by the setting that can be perceived directly and that can be relevant to the wayfinding task. These elements comprise: (1) the architectural and spatial characteristics of a setting, which may range from the interpretation of elements like doors, wall finishes, and so on, to the spatial organization of whole complexes; (2) the signing of the setting as expressed by the different types of signs, maps, and so on; and (3) the people in the setting who provide cues through their spatial and verbal behavior.

The definition specifies that sensory information is to be perceived directly, and the information has to be relevant to the task. The important qualification of this coding category is that the information is perceived directly. The second qualification is included to reduce irrelevant data points. In the case of doubt about the second qualification, a statement should be coded as sensory information. If a person decides to look for information on a map, for example, and finds that no information exists, we will consider "no information" as an element of this category.

In the transcription of raw data, the relevant message on signs is given integrally. Information obtained from maps, from architectural and spatial elements, as well as information obtained from other people is summarized in terms of origin and content. All sensory information will be symbolized by Is.

Memory information

We define as memory information the stored information a person has about the setting or similar settings. The first type of knowledge is particular, such as, for example, the knowledge that the information booth at a shopping complex is located in the center of the main floor. The second type of knowledge is general, such as knowing that information booths are usually located in the center of the main floors.

The important qualification that differentiates this category from the previous one is that memory information cannot be perceived directly, while sensory information must be perceived directly. Given this definition, statement-coded sensory information may have to be recoded later as memory information if it recurs in a place where the information is no longer directly perceivable.

A short summary is given when transcribing memory information, and Im will be used to symbolize it. The accuracy of the information statement is obviously not considered when coding.

Inferential information

In the data of the studies, we came across statements that were related to memory information in that they were not perceived directly but that deviated from the definition in that they were not stored but generated on site. The information was obtained by inference. These inferences or conclusions can be based on any combination of sensory and memory information. Ii will designate inferential information.

The directly perceived sensory information, memory information, and inferential information sums up all the information that a person can have to assist in wayfinding.

The Coding of Sequence and Relations among Units

The time sequence

A continuous numbering system is used to code the time sequence of statements. If, for example, a decision is made following the perception of sensory information Is_n, the decision is to be coded D_{n+1}. In situations where

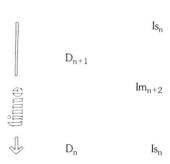

the sequence is not evident, the same index is used for the statements in question. The number system also serves to locate elements (decision points and spatial information) in space.

Relations among decisions

In order to find out if and how decisions are linked, we start by identifying the lowest order of decision in the assumed structure. Lowest-order decisions are those that lead directly to a behavorial action. As the second lowest order, we define the decisions that have led to the lowest-order decisions described above. This ordering can be repeated until we reach the most general decision to complete the task. What we are doing is identifying subdecisions of higher-order decisions.

If D_m is a subdecision of D_n, we are making decision D_m in order to be able to execute decision D_n. If, for example, "to look at a map" is a subdecision of the decision "to go to upper floor," we can say that we "look at the map" in order to "go to the upper floor." When coding, set sentences should make sense in the following manner: if D_m is a subdecision of D_n then we do D_m in order to do D_n, or in order to do D_n, we do D_m.[2]

Relations between decisions and spatial information

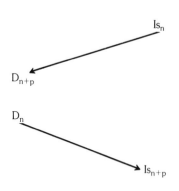

A relation between spatial information (Is_n, Im_n, or Ii_n) and a decision made at a later instance (D_{n+p}) exists if the decision D_{n+p} is based on the perceived information Is_n, on the memory information Im_n, or on the inferential information Ii_n. The decision does not have to follow immediately after Is, Im, or Ii.

A relation between a decision (D_n) and sensory information perceived at a later instance (Is_{n+p}) exists: (1) if Is_{n+p} is a direct result of a decision D_n (for example, looking for Is); or (2) if Is_{n+p} is necessary or useful to the execution of D_n (for example, if the person wants to go to a given destination and then sees the relevant sign).

Notation of the execution of a decision

Decisions cannot always be executed successfully. In an example from the study, the decision "to go to the office building" was often followed by the decision "to go to the elevators" because of the subject's knowledge that office buildings usually have elevators. The decision "to go to the elevators" was made in a number of cases on the metro and fashion level of Alexis Nihon. The elevators on these levels were not positioned so as to be accessible to the public, so that the decision could not be executed at this point.

The notation of the execution of decisions is useful in various parts of the data analysis and is used when transcribing coded data into decision diagrams. If a decision D_n is successfully executed, we use the symbol $\boxed{D_n}$ to designate its execution. If a task is not completed (the decision was not executed), we use the symbol $\boxed{O_n}$.

In some cases, I discovered that two decisions were expressed in one statement, and only part of that statement was executed successfully. For example, when a subject perceived an indicator, he may have stated the decision D_n as "to look for the office building." Assuming he does not find the information, we would still have to indicate that the decision "to look for" was executed successfully, while the unexpressed decision "to find information about the office building" was not executed successfully. In establishing the decision diagrams from the coded data in such cases, we have dissected the decision D_n into its two components, called D_{na} and D_{nb}. This differentiation was not made in the initial coding of the data but was used in the transcription the coded data into diagram form.

In the diagrams, spatial information is also linked to the decisions so that one can read what information is crucial in bringing about important decisions and what information is valueless or misleading.

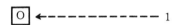

Working through a coding example

To illustrate the coding techniques, we will apply it to a small data sample taken from the second task at Alexis-Nihon. The sample reflects the first instances of a subject trying to find the office building once he had reached the plaza of Alexis-Nihon. To begin with, I will present the original protocol and the coded statements; then I will show how to transcribe these coded statements into decision diagrams.

Coding the protocol

In the protocol, the subject's statements are written lower case and the interviewer's comments are upper case. Material within brackets is descriptive and was not part of the conversation. Messages in single quotes, for example, 'elevators,' were read directly from signs. Statements in double quotes were made by third persons.

ORIGINAL PROTOCOL	**CODED STATEMENTS**

Ah, here I can see maps of the place, maybe that will tell me something.

Is_1 maps on indicator
D_2 to look for information on indicator

ALLRIGHT

'Alexis-Nihon; ground level . . .'

THERE ARE THREE MAPS HERE . . .

'Metro level, Miracle Mart,' metro . . .

"EXCUSE ME" (a third person looks at maps but does not interact with the subject).

WHAT ARE YOU LOOKING FOR?

I am looking for the office building.

D_2 to look on indicator for office building

Parking, ah . . . , 'Office Building—Immeuble à bureaux.

Is_3 'Office Building'

IS THAT IT?

Yes, 'Ground Level-Rez-de-Chaussée,' that's it.

'Ground level'

Now, I am at the metro level; I have to go to the ground level; I have to go up one level.

Im_4 to be at metro level
Ii_5 has to go up one level to go to the ground level

So, 'Steinberg . . . , Office Building,' it's badly indicated.

IT'S BADLY INDICATED?

'Parking P1, P2, P3, washroom,' 'Office Building Lobby,' ah no . . . , all that's at the metro level; eh no . . . , that's not true, it's on the ground level.

Ok, altitude 3 is this one, altitude 2 is the ground level, and metro level is this one, so I have to go to the other floor above.

D_6 to go to upper floor

So in order to go up or down . . . , they don't say much, do they? (leaving indicator and maps).

D_7 to look for information how to go up
Is_8 no information on indicator

YOU DID NOT FIND WHAT YOU WERE LOOKING FOR, BUT YOU KNOW THAT IT IS AT THE FLOOR ABOVE?

But I want to find a place to go (looking around in setting).

D_9 to look for a place to go up

WE ARE NOW WALKING ON . . .

Yes, and here in the center one can see people who go up the escalator.

Is_{10} escalator and people

SO YOU SAW THE ESCALATOR?

I saw people going up, I can only see their legs, one can even see people going up by moving their legs, and here it is indicated . . .

WE ARE NOW WALKING TOWARD THIS PLACE

There is an indicator.

Is_{11} indicator kiosk

AH, AN INDICATOR, YOU SAW IT THROUGH THE GLASS OF THE STAIRWELL.

Yes, 'Office Building—Entrance Atwater,' ok, that's something that interests me.

Is_{12} 'Office Building-Entrance Atwater'

Ah, that's a different thing . . .

ORIGINAL PROTOCOL	**CODED STATEMENTS**
A DIFFERENT THING?	
'Office Building—Entrance Atwater,' so we have to go to the entrance Atwater.	D_{13} to go to entrance Atwater
HERE YOU STUDY THE PLAN, WHAT ARE YOU LOOKING FOR?	
Yes, 'Metro . . . ,' it does not give me anything, I am not at the right floor.	D_{14} to look for entrance Atwater
IT'S NOT THE RIGHT FLOOR?	Is_{15} no information
No, let's go up.	D_{16} to go up [escalator]
OK.	
[on escalator]	
WE HAVE ARRIVED ON TOP.	Is_{17} upper level
Yes, and we turn to the right.	D_{18} to turn right to go to the center
WHY TO THE RIGHT?	
Well, to go somewhere, to go to the center.	
Ah, ah, here I see 'Atwater.'	Is_{19} 'Atwater'
WHAT ARE YOU SEEING?	
I see that beautiful sign, it says 'Office Building,' and I see 'Atwater,' so that confirms everything, and there are also elevators, so it has to be above.	Is_{20} 'Office Building' and 'Elevators'
WE ARE WALKING TOWARD THAT SIGN?	
And we turn to the left, there is an arrow.	D_{21} to turn left following arrow on sign I_{20}
We are at the office building lobby.	Is_{22} office building lobby

From the subject's first remark, "Ah, here I can see maps of the place, maybe that will tell me something," we can identify "maps" as being a unit of spatial information. The maps being directly perceived, we must code them as sensory information (Is). As it is the first unit mentioned, we index it by the number (Is_1). When the coded statement is rewritten, the descriptor "on indicator" is added to differentiate it from other maps, for example, the maps on the kiosk. The second part of the subject's statement ("maybe that will tell me something"), indicates the subject's desire to obtain some information. At this point, he is not specific as to the kind of information desired. This statement and the following behavior of reading the indicator contains the underlying decision "to look for information on indicator." As this decision is taken after the maps were perceived, the decision is indexed by the number (D_2).

The subject's second and third statements ("Alexis-Nihon; Ground Level") and ("Metro Level; Miracle Mart") could also be coded as sensory information, but they have not been included in the coded statements because they did *not* appear relevant to the subject.

The investigator's statement ("what are you looking for?") aimed at eliciting the reason for the subject's reading behavior. The subject's response ("I am looking for the office building") is a description of a behavior that contains the underlying decision "to look for office building." This decision could have been indexed D_3, but because it was expressed in response to the investigator's probing, we are not sure of when the decision was taken. As the decision is a specification of the previous decision in that it only indicates *what* information is looked for, I have used the same index as in the previous decision.

The subject's following two statements, "parking, ah . . . 'Office Building/ Immeuble a bureaux,'" and "yes, 'Ground Level — Rex-de-chaussée,'" shows that the subject has found the desired information, which is coded Is_3. The first part of the subject's subsequent statement, "now, I am at the metro level," is again a unit of spatial information, but this time it is *not* perceived directly and has to be coded as memory information (Im_4). The second part of the same statement, "I have to go to the ground level; I have to go up one level," shows that the subject has made the inference (Ii_2), "having to go up one level," on the basis of Is_3 (the offices being at ground level) and Im_4 (the subject being at the metro level). This inference is also a unit of environmental information that leads, after a series of hesitations, to the decision D_6, "to go the upper floor."

Establishing Decision Diagrams

The decision diagrams (Fig. B.1) are based on the data coded in the previous section. The diagram on the left indicates the structural links among decisions. The diagram on the right indicates the sequential links between decisions and their relation to the available information. The two diagrams are complementary. They have been separated in order to facilitate the reading. The characteristics and the content of the diagrams have been discussed in Chapter 3. Here I will only illustrate how the diagrams are arrived at.

The first step in determining the structural links among decisions is to identify the decisions leading directly to behavioral actions, that is, the lowest-order decisions. Let us recall that a decision of this order does not require any further decisions in order for it to be executed. Reviewing the subject's statements, discussed in the previous section, we have a typical statement containing more than one decision. D_2, which might be expressed as "to look for information," contains two components: D_{2a}, "to find information," and D_{2b}, "to look somewhere" (on an indicator). Whereas D_{2b} can be directly executed if the person is at the appropriate location. D_{2a} is executed only after D_{2b} had been executed *and* the information has been found. We can see in this case that the breakdown is necessary in order to arrive at the lowest-order decision.

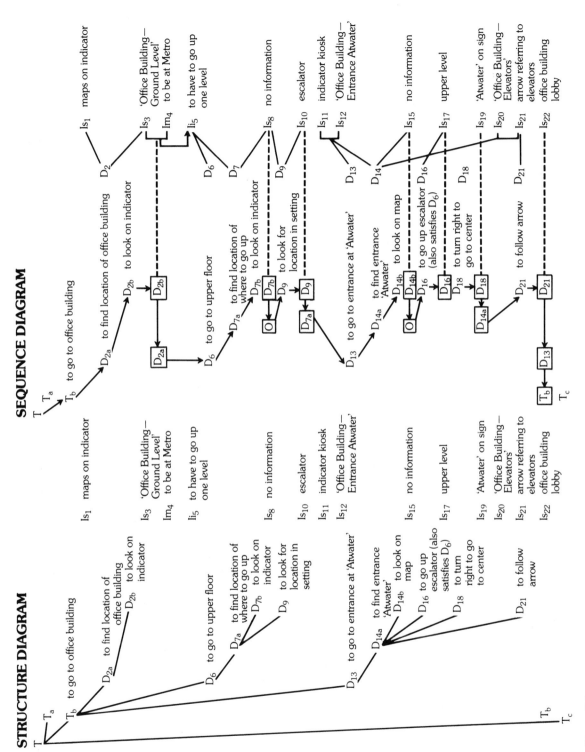

Figure B.1
Decision diagrams.

Once the lowest-order decisions have been found, the linking process is a simple application of the coding rules. Progressively, we indicate *why* decisions were taken. So, D_{2b}, "to look on indicator" was taken *in order to* execute the decision D_{2a}, "to find information for the office building." This decision was taken *in order to* execute the task decision T_b, "to go to office building." This decision was taken in order to execute the task decision T, "to go to Montrad."

The links between decisions and spatial information is established by direct application of the coding rules. So Is is linked to D_2 because Is_1, the maps, led to D_2, "to look for information." D_2 is linked to Is_3, because D_2 led to Is_3, the information that the office building (entrance) is located on the ground floor. The diagram also links the spatial information unit to the executed decision. So, we indicate by the horizontal line that, for example, Is_3 allowed for the execution of D_{2b}, or Is_8 led to the execution of D_{7b} but not to the execution of D_{7a}.

This coding example is typical of the cases encountered. Although the coding is a direct application of the coding rules, it can be seen that coding is demanding both in the attention and in the time it requires.

NOTES

1. The metro lines have since been extended.
2. Lichtenstein and Brewer (1980) used "in-order-to" relations to code goal-directed actions. They report very high coding concordance. In a particular experiment only 10 out of 1,752 responses (0.6 percent) deviated from the model response.

REFERENCE

Lichtensten, E. H., and W. F. Brewer, 1980, "Memory for Goal-Directed Events," *Cognitive Psychology* **2**(3):412-445.

Author Index

Subject Index

About the Author

ROMEDI PASSINI, associate professor at the School of Architecture of the University of Montréal, bridges environmental psychology and architectural design in his teaching and research activities. He completed his architectural training in 1964 in Zurich, Switzerland, at the Eidgenössische Technische Hochschule, and practiced for over six years, an experience that exposed him to the design problems of large-scale buildings. Attracted by the emerging interdisciplinary field of environmental psychology, and owing to a grant from Canada Council, he attended graduate school at Pennsylvania State University where he obtained the M.Sc. in 1973 and Ph.D. in 1977.

Presently, Dr. Passini is researching two major subject areas: mobility and wayfinding problems of the visually handicapped, and architectural communication and meaning as viewed from a cognitive perspective.

Randall Library — UNCW

NA2765 .P37 1984

NXWW

Passini / Wayfinding in architecture

3049002896075